Daniel Start

THE OPEN CAGE

The Ordeal of
the Irian Jaya Hostages

HarperCollins*Publishers*

HarperCollins*Publishers*
77–85 Fulham Palace Road,
Hammersmith, London w6 8jb

Published by HarperCollins*Publishers* 1997
1 3 5 7 9 8 6 4 2

Copyright © Daniel Start 1997

The Author asserts the moral right to
be identified as the author of this work

A catalogue record for this book is
available from the British Library

ISBN 0 00 255848 3

Set in Bembo by
Rowland Phototypesetting Ltd,
Bury St Edmunds, Suffolk

Printed and bound in Great Britain by
Caledonian International Book Manufacturing Ltd, Glasgow

THE OPEN CA[E

For Navy, Tessy
and the Nduga people

Contents

LORENTZ 95

The Flora & Fauna of the Nduga • Lorentz Reserve • Irian Jaya • Indonesia

September to December 1995

An Anglo-Indonesian Rainforest Conservation Project

PROPOSAL

<u>Patron:</u>
HRH The Duke of Edinburgh KG KT

Birds of paradise illustrating the cover of our expedition proposal

ILLUSTRATIONS

Nduga warriors (© Ben Bohane, Wildlight)
In ceremonial dress
With metal axe (© Ben Bohane, Wildlight)
Nduga and Dani OPM
29 February – contact with the ICRC
Huts in the pig village
Yudas and Murip (© Ben Bohane, Wildlight)
Kelly Kwalik makes his speech
OPM wait in ranks

Between pages 258 and 259

Tessy, Lita and 'Little Brother' on the roof (© Navy Th. Panekenam)
The house at Elmin's gardens (© Navy Th. Panekenam)
Inside the house (© Navy Th. Panekenam)
Murip watching the troops (© Ben Bohane, Wildlight)
Headwear on parade (© Ben Bohane, Wildlight)
The most wanted men in Indonesia
OPM raise the West Papuan flag (© Ben Bohane, Wildlight)
Tabril, with Navy and Mark
Looking happy, with the Red Cross
Martha
Petrus holding hands with Anna
Our group, flanked by the OPM
Annette and Anna
Mark and Bill
Murip and Kwalik handing out leaflets
Daud, in tradition garb
The Dani man
Nduga men and OPM
Lined up to watch the slaughter of the pigs
Eating pig stew
The pig slaughter
Last moments before the helicopters took the ICRC away

AUTHOR'S NOTE

The opinions and perceptions expressed in this book are my own and not those of Anna, Annette, Bill or anyone else who was present. For reasons of security the names of some people and places have been changed. The reader's attention is drawn to the correct Indonesian pronounciation of Navy. The 'a' is short as in 'have' not long as in 'cave'.

GLOSSARY

INDONESIAN WORDS

pandana	*species of genus* pandanus *found in the highlands*
ubi	*sweet potato*
mantri	*nurse or health worker*
buah merah	*red fruit, a species of genus* pandanus *found in the low foothills*

NDUGA WORDS

Wa	*greetings*
wam	*pig*
kopi	*a pear-shaped vegetable tasting of cucumber*
nokin	*string bag*

ABBREVIATIONS AND ACRONYMS

ABRI	*Indonesian army*
ICRC	*International Committee for the Red Cross*
Unesco	*United Nations Educational, Scientific and Cultural Organization*
MAF	*Mission Aviation Fellowship*
SB	*Short Band/Wave (Radio)*
WWF	*World Wide Fund for Nature*
BScC	*Biological Sciences Club*
Kopassus	*Special Forces troops*
OPM	*Organisasi Papua Merdeka*
Komnas Ham	*Komisis Nasional Hak Agasi Manusia (Indonesia's National Commission on Human Rights)*

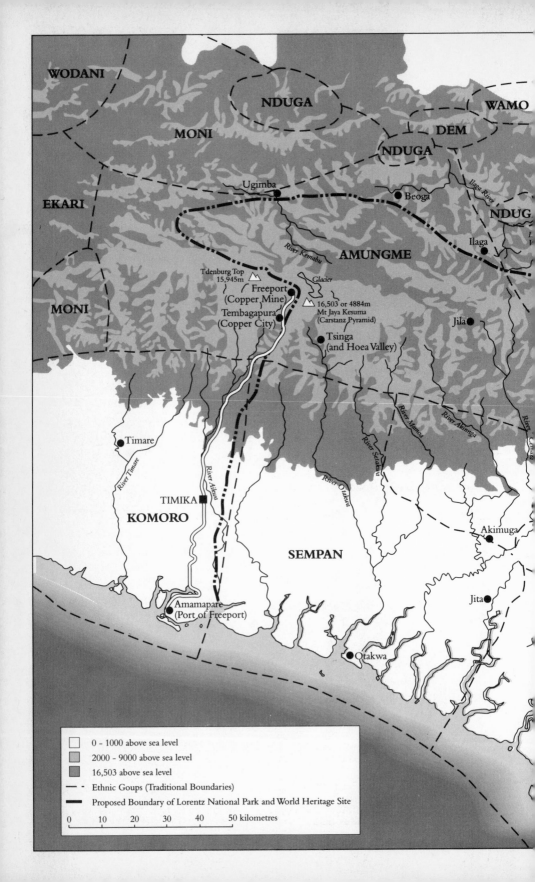

WODANI

NDUGA

WAMO

MONI

DEM

NDUGA

NDUG

EKARI

Ugimba

Beoga

River Ilaga

Ilaga

AMUNGME

River Kemabu

MONI

Tdenburg Top
15,945m

Glacier

Jila

Freeport
(Copper Mine)

16,503 or 4884m
Mt Jaya Kesuma
(Carstanz Pyramid)

Tembagapura
(Copper City)

Tsinga
(and Hoea Valley)

River Mamoa

River Akimoa

River

Timare

River Otakwa

River Saidetea

River Timare

River Aikwa

TIMIKA

KOMORO

Akimuga

SEMPAN

Amamapare
(Port of Freeport)

Jita

Otakwa

0 - 1000 above sea level

2000 - 9000 above sea level

16,503 above sea level

- - - Ethnic Goups (Traditional Boundaries)

━━━ Proposed Boundary of Lorentz National Park and World Heritage Site

0   10   20   30   40   50 kilometres

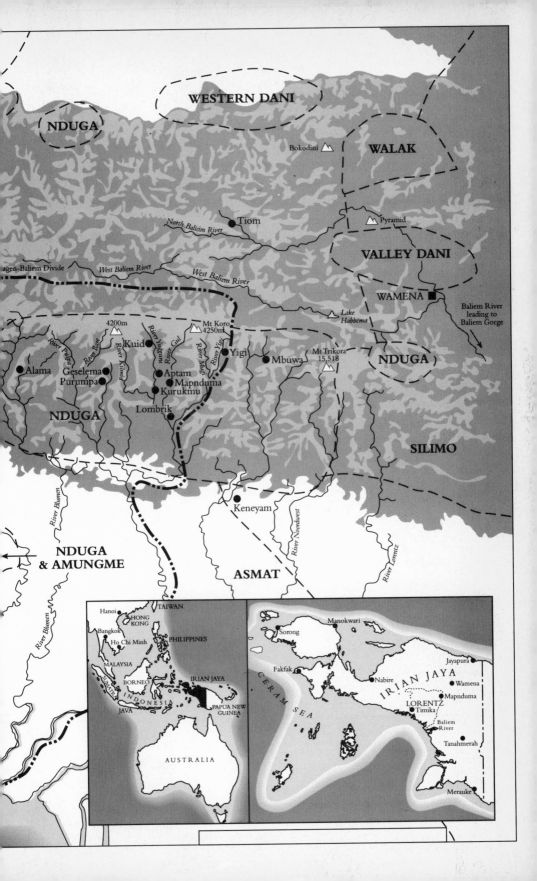

WESTERN DANI

NDUGA

Bokodini △

WALAK

North Balicim River   ● Tiom

△ Pyramid

VALLEY DANI

agen-Baliem Divide   West Baliem River   West Baliem River

WAMENA ■

Baliem River
leading to
Baliem Gorge

△ Lake
Habbema

4200m △   Mt Koro △
4250m

● Kuid

River Pulpa   River Ilaxe   River Kilmit   River Baguun   River Gul   River Mug   River Yigi   ● Yigi   ● Mbuwa   △ Mt Trikora
15,518   NDUGA

● Alama   Geselema ●   ● Aptam
Purumpa ●   Mapnduma
Kurukmu

● Lombrik

NDUGA

SILIMO

River Blumen

← →

NDUGA
& AMUNGME

● Keneyam

River Noorduest

River Lorentz

ASMAT

River Blumen

TAIWAN
Hanoi ●   HONG
KONG
Bangkok ●
Ho Chi Minh ●   PHILIPPINES

MALAYSIA

BORNEO   IRIAN JAYA
INDONESIA
JAVA   PAPUA NEW
GUINEA

AUSTRALIA

Manokwari ●
Sorong ●

Jayapura ●

Fakfak ●   IRIAN JAYA
Nabire ●   ● Wamena
● Mapnduma
CERAM
SEA   LORENTZ
Timika ●
Baliem
River

Tanahmerah ●

Merauke ●

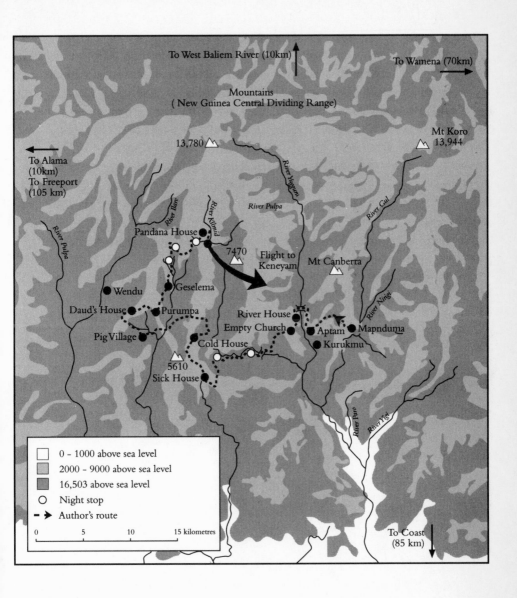

To West Baliem River (10km)

To Wamena (70km)

Mountains
(New Guinea Central Dividing Range)

To Alama
(10km)
To Freeport
(105 km)

13,780

Mt Koro
13,944

River Yiggni

River Gul

River Pulpa

River Ilare

River Kilimid

River Pulpa

Pandana House

7470

Flight to
Keneyam

Mt Canberra

River Ningi

Wendu

Geselema

Daud's House

Purumpa

River House

Empty Church

Aptam

Mapnduma

PigVillage

Cold House

Kurukmu

5610

Sick House

River Paso

River Ygt

	0 - 1000 above sea level
	2000 - 9000 above sea level
	16,503 above sea level
O	Night stop
- ➤	Author's route

0   5   10   15 kilometres

To Coast
(85 km)

THE OPEN CAGE

PROLOGUE

The information presented below is adapted from eye witness testimonies published in July 1995 by the Bishop of Jayapura, Herman Munninghoff. His report has since been broadly verified by an independent enquiry of the Indonesian government's Commission on Human Rights (Komnas Ham).

Late in the night of 6 October 1994 five heavily armed soldiers, guided by a village man, came and surrounded the small tin-roofed hut. The first soldier pushed open the door with the muzzle of his gun and flashed his torch across the bare wooden walls. Inside was a rickety table, a cooking pot on the floor and a collection of string bags hanging from a nail. A Papuan woman, Maria, and her two young children were sleeping in a huddle of blankets in the far corner.

'*Bangun*, get up,' the soldier barked in Indonesian. He moved towards her as the others followed him, filling the hut. 'Where is your husband?'

Maria sat up sharply, gathering her children to her and trembling in the bright light of the torch. She was very afraid. 'Down by the incubator, working,' she stammered. 'Why do you . . . ?'

'Shut up,' the soldier snapped. 'Take us there now.'

The chicken incubator was just a few kerosene lamps rigged up in an old steel cargo container, about head high, three yards wide by six long. There were several of these containers in the area. They belonged to the Freeport gold and copper mine which used them to take goods from the port in the coastal swamps up to the mine site, high under the tropical glaciers of Mount Jaya, New Guinea. The mountain, the highest point between the Himalayas and the Andes, contained the largest combined reserves of gold and copper in the world. It was also a sacred site of the Amungme tribe.

When Maria and the soldiers arrived at the steel box her husband had finished his work and was sitting on top, playing cards by lamplight with his three younger brothers. The soldiers ordered them down to the ground and pushed their faces into the earth.

'You are the brothers of Kelly Kwalik? Yes?' shouted the soldier. They cried out, saying they knew nothing about him but they were pulled up again and escorted to the nearby cars. Maria pleaded to be allowed to go with her husband and brothers but the soldiers pointed their guns and told her to stay. Weeping quietly, she followed at a distance and stood watching as the cars drove into the night.

Early the next morning, Maria gathered the other wives and children and walked for several miles up the dirt road that linked the resettlement site with the town of Timika. Twenty years ago there had been little there, just forest and the Freeport airfield, but as the mine had grown so had the town. Now there were transmigration sites nearby which provided new homes for the Indonesian settlers who came from over-populated Java. And there was the regional military command centre, one of the largest in Indonesia.

The land around was flat and dusty. Thirty miles to the north the mountains rose steeply into the cloud. Although her children knew no other home, she could still remember her small Amungme village. There were clear mountain streams, forests filled with good things to eat and sweet potato gardens with views out over the world. When the mine had opened thousands of them had been resettled in camps in the lowlands near Timika. At first they had thought the new life would bring them riches like those of the white men and the Indonesians; instead it had brought them malaria and rivers poisoned with copper effluent. And now Timika was filled with many Indonesians who treated the indigenous black Papuans with little respect.

'What is the use of coming to see your husbands,' the guard said at the gate of the military base. He laughed. 'You think we have eaten them! The brothers of Kelly Kwalik would not taste good!' Outside, on the road, the women stood waiting for several hours.

Eventually, they were called and taken inside. In the corner of the ground stood two Freeport containers, baking in the sun. In the hot dark interior were the men, shackled by their feet and hands. Maria and the women wept.

Kelly Kwalik, Maria's notorious brother-in-law, had been born in the 1950s to a large family. He was brought up in a highland village long before the coming of the Freeport mine. In his late teens, Kelly had excelled at the tiny mission school and won a scholarship to the Catholic seminary in Jayapura, the capital of what was then West Papua. After graduation he had been a teacher for a while, but in the early 1970s he had left to join the newly formed OPM (Organisasi Papua Merdeka) or Free Papua Movement that, with bows and arrows and a handful of guns, was resisting the Indonesian annexation of West Papua. He made the 250-mile journey home to the highlands by foot and was involved in several attacks on the new Freeport installations there before taking up the position of OPM regional commander.

In August 1994, two months before his brothers were arrested, Kelly Kwalik had initiated a new series of rallies and protests in Amungme villages in the valleys of Tsinga and Hoea to the east of the Freeport mine.

'No Amungme land is safe. No Amungme family can sleep easy,' Kelly Kwalik cried out to the crowd of one hundred or so men who had gathered in the steep, forested valley to raise the West Papuan independence flag, eat pig and bake potatoes in pits. 'The Indonesians will continue to dig our mountains, take our land and discard the people like dirt. Then they will move on to the next tribe, and then the next, until they have dug up every mountain and killed every Papuan from here to Papua New Guinea.'

There was plenty of support in these remote highland communities for Kelly and the rebels. Everyone was bitter about the mine and the aggressive military rule that had come with it. In Indonesia, the military was strict. The law stipulated, for instance, that anyone found raising the West Papuan flag was to be shot on sight. Eventually news of the demonstrations leaked out and it was suspected that Kelly and the rebels in the forest were planning an uprising.

Troops were ferried into the Tsinga and Hoea valleys by heli-copter to suppress the dissent. Hundreds of people fled into the forest and the army searched every corner of the villages, capturing anyone who remained, burning houses, destroying the gardens and looting the churches. In Timika and the resettlement camps the Papuans, particularly the Amungme, were under intensive surveil-lance. The army employed people to spy and inform on each other; checkpoints were set up to monitor their movements and many were detained, tortured or killed. While the people lived in fear, Kelly and his rebels were safe, hiding deep in the forest. They planned to demonstrate again on Christmas Day, this time right outside the Freeport mine.

After her first visit, Maria returned to the army post in Timika every day and asked to see her husband, but it was not until over a month later, on the 10 November, that she was given permission. He was sitting gaunt and yellow, shackled in the dust outside the container, holding a bloody cloth.

'This was drenched in my blood when they tortured me,' he cried, 'and now I am sure I have no hope of staying alive. I can't stand it!' Maria tried to comfort him although she was also crying. He pointed to a large bloody bandage on his calf. 'I tried to run away so they would shoot me rather than torture me but they shot me in the leg and dragged me back.' Before he could say more, soldiers surrounded Maria and told her to go home and come back in one week. When she and the other wives returned the containers were empty and the army said they knew nothing of the Kwalik brothers. Maria knew then that the men were dead.

More people were being rounded up, and Maria herself was soon taken.

'We have been told that you have connections with Kelly Kwalik and the rebels in the forest,' shouted an army corporal looking at his notebook. 'You give them salt, monosodium glutamate, blankets and sugar!'

'I don't know anything about this,' pleaded Maria. 'I only know the village people who hid in the forest when the army came to Hoea and Tsinga. Some of them have been resettled at the new transmigration camp. We asked them to become members of our community co-operative and, yes, we helped them with salt and blankets. In my culture we are taught to share if you have more than enough. That's true, but if you mention Kelly Kwalik and his men in the forest then I don't know about it.'

On Christmas morning 1994 it was clear and bright. A crowd of about three hundred people had gathered on the Freeport road wearing penis gourds, head dresses and leaves in their arm bands. They were singing, shouting, marching and dancing around a pole bearing the West Papuan flag and waving bows and arrows. It was not long before troops arrived on the scene.

'Don't shoot, don't shoot!' the men cried out. 'We have not come for a bloody war. We just want to speak to Freeport and government officials about our land rights.'

The army began shooting. Several people fell, while the rest scattered into the nearby forest. The rebels were chased and the army entered all the villages around the mine, breaking into the Christmas morning services and interrogating the congregations at gunpoint.

'How can there be three hundred rebels in this area if none of you are feeding them and collaborating with them?' demanded the regional commander of one church congregation. 'You will help us find these men or my soldiers will not be responsible for their actions.' For four hours the men, women and children were held. Among them were a group of eleven men who had come up from Timika by bus, a journey of about thirty miles along the Freeport road. When the congregation was finally released these men were worried that they would be late returning to their families. They hurried to the army post where the return bus would collect them. The soldiers were still tense and angry about the demonstration that morning. They checked the men's papers to see if they had the correct permits to allow them to travel outside their home area. Then they beat them, stripped them naked, stole their money and detained them in containers, accusing them of being rebels. By the afternoon, the soldiers had relaxed and agreed that the men should be allowed to return home.

The road from the mine to Timika passed through several army checkpoints. When they stopped at Mile 66 thirty new soldiers boarded the bus, separated the men and taped their hands. They knew now they were being taken for questioning at the army post in Timika and had heard stories of what went on there. As the bus continued down the winding mountain road one man tried to escape by wriggling through the window. The bus screeched to a halt and the soldiers ran after him as he staggered along the concrete. They shot him in the head then dumped his body down a ravine that was close to the edge of the road.

Those remaining on the bus were terrified. They were taken to the military base at Timika. They were ordered to confess that they were rebels. Their bodies were beaten with boots and their necks were beaten with sticks until several lay dead on the ground. The soldiers brought in black sheets to wrap up the bodies and the others were moved into the corridor while the soldiers mopped down the cell.

'I am not an educated person,' said one of men, weeping on his knees, 'nor am I a government official or a police or military man. Is that why my blood is regarded as animal blood? I tell you it is not animal blood, it is human blood. It is for my community that I am sacrificing this blood, for my children and grandchildren so that they can be "people" like other tribes.'

In the first days and weeks of 1995 many more men, women and even children were brought from surrounding villages to the army post for questioning. All were tortured until they confessed to being rebels. Back in the villages near the mine the people were angry and went to the commander of the army. He asked for proof that they had not been involved in the Christmas Day demonstration, so a group of them, armed with bows and knives, went into the forest and found some of the OPM rebels hiding. They caught one man and, although they knew him, they killed him, chopping his body into pieces and taking a portion of his arm to show the military commander and members of Freeport who had gathered to meet local representatives.

An elderly Amungme leader cried in grief and then began to talk: 'Everyday I ask God in my thoughts and prayers why He had to put these beautiful mountains on our land. And why there had to be so much richness inside to attract the army and Freeport and all the other outsiders who have come to use us and leave us suffering. I am old now. Many of the other elders who helped in those first surveys for Freeport are dead or very old like me. And you should be aware that we have received nothing from Freeport, except the suffering we have to deal with today. Why don't you just destroy us all? It is easier that way, then you can take everything. So it is true I am angry at God.'

He took his knife and offered it to the head of Freeport security. 'Go on, take it, kill me. Because I can't stand to see this suffering any more. Do it. Cut off my head. Chop my body in two and take out my stomach and put it with my head and cut the left half of my body and bury the pieces from here up to the Grasberg copper mountain and take my right side and bury the pieces along the road from here to Timika and the port. And on your way back round up all the people you have detained, and all the others still in the villages and those hiding in the forest and all our pigs and bury us in a huge hole and cover us up and then you can do anything you want.'

It was quiet for a while. Then the security chief thought of a way to defuse the situation. 'I, too, am a Christian and had a missionary education. Jesus, too, went through much suffering. He, too, was tortured and finally crucified. But he was never angry at anybody. Instead he loved and forgave those who hurt him. So for those people who have been detained and tortured, God is hearing their cries, you do not have to be angry for them.'

As 1995 progressed Kelly Kwalik and the OPM retreated while the military continued their crackdown in Hoea and Tsinga. Hundreds of innocent villagers were still hiding in the forests. There was little food or shelter and many were ill but they were too frightened to return to their army-occupied villages. On 31 May 1995 a small group of these families gathered, as they had every day for many months, to pray for safety in the uncertain times ahead. Unknown to them, soldiers from 752 Trikora battalion had found their remote forest location. As the people knelt in prayer the soldiers opened fire, killing eleven, including two women and three children.

Although our group knew there were serious troubles in Amungme villages adjacent to the Freeport mine we had not had access to Bishop Munninghoff's detailed report when we left for Indonesia in October 1995. One study site was Mapnduma, almost one hundred miles to the east of Freeport in the Nduga region. The advice from people on the ground was that this area had never been troubled by the military or the OPM and was safe and peaceful.

ONE

THE AMBUSH

I sat looking down the gorge from the bitter end of the grass airstrip.
It was my favourite place to come and think. Only five miles to
the north a sheer black megalith loomed over the valley. At over
14,000 feet it was just one peak among the mountains of New
Guinea, the most remote and unknown tropical region left on
earth. To the Nduga people of Mapnduma, it was a worthy home
for their ancestors. This morning it was free of cloud, proud and
forbidding in the bright sun.

A faint trace of smoke caught my eye, curling lazily upwards
from the forest high on the ridge above me. I nudged the naked
young boy sprawled out next to me. He was fiddling with the
material of my T-shirt, alternatively smoothing it and twisting it.
I pointed at the smoke, shrugged and looked as questioning as I
could.

For an instant he was puzzled, then he smiled. I pointed again
and there was a flash of understanding.

'*Mburo*,' he said quickly in the Nduga language. He laughed
excitedly. '*Nggwil purak mburo*.'

'Ah, *mburo*.' They were the local variety of sweet potato. I held
my fist to my mouth, chomping like a donkey. '*Wasing*,' I said,
diplomatically, 'delicious'.

The boy collapsed in a fit of giggles, and rolled about in the
grass.

I propped my chin on my hand again, crossed my legs and
looked back at the smoke. It was a strange place to be burning the
undergrowth to make a garden; surely too high to grow potatoes

– the soil would be too thin. Lower in the valley, the soil was much richer and thicker and, though the slope still looked too steep for cultivation, there were rows of perfect green dimples clinging to the sheer face of the mountain. Unlike Asian farmers, the Nduga did not hem their unstable hillsides with terraces, they buttoned them with heavy mounds.

I had worked in the gardens, in the scorching mid-day sun, digging with sticks and carrying mud in my bare hands. I had helped build and mould the mounds. Each was about three feet wide and protected the soil, and the potato plants, from being washed down the slope by the frequent rains. Every family had to make these gardens. An area of forest would be laboriously cleared and burned before the soil could be dug over. It was back-breaking work, but nobody who worked went without.

I heard singing and the swish of grass skirts on the steep path below. A group of women were climbing up to the village from their gardens on the slopes down by the thundering river below. String bags made from bark were suspended down their backs from straps stretched across their foreheads. They were bulging with potatoes, with *mburo*. I looked at my watch. It was half past eleven and still I was musing and worrying.

Walking back to the house, the smell of fresh bread drew me into the kitchen where two loaves were cooling on wire racks. There was no one about. Maybe a little indulgence would help me make my decision. Taking a thick slice topped with chocolate spread into the drawing room, I sank into the sofa and stared out of the large bay windows. It was like sitting in front of a wall-to-wall cinema screen.

A couple of men ran by with bows and arrows and went inside one of the village's huts. They were naked except for their penis gourds, the long narrow sheaths made from a yellowish local gourd that protected their masculinity. Like all the huts, this one was raised a few feet off the ground on stilts, with bark walls and a roof made from thick layers of palm leaves. Inside there would be a central fire, room for several bodies to sleep and, at the back, hutches for the pigs. It would be warm, dark and smoky. Just as it had always been.

The expedition house set us apart. It belonged to the missionaries who had worked in the village for thirty years. Over the decades tiny missionary aeroplanes had bounced on to the airstrip they had cut from the precipitous jungle and brought in tea cups, window panes and roses, kitchen sinks and coffee tables, solar panels, a wood-burning stove and a bathroom suite. From our haven of Western domesticity, only the primeval view from the window reminded me that I was in a different world.

I heard Bill coming down the stairs and I hastily hid the plate under the sofa and wiped my lips.

'I've been outside thinking, Bill,' I said.

'Well done.'

'About my dilemma.'

'No kidding.'

'How about if I go back over to the next valley, and repeat the tree surveys. Then I could double the data from that vegetation type. Do you think that would be enough to complete a statistically significant study?'

Bill, Anna, Annette and I had been working in the village of Mapnduma for eight weeks with several Indonesian and Papuan scientists. We were due to pack up and fly out in five days but I had weeks of research left to finish. I dearly wanted to stay longer but the others were ready to go. Somehow I had to cut my losses. But I didn't know where to cut. The more I worried the less I got done.

'Come on, Dan, the headman already told you that you can't go down there again,' said Bill exasperated. 'You'll cause mayhem if you do.'

I got up and paced the drawing-room floor. It was a very pleasant floor, panelled and polished. I had paced it many times that morning bothering people with my worries. Bill had already had his turn.

'What about the lowlands? Do you think I could get down there again in a day? I could get some more pictures of the birds of paradise. What do you reckon?' I paused. 'Or do you think I could stay on by myself for a bit, to finish off everything properly?'

Bill sighed. I might just have started to irritate him. 'For God's

3

sake, Dan, I couldn't give a shit,' he snapped. 'You sort it out, it's your bloody fieldwork.'

• The sudden whooping and howling from outside was a welcome distraction for both of us. There was constant fighting and arguing between families, clans and villages. It was the Nduga's favourite sport. Last week a man had allegedly dragged off a young woman into the forest where she had beaten him up when he had attempted to have sex with her. Her family demanded one of his family's pigs in apology. His family was furious and in turn demanded compensation for his wounds. It had almost started a war. The week before that the headman from the village up the valley had come to Mapnduma to debate the ownership of a piece of forest midway between the two villages. The argument had become very heated and ended in a fight between two of the men, and some of the women who had tried to stop them. Everyone had gone home in good spirits, pleased with the day's entertainment.

There was more whooping and I went to the window and peered out. About fifty men were running down from the ridge above, past our house and into the village. They had painted faces, pig tusks through their noses or feathers in their hair. They bristled with leaves and greenery stuffed into their arm and head bands. And each was armed with a bow and arrows or a machete.

I rushed to the chest, grabbed the video recorder and ran out of the door. Bill was ahead of me talking excitedly into his tape recorder.

'What's going on?' I called to him.

'Search me, they've gone up to the church, where the WWF guys are.' Three consultants from the Worldwide Fund for Nature and Unesco had arrived in the village two days before. Their team of three and our team of eleven combined to make more outsiders than most of the villagers had seen in their entire lifetimes.

'*Masuk*! *Masuk*! Get in!' a local man screamed in Indonesian. He was waving frantically and running towards our house. In the centre of the village, about a hundred yards away, the crowd of warriors had congregated. The clatter of arrows and stamping of feet filled the valley, sending clouds of dust into the bright haze of the day.

4

They began to chant and wail, jostling to attack. I had no idea what was going on but I went quickly back to the house.

Inside, Adinda and Lita, the two young Indonesian women on the project, were crying softly. Anna and Annette were standing at the bay window looking apprehensive but calm.

'It's okay, it's okay. It has nothing to do with us,' I said, although I was no longer so sure.

'Oh my God, they're coming over here.' Anna had paled. The man from the village who helped us with the cooking had found the keys and locked the door. We looked to him anxiously but he only shrugged his shoulders.

'Get upstairs,' Annette shouted. We all clambered after her to the bedroom where I stood behind the curtain, my video camera still recording. Men began to mass around the house. My mind raced and I scrunched my trousers, rubbing the sweat from my hands. Had they really come for us?

Reinforcements were pouring down from the ridge where I had noticed the smoke trails earlier. They ran straight across our garden, hooting and shrieking in unison, obliterating the fence, crumpling the flowers. They filtered in with the others until over a hundred of them were circling the house, smashing everything with machetes, rocks and axes.

There was a loud crack outside and a bullet whizzed straight through the wooden wall, just where I had been standing. It made a little patch of sun about a foot away from my head. I was outraged.

'Oh Lord Jesus, they have guns,' Lita whimpered in Indonesian.

'Get down, Dan!' shouted Annette.

I dropped to the floor and crawled to the middle of the room. We huddled together, whispering quietly and breathing noisily.

Surely they had not meant to shoot at us. It was probably a warning shot gone astray.

'Adinda, do they definitely know we're up here?'

'I don't know. I don't know. I think they saw me, at the window.' She was having difficulty breathing.

'Don't worry, they won't hurt us,' I said, holding her arm. I sounded more optimistic than I felt. During our time in Mapnduma we had been treated with the utmost respect and considered many of the local families as friends. But given the gunshot there was no doubt that this was the OPM, the guerrilla independence movement. It had no history of operating in this area but I knew it had attacked Indonesian civilians before.

We made a tangled heap in the middle of the floor, as far from the wooden walls as we could get. I tried to identify the limbs: Anna and Annette; Navy, Tessy, Lita and Adinda, the four Indonesian biologists. Shit, where was Bill? I couldn't remember if he had followed me back into the house. Was he inside when the door was locked? Maybe the OPM had already found him. Hopefully he was hiding somewhere in the village.

There was loud banging below. It sounded like the front door. Then talking and shouting. How many people were in the house? There were smashing sounds, possibly of furniture. We held our breath, straining to hear and identify the noises. They would find us soon and for the first time it crossed my mind that they might kill us.

I closed my eyes. The six of us were holding on to each other. I could smell sweat and fear. Could I hide, or fight or run?

The chanting in the garden was getting louder and louder. More people were inside. They were on the stairs now, shouting.

Then there was a crash against the door.

'They know we're in here; just let them in, let them in,' Anna screamed. Navy crawled over to the heaving door, shouted something in Indonesian, and then opened it.

I looked up and swallowed hard. Yudas was standing there in his tight shorts and green beret with a musty Second World War rifle in his hand.

'The bastard,' I whispered to myself. Then, 'Thank God.'

We knew this man. He had worked for us for almost four weeks. He had drunk coffee with Anna and Annette in the drawing room while identifying parrots and tree kangaroos from books. He had laughed and joked with Bill and me as we collected plants and counted trees in the forest. I knew he had worked for the OPM. But he knew us and he liked us.

His eyes now were wild but he was in control – he had the gun. He waved us downstairs with the barrel and the men behind him watched us carefully.

The drawing room was still. Chairs lay on their sides, books were scattered along the shelves and a mug, left over from breakfast, was smashed to pieces on the floor.

Outside, the seething crowd pressed against the door, jumping up at the windows and banging the walls. Their muffled clamouring seemed a world away from the cool calm of that room.

'*Ke luar.* Get outside,' ordered Yudas calmly in Indonesian.

Adinda began pleading but he grabbed her arm and threw her to the front of our group. '*Ke luar! Ke luar!*' This time he screamed, jabbing the gun close to my face. I turned my head away from the barrel and he fired between my feet. The crack ripped through the air and the smell of powder made me retch.

We pushed forward towards the door. Two men were holding it shut with their backs as the crowd heaved outside. Yudas shouted again and they manhandled us out on to the porch, a small roofed area with waist-high walls and two steps dropping down into the garden. Two OPM men were at the front holding Navy's and Adinda's wrists as if they were trophies. The shouting filled my head. A tangle of arms, reaching up from the crowd, tried to thump and grab us from our podium as we cowered, burying our heads, bunching together and crying out with each blow. A hundred lurid faces blurred around us with large, ecstatic eyes.

Navy and Adinda were being beaten, punched in the face. Adinda fell to the floor. And then men – I thought from our village – climbed into the porch area with us and on top of us and began fighting against the warrior group in front.

An old man, with a long twirly penis gourd and broken teeth, the headman from Kurukmu in the next valley, was holding my wrist, shouting hysterically to the crowd. I wrestled against him but then it dawned on me he was trying to help. Now more warriors were trying to climb into the porch but they were thrown down by our protectors.

7

The fighting was frenzied. A man pulled a hanging basket from the wall and hurled it towards us, sending hard clods of earth smacking across our faces, littering the floor with pansies. Small stones and rocks followed and then a machete slammed into the wood of the porch. There were several men holding them high in the air, about to charge. We screamed at them in terror, then fell to our knees, scrambling to hide among the legs of our bodyguards. A blade came down at speed towards Annette's shoulder, her face froze in horror and the edge stopped millimetres from her body. She grabbed me and I pushed closer to Anna covering my head with my hands. More people pushed forward, shouting and wailing, knives slashed the air and larger rocks landed around us. The chaos was coming closer and it seemed nothing and no one could stop it. I cringed, waiting for a blade or rock to make contact for the first time and braced myself for the pain.

Then Yudas towered above us again. We shouted up to him, begging that the crowd should not kill us. He began hammering our bodyguards away with the butt of his gun, beating them about the face and the hands. He shouted into the bedlam of the crowd and we were pulled down on to the granite flagstones of the garden.

We stood together, shaking and aching from exhaustion and fear. Some men ran in circles around us, dancing and jumping. Others cried orders, holding their bows high in the air. I looked up and saw Nlam. He had worked for me as a guide, and only days before I had helped him carry potatoes from his gardens as we talked innocently about our adventures in the forest. Now he had painted his body and face with soot, and daubed it with white streaks of mud. He seemed full of hate, hopping trance-like in a line of men on the low garden wall whose bows were primed and aimed directly at us. He turned to me and I tried to meet his eye but his glazed stare looked straight through me.

Suddenly, the crowd quietened and we shifted in the threatening silence.

'Will they kill us now? Is it now?' sobbed Lita softly. They tied our wrists tightly behind our backs with tree rattan and the cable from our radio relay station. They fumbled to remove our watches and jewellery and began to argue over them. Navy – his face bruised and cut – directed the women to the centre of the group so the men would take the brunt of any new attack. I searched for some strength to keep myself calm.

Then the marksmen on the wall began to whoop excitedly again. Others leapt up and joined the line, drawing arrows and priming their bows. Yet more began to stamp and cry, brandishing machetes and jerking them across their throats.

The mood of the crowd rose and fell in waves of nausea, and during these terrifying moments I saw Ayup, who I knew well, leap in front of the warriors. He stripped off his T-shirt and passionately threw open his arms. With tears pouring down his face he shouted: 'Kill me. Take me instead.' Philipus, the village preacher, was running among the crowd crying: 'Be calm and peaceful,' as the women and children of the village fled down to their gardens and the river.

The sky was filled with a swirling mass of black afternoon cloud, descending to cover first the high peaks of Dobo Koro, then Mount Canberra which towered above the village and, finally, the ridge above the house from where the men had come. The first drops of rain sizzled on the sun-baked flagstones and seemed to quench the mob. As it began to pelt on their bare skin, the men disbanded. Some sheltered in a long line under the narrow eaves of the house. Others brought out rain mats from their string bags and crouched under them in circles. The brave line of marksmen ran with their bows to the airstrip and the shelter of the huts. The driving rain drenched us, dribbled from our hair, and dripped from the tips of our noses. I sucked the cool water into my dry mouth and began to shiver in the sudden cold.

Yudas reappeared and motioned us inside with his gun. Relieved, we shuffled up through the porch and congregated, wet, miserable and silent, in the kitchen area. People were all over the house. We could hear them uprooting furniture and rustling through bags. Markus, Bram and Yakobus, the Papuan members of our team, had been hiding in the back rooms and were now led in.

✒ 'Where is Bill?' demanded Yudas. He had worked for Bill more than anyone and knew him best.

There were blank looks all round. 'He ran away, maybe. He was scared.'

Yudas shouted upstairs then one of his companions looked towards the room where Bill and I slept. He tried the handle but the door was locked.

'Open it!' Yudas screamed.

'We can't. It bolts from inside,' I said.

Yudas threw himself against it.

'No! I'll see.' I went up to the door, my hands still tied.

'Bill, are you in there?' We waited. 'Bill, they know you're in there. Come out now, it's safe.'

Seconds passed as I thought of him fleeing the village, running through the forest alone. The door clicked open and there he stood, pale, gaunt and trembling.

'What is it?' he stammered.

'It's okay, no one's hurt. We're all here.'

And with frightened eyes he joined us.

He had gone straight to the bedroom, tape recorder in hand, as the rest of us had run upstairs. The only place big enough to hide was under the bed among the dead cockroaches and banana skins. From there he heard the breaking of the house, the chanting outside and the screaming as we were attacked on the porch. He thought we had been murdered and that he was next.

Men were coming and going, stamping their wet feet across the mud-slicked floor. There seemed to be four leaders, including Yudas. The first, Murip, in green clothing and a tatty blue anorak, was standing in the far corner, watching us in satisfaction through beady eyes. One hand stroked his large furry beard while the other was in his pocket, helping to balance the rifle that was wedged under his arm and pointing to the floor. A small brown dog scampered over from the door and yapped up at him. He scooped it up and sat down with it on the sofa by the coffee table, propping the gun by the wall. In his jacket was a plastic bag filled with cash, probably ours. He pulled it out and counted through it, pencilling numbers into a scrappy Bugs Bunny exercise book.

Daud was the eldest and skinniest of the four. He hopped in the middle of the drawing room from leg to leg, waving his machete in one hand and a huge plume of black cassowary feathers attached to a loop of rubber tubing in the other. Grinning and humming, he continued his dancing well into the afternoon, stopping only occasionally to talk to Murip or the third leader, Silas.

This man strutted about the room giving everyone filthy looks. He wore a white balaclava and held a small knife, with serrations cut roughly from both edges. He looked the most aggressive and began to take charge of the afternoon's proceedings.

'Where are the guns?'

People had been searching the house for some time now. We explained there were no guns, but the searching continued as rooms that even we had never seen inside were smashed open.

'Where is the money?' was the demand, once the absence of firearms had been established. Annette described the hiding place, but the cash had already gone, into Murip's bag no doubt. Silas shouted furious orders to his lieutenant, who stood to attention with his long straight gourd pointing up and his white whistle dangling down around his bare chest. He trotted off, shouting and whistling, and minutes later, over at the airstrip, some thirty men stood in two lines being frisked in the rain. It was impressive. The lieutenant returned. None of his men had the money but heated accusations were being exchanged in every corner.

The old village chief with the twirly gourd, the one who had tried to protect us on the porch, came into the house. He held his right hand up and smiled bravely as blood ran down his arm and dripped from his elbow on to the slippery floor. His middle finger had come between the butt of Yudas's gun and the concrete floor of the porch. It was smashed to red pulp and he was looking for a knife. After some debate, Naftali the village nurse was called. There was no option but to chop it off, said Naftali, and the gathering audience agreed. They found the bread knife and we watched them flush the pieces down the sink.

Marc and Martha, a Dutch couple in their thirties, and Frank, a German, were led into the house. They were the Unesco and WWF representatives who had arrived in the village just two days before. They had not been tied and they positioned themselves at an obvious distance from us.

Fourteen of us now stood in the kitchen area, shivering and humiliated, watching the proceedings in dazed silence. Anna, twenty-one and the youngest of our group, was part hidden behind the fridge. Her beautiful, long dark hair and colourful braids were plastered against her face and she was peering over the top of her greasy, steamed-up glasses, which had slipped to the end of her nose. 'Are you cold? You can have my top when I get undone,' I whispered, feeling the need to be chivalrous. I began to wriggle my wrists and the tree rattan came apart easily.

'No, no, really, don't worry.' She forced a smile, snivelling and shaking her head.

Some friendly village men loosened our bonds and looked at us kindly.

'Where's Annette?' I asked.

She heard her name and glanced up from behind Tessy's legs on the kitchen floor where she had sat down. Her eyes were wet and bloodshot. I think she had been crying. Her hand slid out from behind her back and wiped away some grit from her face then quickly returned. She had got loose too.

Bill was standing at the end of the kitchen. His brow was furrowed and his chin rested on his hand as he stroked his pursed lips. I tried to catch his eye but he was staring anxiously into oblivion.

Navy stood proudly, though one eye was swollen and bloody where he had been hit. Adinda's face was buried in his chest. Lita and Tessy were whispering to each other but they were clearly still very scared. Bram and Markus were standing separately with their heads bowed. Yakobus, I could no longer see anywhere. We waited.

Philipus, the preacher and our host in the village, was tied up like us. As we stood unmoving he began to whimper on the far side of the room. He curled himself into the corner, his head wrapped in his arms. He wept, ashamed that he had been unable to protect his guests. He cried for everything he had wanted for his village. He grieved for his people and the tragedy that was to unfold.

TWO

PREPARATIONS

One August morning, with the sky a deep blue and the day already hot, I spread out my Ordnance Survey map and scanned it for new places to visit. A few miles away, in the folds of the nearby Downs, there were burial mounds in woods on the side of a hill. Packing sandwiches, I pedalled off on my bicycle in search of these mysterious and lonely antiquities. But the woods were filled with picnic makers and the burial mounds were strewn with litter. There was no splendour and I left feeling sad

Set well back from the track was a rickety old gate. A sign had been nailed to the wooden bars with Keep Out scrawled on it in red paint. I dropped my bike in the hedgerow and climbed over. The overgrown path took me deeper and deeper into the woods. The smell was dank and earthy. Light filtered down through the leaves, dappling the soft needle floor. I was surrounded by old and magnificent yews. I walked further, then I sat down. The trees seemed to hold me in a spell. I felt I belonged to something lost and ancient and I was filled with serenity.

I never stopped searching for that feeling. On holidays and at weekends I would pour over my maps and go walking, cycling and camping with friends. We would explore old ruins, climb church towers or just sit at the top of the highest hills. Meanwhile, at school, I worked with a vengeance, determined to achieve the best. After sixth form, I set off for Romania to cycle across the Transylvanian Alps before deciding to raise funds to join a conservation and community project in Uganda. Two months later I had two and a half thousand pounds and stood at Heathrow airport laden down with fifty kilograms of luggage and A levels in maths, physics and chemistry. The mountains, forest and people of Uganda were a revelation to me. I walked alone in the rainforest, I break-fasted with chimpanzees and felt at one with nature.

My most lasting memory of Uganda was of the Ruwenzori mountains, the Mountains of the Moon and the true source of the River Nile. In an awe-inspiring fortnight I climbed up through lush tropical foothills, across vast alpine swamps, past lakes by which plants grew to freakish proportions, until I reached the shrouded peaks. As the clouds cleared, I stood astride the equator on a pile of snow; gazing out on Lake Victoria and the Indian Ocean to the east, the Congo basin to the west.

In October 1992 I began my first year at Cambridge and forgot Uganda in the social whirl. By the end of the year, I had split up with my girlfriend, wasn't sure who my friends were and found my course a torment. Cambridge, which had seemed so large and impressive, was shrinking rapidly around me. As claustrophobia set in, I remembered the incredible equatorial snow-capped mountains.

Equatorial snow-capped mountains. I wondered if there were many more in the world. From Africa on page thirty-seven I followed the equator east across the Indian Ocean until I came to the island of New Guinea. The eastern half made up the independent country of Papua New Guinea but the western part, Irian Jaya, was the most easterly province of Indonesia, a band of equatorial islands forming a country wider than the United States. Irian Jaya looked about the size of France but seemed to be almost entirely covered in forest with few roads or towns. There were plains and hills to the north, swamps to the south, and rising between them the backbone of New Guinea, a mountain range which reached 16,400 feet. That had to be high enough for snow, even on the equator.

The encyclopaedia had a picture. The glaciated top of Mount Jaya towered above mist-filled ridges and steep, forested valleys that fell away into thick lowland jungle and crocodile-infested man-grove swamps, down to the Arafura sea. It was the highest peak in south-east Asia and in its shadow were some of the richest mineral deposits in the world and many distinct tribal peoples. I was spellbound.

I spent several wet afternoons in February 1994 searching the University library's book stacks to find out what conservation work was being carried out in the area. There didn't seem to be a lot published about Irian Jaya, or Dutch New Guinea as it had been known. Only when rummaging through old Worldwide Fund for Nature (WWF) reports did I, at last, find something concrete. WWF had been working in Irian Jaya for over ten years and had proposed a series of National Parks to cover some of the most outstanding areas of natural diversity. The maps showed various large blobs and there was a small description and bibliography on each proposed site. All the areas looked interesting, but the most impressive was Lorentz, a huge area eighty miles square running from Mount Jaya and the craggy mountain range in the north right down to the coast in the south. With so many different physical environments packed into such a small area, it was suggested that Lorentz contained more ecological zones and more different species than any other comparable region on earth. I knew a little about New Guinea's flora and fauna already: spectacular birds of paradise and bower-building birds, giant nest-building turkeys, tree-dwelling marsupials, carnivorous pitcher plants. But in the Lorentz area little biological work had been carried out since it had first been explored in 1911 when Dr H. A. Lorentz himself had tried to conquer the eternal snows. Since then the area had remained one of the least known tropical regions in the world.

I rang WWF in Geneva that afternoon and persuaded the librarian to send over the most recent reports on Lorentz. Environmental threats included logging, petroleum exploration and the huge US-based Freeport mine under Mount Jaya. WWF were trying to secure conservation status for the area and were also hoping to involve the local communities in the long-term management of the land. Missionaries had been in contact with most of the tribes since the 1960s but access was difficult: by light aircraft in the highlands or canoe in the southern planes. According to WWF, the remote terrain and the lack of good biological data was hampering the area's formal protection.

I began looking into the possibility of organizing a small team of biologists to carry out some much-needed research in Lorentz. My uncle, who had worked at the British Embassy in Jakarta some years before, was enthusiastic but he warned me that Indonesia was steeped in bureaucracy and that official application procedures were lengthy, especially for foreigners. I would need a great deal of patience and determination. I visited specialist libraries in London and began talking to people, organizations and institutes which had links with Irian Jaya. It was an incredible place, they said, and it badly needed more study. The problem was that nobody could get in to do it. For several decades Indonesia had kept much of the interior closed off to all but the missionaries, mining companies and the military.

Irian Jaya, its geography, flora and fauna, was, quite literally, a continent apart from the rest of Indonesia, lying on the Australian tectonic plate, separate from the continent of Asia. Its people, the Papuans, dark skinned and curly haired, had more in common with the aborigines of Australia than the lighter-skinned, straight-haired Malays of south-east Asia. The Indonesian government, 2,500 miles away in Jakarta, claimed that as part of the Dutch colonial empire Irian Jaya now formed a natural part of Indonesia. But Dutch New Guinea and the Dutch East Indies had been separate colonies. After the Second World War when the Netherlands finally ceded the Dutch East Indies, Dutch New Guinea was withheld and prepared for self-rule as West Papua. Indonesia, rapidly becoming the fourth most populous country on earth, was furious, and the UN declared that a plebiscite should be held to determine the Papuans' view. Sadly, this 1969 UN Act of 'Free' Choice provided no choice at all. It is well documented that many of the 1,025 representatives who were chosen to represent the one million West Papuans were threatened by the Indonesian military who were already well established in the region. With communism sweeping Asia, and lucrative mineral opportunities to be found in West Papua, the United States sided with the Republic of Indonesia and pressured the United

Nations to ignore any anomalies in the Free Choice vote. The fate of the West Papuans was legally sealed and Indonesia renamed their land Irian Jaya, the Victorious Hotland.

The Papuans resisted. The OPM (Organisasi Papua Merdeka or Free Papua Movement) was formed, but their bow-and-arrow resistance had little positive effect. Unable to distinguish between rebel and civilian, the military strafed, napalmed and bombed entire villages over large regions. Thousands, possibly ten of thousands, were killed; thousands more fled to Papua New Guinea as refugees, and detentions, torture and terror became commonplace. Nevertheless, a decade on, the army still had not quelled the insurgency. In the early 1980s the government adopted a new policy known as the Smiling Campaign. The air attacks were stopped and development projects were slowly introduced to the remote tribal interior using the missionary networks and infrastructure already in place. At the same time a transmigration programme funded by the World Bank was promoted as bringing the benefits of Javanese civilisation and progress to the primitive Papuans. The programme aimed to take over five million people from Java, by then the most crowded place on earth, and resettle them in other parts of Indonesia. Irian Jaya was a major target, along with other provinces which opposed the rule of the Java-dominated state. Many saw transmigration as a disguised invasion force. If so, it was one of the largest in history.

I was angered by what I learnt but those I talked to seemed to think Irian Jaya was becoming more peaceful and open. Transmigration had only had limited success. There had been little activity from the OPM for over ten years and the government was much less sensitive about foreigners working in the area. There was even some tourism: the Baliem valley in the highlands, which had been at the heart of many uprisings in the late 1970s, had now become an exotic destination for foreign travellers keen to trek and to meet the Dani tribe, a remote highland people, noted for their ritual warfare and elaborate gardens.

I was convinced that a small team of biologists could be highly effective in documenting the presence of rare or threatened species.

This data would support the area's conservation status and help protect the lands and forests of the indigenous communities. If the team had an Indonesian and Papuan component it might initiate a programme of long-term work and raise awareness within Indonesia about the area and its people. To work safely and effectively the project would have to be meticulously planned, and to gain the permits and funds it would need unprecedented support. As the first half of 1994 proceeded I amassed reports, sent letters and met more people. It became clear that if I was serious I would have to fly to Indonesia itself. In late June I boarded a plane to Jakarta with briefcase in hand. The plan for the project had evolved. It had a name – Lorentz 95 – and its first objective: fish. No one had studied the highland rivers of Irian Jaya and there were likely to be new species or those of conservation significance. The Director of the Indonesian Institute of Biology was a fish specialist and it was this institute that I hoped would sponsor our research.

'Out of the question,' said the Director leaning back in his chair behind a heavy cloud of clove cigarette smoke. He picked up my name card and stared at it again. 'I am afraid, Mr Start, you must chose another location in Indonesia for your work. Sulawesi is a very nice place, with very interesting fish, perhaps. Java is also nice, and there you have no problem from strange food.'

We sat at a table in the middle of the bare-walled room as typewriters clattered and a brown Bakelite telephone rang un-answered on his table. I straightened my back and gave him a determined stare. He had to be impressed that I had come all the way from Britain to see him. 'I am only interested in Irian Jaya,' I said simply. I added some facts about the importance of the fish in the region.

He explained that no one had been to the area, not even Indonesians.

I explained that I would have Indonesian colleagues from Jakarta and Irian Jaya.

He looked glumly at the telephone then back at me. 'Okay,' he said, 'I will raise your proposal with representatives from the military next week. Depending on their response, the Institute of Biology may back you, but only if I meet your Indonesian team before you leave.'

I walked down the corridor elated. But hunched in the back of a tiny three-wheeled scooter taxi, I worried about finding this team of Indonesian scientists. I had only three weeks to do it.

We bounced along the pot-holed roads, careering around corners and between lines of traffic as I directed the driver through the back streets, my finger tracing the route on my city map. Finally, I unfolded myself from the taxi and walked down a series of alleys. The houses were identical two-storey breeze-block boxes, rows and rows. I was staying in one with an Indonesian family whose thirteen-year-old son was due to be circumcised in a fortnight. They were organizing the traditional party that accompanied the event. Everyone was very excited.

'Mr Daniel, Mr Daniel, please excuse my family they have come for the party,' my landlady said as she stirred two huge vats of noodles simultaneously, a long wooden spoon in each hand. 'They were worried about getting lost on the way to the house and so they decided to leave early.'

I couldn't believe it. They lived sixty miles outside Jakarta: a day's bus journey at the most. They had arrived almost two weeks too early. At least twenty of them. The two-bedroom house was filled with frenetic children and hobbling grandparents. The heat was oppressive and the smell from the lavatory was starting to rise. I needed a drink.

From the telephone kiosk down the road I called an old friend of my uncle. He took me out to a downtown bar where dancing girls served the local Bintang beer in huge pitchers. We joined a table of middle-aged expatriates. Among them was a young man of about my age. James had organized a university expedition to a remote island only a few hundred miles from Irian Jaya. Due to leave for the field later in the week, he and his team would spend three months in the forest making zoological surveys. I told him my story and he suggested that I join him at a meeting with a small conservation organization based in southern Jakarta. There, he said,

I would find excellent biologists, all young, experienced and highly motivated. They were the type of people who would be running Indonesia's National Parks and wildlife sanctuaries within a couple of years.

We arrived at BScC, the Biological Sciences Club, late the next afternoon, and scrambling over piles of concrete and rubble made our way into the main office. A family of terrapins swam in a fractured aquarium, held together with sellotape and balanced precariously on a pile of books. Curling posters of parrots and orangutans covered the open cracks in the walls and large brown stains on the ceiling oozed a sticky-looking fluid. We took our seats at a table with various members of the BScC. A large man in his late twenties, with thick glasses, strode across, plonked down some papers and shook our hands. 'Navy W. Th. Panekenan, International Liaison Officer. Good afternoon,' he said.

After James had conducted his business I introduced myself. When Irian Jaya was mentioned there was a good deal of murmuring. I pulled a map from my bag and laid it over the coffee cups scattered across the table. It was the US Air Force map from 1964 and huge swathes of land were marked 'Relief Unknown'. I began to explain my ideas for Lorentz 95 as Navy translated my speech, waving a ruler around and conducting the crowd that was growing around us. I began to describe the tribal regions. The northern tribes were highlanders: the Amungme in the north-east near the Freeport mines and the Nduga in the north-west, closer to Wamena and the Baliem valley. The southern tribes were coastal people: the Sempan to the south-west and the Asmat to the south-east.

Navy was peering over the map, his nose about an inch from the surface. 'Well, we should stay away from Freeport,' he said, leaning back in his chair, wiping his glasses with his T-shirt. 'That would leave the Nduga or Asmat regions.' He looked to me for confirmation and I knew the project was sold.

In broken Indonesian and English we talked into the night. James had left hours before. People came and went, the ashtrays filled and more coffee cups accumulated. BScC had been carrying out conservation and community projects in Indonesia for twenty years but they had never worked in Irian Jaya. There was great enthusiasm and they wanted to add bird, plant and community studies to the highland fish research. It was about ten o'clock, while I was saying my goodbyes, when a tiny, quietly spoken, young woman asked, 'Do you think it is a safe place to work?' She stood peering primly at me over her gold-rimmed spectacles with her hands clasped behind her back. She looked about fifteen, but I was told she was twenty-four. This was my introduction to Adinda.

'I think so,' I answered. I had no reason to suppose otherwise.

I wandered out into the alley and was engulfed by the pungent night air. I considered Adinda's comments again. There was the serious danger of breaking a leg miles from anywhere. And there were disturbances at Freeport. But far to the east, one hundred miles from Freeport, would there really be a threat from the people and the OPM? After all, we would be there in support of them, not against them. The issue disappeared from my mind as I saw a bus and ran frantically up to the otherwise deserted main road waving my arms in the air. I jumped on as it rattled to a momentary stop beside me, revving furiously. The twelve-year-old conductor tapped the roof, I put my feet up on the seat in front and the tungsten grey suburbs of Jakarta streamed past.

During my weeks in Jakarta I worked myself into oblivion. I would rise at 4.30 every morning and would not return home until 10.00 at night, my time filled with meetings, telephone calls, socializing in clubs and bars and visits to libraries and BScC. I survived on adrenalin. I discussed research ideas at university departments; visited ferry companies, airlines and the Mission Aviation Fellowship; met with Freeport, the Forestry Department, WWF, and tracked down anyone who had ever set foot in Lorentz. People were interested but they were also wary. 'This is a very difficult place to work. You will never get the permits,' they said.

With a week remaining of my stay in Jakarta, it had become apparent that I would have to fly to Jayapura, the capital of Irian Jaya itself. It was an eight-hour flight across azure seas and the 13,677 islands of the Indonesian archipelago. I touched down among green hills and rainforests on the northern coast of New Guinea. Smiling Papuan faces greeted me at the tiny airport and it felt like I had returned to Africa. I had arrived on a Friday and by the end of Saturday I had met people from Cenderawasih (literally Bird of Paradise) University, the Forestry Department, WWF and the regional government. Many of the top positions were held by Papuans but the soldiers and policemen were all Indonesian.

On Sunday when everything was closed I escaped to a beach several miles up the coast. There were palm trees, a coral reef and a couple of Papuan families collecting driftwood. Unfortunately, an unpleasant fat Indonesian businessman decided to befriend me. All of Irian Jaya belonged to him, he explained, while scratching his crotch. The natives were just an embarrassment now that development had come. He began shouting angrily at the Papuan women and children nearby: 'Clear off! Get off the beach! Can't you see we don't want savages near us?' He waddled after them and tried to hit one but he was too slow. I felt deeply ashamed to be associated with him. During my time in Jakarta I had grown to like the generosity, warmth and hospitality of the Indonesians. I returned to Jakarta the next day angry that this man had discoloured my rosy picture.

The board of BScC had met several times to discuss their involvement in Lorentz 95. Navy had been appointed as Indonesian coordinator of the joint BScC–Cambridge project. I was pleased. He seemed someone who would get things done. We agreed that the project should have four components: botany, ethnobotany, zoology and ethnozoology. We would work using conventional methods to sight birds and mammals, study fish and collect flowering plants; and we would complement each of these surveys with a study of traditional knowledge, working with the Nduga to document their nomenclature, knowledge and use of the plants, animals and forest around them. Here was a unique opportunity to compare western science and concepts with those of an ancient culture.

Adinda Saraswati, the woman who had asked about safety, was experienced in aquatic studies and was to work on the fish project.

She also happened to be Navy's girlfriend. The others on the team were Matheis Yosias Lasembu, or 'Tessy' an ornithologist and Navy's field partner, and Lita Tanasale, an ethnobotanist. A few days before I was due to fly home we visited the Institute of Biology with our plan to work in the Nduga region of Lorentz. The Director offered the full support of his institute. All he needed to begin the permit application process, he explained, was a full proposal, proof of funding, details of the full British team and references from leading professors in our field. The sooner all that could be arranged the better, as the permit application process could take up to a year.

I returned to Britain overcome by exhaustion and my body erupted in boils. I felt nauseous at the slightest thought of Irian Jaya and I could not bring myself to talk about my time in Indonesia. I was sure my dream would be crushed by the enormity of the task ahead, despite the progress I had made. I slept for a week and then, in a state of rebellion, spent the summer working for a petroleum company whose fuming juggernauts, sprawling refineries and contaminated effluent were blissfully removed from the virgin forest of Irian Jaya. By the end I felt the old enthusiasm stirring again. I returned for my final year in Cambridge and converted my bedroom into an office, installed telephone lines, computer, e-mail, fax machine, printer and answerphone. I set up shelves for the large library of reports and books that had accumulated and soon there was headed notepaper and envelopes. I printed a hundred fluorescent posters advertising the expedition and plastered them around the university. Application forms were sent out and people interviewed.

Bill Oates, a final-year botanist, was the first to join the British team. He was a tall Scotsman, with hazel eyes and short brown hair, who in his own words had 'lived on a farm in the borders all my life, putting up fences, milking cows, so consider myself to be of a practical nature'. He seemed friendly, reliable, of a basically conservative and serious disposition and, most importantly for the project, he had a rigorous scientific mind. We set to work immediately, contacting professors at the Royal Botanic Gardens at Kew.

There was a good deal of enthusiasm and we were thrilled when the Director, Professor Sir Ghillean Prance, agreed to be the British patron. Bill and I drew up methodologies, prepared budgets and began drawing up the thirty-page preliminary proposal. We worked well together and made rapid progress. Each morning I would cycle madly through Cambridge, scarf flapping in the wind. Grabbing the cold toast from my front basket I would run up to the top of the Old Cavendish for my lectures, and by quarter past eleven I was home, ready to begin correspondence and telephone calls. Bill would usually call by after lunch to discuss the day's business.

'Dan, when are we going to choose the other two team members?' he asked one day as we sat drinking coffee on the lawns of Emmanuel College. 'We've got to apply for those permits soon and start the fund-raising. If you don't like any of the ones you interviewed what about someone from the third-year ecology or zoology courses?'

'Do you know many of them?' I asked. 'They do need to be female. There's no way we're going there with an all-male team.'

He fell back laughing. 'I don't believe you. You can't be serious?'

'Come on, Bill, we need a mixed team. The female Nduga hold certain cultural knowledge and the males other knowledge. There's no way the local women will talk to us. You know all this. Anyway, it makes the whole project more balanced.'

Bill shrugged his shoulders and then looked at his watch. 'Shit, Dan, I've got to go, I'm late for rowing, they'll kill me.' He had scooped up his papers and was already away.

'Go and sort out some girls who want to go to Irian Jaya,' I shouted to him as he ran off across the grass. 'And make sure they're good looking.'

Annette van der Kolk was the first person Bill introduced to me. She had short dark hair and shining brown eyes.

'This is worse than a job interview. How much do I get paid?' she teased. 'No, you're right, I understand what you're saying about commitment. I'm on top of my degree and I've got time this year. I want to get some experience of field biology and I'm very interested in New Guinea. When Bill asked me, I couldn't believe it. I've been really excited all day. If you decide you want me, I'll take twenty-four hours to reply. And you can trust the answer because I'm not in the habit of letting people down.'

We talked about her dissertation on freshwater mussels and then moved on to the possibility of her studying highland fish. Like Bill, she was rigorous in her scientific approach, showing sparks of considered enthusiasm. She had experience of overseas conservation work and of fund-raising. She was perfect for the job.

I saw two other undergraduates before I met Anna McIvor. She arrived out of breath, in a long patchwork dress with three juggling clubs sticking out of her knapsack. She had been earning some money that afternoon making hair braids for the tourists and had several in her long flowing hair. She was slightly plump, full of smiles, and immediately likeable.

'Would you like a cup of tea?' I asked.

'Er, no,' she said eyeing a box of crunchy oat breakfast cereal left on the table since the morning, 'but can I possibly ask for some of those?'

'These?' I said surprised. 'I'll just wash up a bowl.'

'No, no, it's okay. I don't need milk.' She smiled, took the packet, rummaged inside and began crunching, dropping crumbs everywhere.

Anna was Annette's dissertation partner and it seemed they already worked well together. They had spent many hours standing in cold murky fen water up to their waists collecting mussels. We talked about the expedition. She was warm and impassioned and it became clear that it was the people of Irian Jaya, the Papuans, that drew her most to the project.

I got up and went to the library shelves in the office and came back with a thick report.

'These are Nduga language sheets. I borrowed them from the missionary office in Jakarta. They were typed up in the late 1960s by the first linguist to work in the area. She worked mainly with the missionaries getting the Bible translated into written Nduga. It has never been a written language, of course. It's all done phonetically. There's enough stuff here to begin learning the language so that we can at least get by when we arrive.'

We looked at the faint blue type on the fading yellow paper.

'*Mburu nere-o*' equals 'I am hungry for sweet potatoes.'

'*Angga wene mbi jakyndejag-o*' means 'I want to teach you some Bible verses.'

Anna laughed. 'I won't be doing that. Juggling maybe, Bible verses, no.'

'There are Indonesian speakers as well in the main village of Mapnduma,' I said. 'There's a small school there and some have worked at the Freeport mines.' I paused. 'Would you like to be responsible for learning Nduga, and for coordinating the people-oriented research?'

She pondered the question for a moment. 'You think I should?' she asked tentatively.

'Not should, *want*. Do you want to?'

Her face lit up and she smiled as she nodded. 'I'd love to.'

I gave her some language sheets and she went off down the stairs, muttering Nduga to herself. It was clear that Bill, Annette, Anna and I were very different people. Bill and Annette would be good at keeping the project firmly down to earth and the scientific side on track, while Anna and I were inclined to work with the people and be a little more flexible. I hoped it would be a good balance.

It was in December 1994 that we first heard from Adriaan and Elfrieda van der Bijl, the resident missionaries in the Nduga region of Lorentz. Their letter was the beginning of much correspondence. These extraordinary people had lived and worked in the Nduga areas for over thirty years and they told us about food, language, air transport, accommodation and, of course, the people themselves, with whom they had discussed our plans. As for safety, they said there would be no problems. With the assurance of the van der Bijls, and with all the advice I had gathered in Indonesia and Britain, I was confident that we had chosen a peaceful place to work.

Other letters began arriving from institutes in America, Australia, Indonesia and the UK supporting our objectives. The British

Ambassador in Indonesia suggested that he might visit the team in the forest, during his forthcoming visit to Irian Jaya in early 1996. We received a letter from the Director of the Indonesian Institute of Sciences offering his personal patronage. I even met representatives of HRH the Duke of Edinburgh, the Chancellor of Cambridge University, and answered their questions as eloquently as I could. The Chancellor also agreed to give his patronage to the project, which was a very rare honour. With all this support behind us, we began writing our final proposal, full of explanations, references, quotes and pictures. It had to secure our permission from Indonesia, convince us and everyone else that we were immaculately prepared, and raise at least £20,000 in six months.

Christmas came and went and I returned to Cambridge on 2 January 1995. The college was bleak and deserted with just the porters and their jokes for company. I sat in my cold room wrapped in my coat and scarf, trying to catch up on my academic work. Thankfully our fund-raising campaign was beginning to pay off. The local printer agreed to produce our proposals in colour, free of charge, British Airways sponsored Club Class flights, Phillips donated VHF walkie-talkies and a relay station, Becco sponsored powerful solar panels. We won a Winston Churchill Memorial Fellowship, the top Royal Geographical Society award and a top British Petroleum conservation award. The bank balance grew, but so did the budget.

Although we were science undergraduates, we still needed to learn as much as possible about the specific methods we would be using. Anna attended a course in Edinburgh about anthropological techniques, Annette and I attended training days with BirdLife International and the Royal Geographical Society in London, and Bill learnt about plant-collecting techniques at Kew. Slowly we began to feel confident that we could carry out the work professionally.

Although money and support were under control, the team was now spread across three continents – Europe, Asia and Australasia – and it was far less manageable.

'I *have* been trying to fax BScC,' I said to anyone in the room who was still listening. It was a Friday night in Cambridge and we were having our bi-weekly meeting in my room. Anna was in the corner doodling. Bill sprawled on the bed staring intently at the ceiling. Annette was on the edge of her chair, legs crossed, with an elbow on one knee and her last cigarette between her fingers. Her packet had run out, and I was partly responsible, much to her annoyance. I knew that she wouldn't have much staying power now. Annette and Bill had been bullying me because we had had no communication from BScC for over a month. Communication with Jakarta was definitely my responsibility, but I wasn't prepared to let it be all my fault.

'I've been faxing them, and writing, and Charles saw them.' Charles, my uncle, went to Jakarta regularly and was meeting with the team on our behalf. 'And they still haven't sent me anything.'

'Well, telephone them instead,' said Annette. 'We need to know what's going on out there. I mean, when are those permits going to come through?'

'Telephone them?' I was shocked. 'Do you know how much it costs to telephone Indonesia? £1.20 per minute. That's £20 for a short chat.'

'Or 2p per word. Look, we've got £18,500 in the bank,' said Bill. He was the treasurer. 'Get on the phone and find out what's going on.'

Anna, Annette, Bill and I had all evolved different ways of expressing our dissatisfaction with each other, although they were usually fairly united against me. Anna hated any confrontation and would withdraw when she was upset. Annette would be civil, although there would be something derisory and short in her tone. Bill was straightforward. He told me what he thought pretty quickly. I had such high ideals that I was always dissatisfied. At times I was bossy and unappreciative and would become the common enemy, but I told myself it was a form of team bonding between the three of them.

Communication with Indonesia improved as soon I picked up the telephone and spoke directly with Navy. He was a brilliant and highly motivated leader. I had originally wanted the Indonesian coordinator to be a Papuan but it was soon clear that so much of the political clearance came from Jakarta that without a strong Java-based team we would have little hope of succeeding. Nevertheless, the Papuan team was evolving well. I had met Markus Warip, an anthropology lecturer at Cenderawasih University during my brief visit to Irian Jaya in 1994. Since then he had written many times asking to join the expedition. Abraham Wanggai, or Bram, from the Forestry Department, had been nominated by his boss. It was important for the Forestry Department to be involved as ultimately they were responsible for conservation areas in Indonesia. Yakobus Wandikbo had been recommended by the missionaries as an Nduga, born in Mapnduma, but who had graduated in anthropology from Cenderawasih University. With his knowledge of the area and people he would be a great asset.

With finals approaching, Lorentz 95 was at last looking solvent after fifteen months of planning. My degree was in a much less healthy state. The expedition was put on hold while reading lists and journals piled up around me and I was haunted by the image of freshly printed exam papers in an echoing hall. I was a biologist turned neurobiologist. The subject, as many people were quick to point out, was not closely related to ethnobotany but I felt that it bred a professional attitude fundamental to the success of any biological work. I graduated among friends and family on a hazy day in late June and the college emptied. The four of us stayed on in Cambridge to continue fund-raising and preparations, collecting together almost £10,000 worth of expedition equipment, from silica gel and sleeping bags to global positioning units and walkie-talkies.

Shortly after we celebrated the arrival of our permits from the Institute of Biology, I noticed a paragraph in *The Times* reporting that the army had shot dead eleven civilians gathered for prayer in the forest near Freeport in the Amungme tribal region. We wondered if it would affect our chances of obtaining security clearance from the military but believed Freeport was far enough away to have little effect on our area. For final approval of our plans we would have to wait until we reached Jakarta.

On 9 October 1995, a convoy of cars packed with boxes, ruck-sacks and family arrived at Heathrow. As I stood at the barrier to passport control, saying my goodbyes, I realised, looking back on almost two years of hard work, that I was very proud. Not so much of what had been achieved, but of the sheer dedication against such difficult odds.

'Good luck with Jakarta,' said my uncle and I knew what he meant. Until we had actually landed on the tiny grass airstrip in Mapnduma, we couldn't be sure of anything. I had dreamt of that flight into Mapnduma many times. The flight back home again, however, had never entered my imagination. Life after the expedition was a haze. Lorentz 95 was my springboard out of university and into the real world. I didn't know where it would take me, but I was confident that it would be just right.

The jumbo jet taxied into Jakarta airport in the late evening. The rarefied atmosphere met a wave of heat and humidity at the aircraft door. I clanked down the metal steps and strode across the tarmac, avoiding the oily puddles, towards the luminous baggage reclaim hall. With six baggage trolleys loaded, and all the formalities over, we took a deep breath and headed into the din of the public arrival hall. There was just a tiny passage through the crowd of clamouring and shouting people. I searched frantically among the cardboard plaques for 'Cambridge', 'Lorentz 95', anything.

'Has anyone seen them yet?' I called back to Bill, Anna and Annette. 'You know what Navy looks like don't you? Big guy, glasses.'

'Eh, mister, you want taxi?' a voice whispered in my ear.

'No, thank you,' I replied firmly.

'Eh, you sure? Good price, good taxi. I no cheat you.' The man began tugging at my arm. I could see him smirking out of the corner of my eye.

'We have friends meeting us. Go away.' I kept going. I didn't trust taxi men and I was growing anxious at the thought of our valuable baggage among all these strangers.

'Friends? They good friends? They want taxi, too?'

That was it. I turned to shout at him but he was laughing. The bastard was laughing at me.

'It's me. It's me,' the man said, patting his chest.

I stared hard at him. He stopped laughing and looked innocently at me.

'It's me, Navy.'

'Shit. Navy!' He had lost about two stone and wore no glasses. It had been over a year. 'Am I glad to see you. Guys, look, this is Navy. Meet Navy.'

'So Navy,' I continued, 'you have a good taxi business?'

'For my friends, I have a very good fleet of taxis,' he chuckled and led us over to the waiting cars.

Early the next day we met Tessy, Lita and Adinda as well. We were jet lagged and exhausted but Navy had already arranged the day's activities. I was due to go to the Police Department to arrange some permits and Tessy, who knew the procedure, would show me how it was done. Tessy and Navy had been friends and field partners for many years but were very different characters. While Navy was tall and heavy; Tessy was short and skinny. Navy loved to be in control and make decisions, Tessy preferred to work behind the scenes. Navy could brag and boss; but Tessy was shy and unassuming. Navy had excellent command of English; Tessy knew about three words.

'Eh, *you . . . like . . . pop music?*' he asked.

We were sitting on the back seat of a bus. It belched smoke outside and smelt of rotting melons within.

'*Kadang-kadang,*' I said. 'Sometimes.' I flicked hurriedly through the pages of my pocket dictionary searching for 'it depends'.

'*Ter . . . gan . . . tung,*' I replied, triumphantly. '*Tergantung.*'

He looked at me with amusement. He had a shock of curly black hair and his skin was pitted with the aftermath of adolescent acne. He was thirty, but with his boyish face and his tiny frame he looked about twenty-one.

'*Tergantung apa?* It depends on what?' he asked, probing.

I couldn't even think of a reply in English for that one so I tried for something simple.

'*Kalau* baik, *saya suka.* If it's *good*, I like it.'

He chuckled at the uselessness of our conversation and started to sing quietly and melodiously in Indonesian. The two women in front glanced round. He had closed his eyes and was moving his head slowly from side to side. The women began to whisper and he stopped, a wide, blissful grin across his face. He took out a filterless clove cigarette, clicked back his Zippo and lit up with the elegance of an addict. Creamy, sweet smoke wafted by. I stared, transfixed by the whole process.

'*Kamu rokok*?' he asked. Whether I smoked or not was a question I rarely knew the answer to. I refused to buy them, but somehow I seemed to end up smoking quite a lot anyway.

'*Tergantung. Kadang-kadang,*' I answered, taking one from his pack. It was my first day and already I had learnt two words which could answer even the most tricky Indonesian questions.

Although the Institute of Biology had approved our work there were many levels of clearance to obtain in Jakarta and Irian Jaya. We continued our permit-collecting trips and began the round of meetings with relevant organizations in Jakarta. We visited Martha Klein in the regional Unesco offices. She was working to have Lorentz declared a Unesco World Heritage Site but it was WWF, together with the Indonesian Forestry Department, who were responsible for managing the area and securing its crucial National Park status. For several years WWF had been trying to organize their own programme of work in Lorentz and were soon to embark on a two-year project. Their Irian Jaya office had been vocal in its support for our proposals over the previous year, but the Jakarta bosses had been more reticent. Mark van der Wal, a Dutch man, was the biologist leading their project.

'So what are you going to offer the people?' he asked me immediately, staring me straight in the eye. 'These people have been dumped on by outsiders. Why should they cooperate with you?'

The room went very quiet as I replied that we had an Nduga man on the team who would explain why our data was important for the long-term protection of the Nduga's forest. We would run projects to repair the airstrip and help the school and clinic. Most importantly, there would be the opportunity for people to earn some money. 'And we're young,' I said trying to end on a lighter note. 'We've brought volleyball and football. At the very least we hope our stay will be fun.'

He swivelled his pencil, deep in concentration, then looked up at me. He was a tall, lean man with an angular face. 'All I can say is that if something is not quite right then sit a bit longer, have another cup of tea, give up for the day, anything. Don't push things. WWF have to work with the impression you leave.'

Some time before I had asked if WWF would second one of their staff to our project. Now we agreed that Mark and his team would visit near the end of our stay to effect a smooth transfer between teams in the region.

The OPM were not mentioned until our third week in Jakarta. The four of us were visiting Colonel Ivar Helberg OBE, the Defence Attaché at the British Embassy. He was an enthusiastic, ex-special forces man, sitting beneath a wall of military memorabilia. We warmed to him immediately, especially when he offered to host a small party for the team and several other people he knew who were interested in the area. The embassy would be the first point of contact in an emergency and we discussed our evacuation procedures, insurance, home contacts and other information in detail. I asked him if he thought there were dangers, other than injuries, that we should be aware of. After some deliberation, he suggested that there was a small chance of kidnap and robbery by the OPM, despite our distance from the Freeport mine, but he thought it very unlikely that we would be harmed. The next day at the Freeport headquarters I mentioned Ivar's comments but they assured me that the OPM were too few in number and too disorganized to be a threat.

We shopped, packed, went to more meetings, collected more permits and even organized a press lunch to launch Lorentz 95, attended by the Minister of the Environment and hosted by British

Petroleum Indonesia. The day before we left Jakarta, Lorentz 95 was in all the papers and on national television news.

When we flew in to Jayapura, it was even larger, hotter and more mosquito ridden than I remembered. After a week waiting anxiously for our final military approval we boarded a twin-propeller passenger plane and headed for the interior of Irian Jaya.

As we rose high between the peaks of the central cordillera the Baliem valley opened up below us suddenly and dramatically. For forty miles the meandering river had cut a flat green swathe ten miles wide through the mountains. The fertile land was watered by irrigation ditches, dissected into geometric, stone-walled garden plots and farmed by the 50,000 strong Dani tribe as it had been for over 10,000 years. These sophisticated stone-age people remained hidden from the outside world until 1938 when a sea-plane from the American Archibold expedition spotted the valley and landed on Lake Habbema above. Now the valley had its own road and Wamena, the capital, had grown into a small town colonized by Indonesian traders and taxi drivers. It had a Mission Aviation Fellowship (MAF), too, which flew its tiny Cessna aircraft and Hughes helicopters to the remote airstrips in the area around, ferrying supplies for the missionaries and their communities.

It was at the MAF office that I first met Elfrieda van der Bijl. She was looking rather windswept as she heaved a generator out of a Cessna and on to a trolley but she wiped the oil from her hand before she shook mine. She was a Canadian of about forty-five and was married to Dutch missionary, Adriaan van der Bijl. Together they had worked with the Nduga since the early 1960s.

Elfrieda and I walked through the market looking for Adriaan. We found him inspecting piles of tomatoes laid neatly in front of an old Dani woman who sat nonchalantly on the bare earth floor. He was speaking Dani and I knew he also spoke Nduga fluently, as well as Dutch, Indonesian and English. He and Elfrieda embraced warmly. They had both returned to Wamena that morning from far-flung mission posts and had not seen each other for several weeks. Looking down to me with his wise eyes and shining white hair he had the air of a Biblical figure. He was a tall, strong man in his late sixties, graceful and gentle in his manner but with a rugged look that spoke of many adventures. When he put his left hand to his face I saw he had lost two fingers. In Dani culture it was normal to amputate a finger each time a close relative died. I asked him how he had lost his.

'Helicopter,' he said plainly, putting his hand in the air to show how.

'Ouch,' I said.

'Ouch, indeed.'

The entire team met Adriaan and Elfrieda later that morning. We would be using their house in Mapnduma while they worked elsewhere: Elfrieda in another Nduga village and Adriaan in Timika.

'Are you ready for everything?' asked Elfrieda. 'Like the naked-ness. It will be a shock, I promise.' As we talked I began to feel the enormity of the cultural confrontation ahead. If the Nduga would shock us, what effect would we have on them? They described their house, the people, the mountains and Mapnduma itself and there was excitement among all of us. But it was as they explained how the short-wave radio worked that I began to understood just how isolated and vulnerable we would be. And with that realization there came a pang of nerves.

'There will be disputes and problems,' said Adriaan. 'Often about money. Just leave the Nduga to sort it out among themselves.'

'But you will have fun,' said Elfrieda warmly, moving forward in her seat. 'Being young people, they will like you and trust you and they will love the football.' She took hold of Adriaan's hand. 'They are a simple people but Adriaan and I have learnt to love them very deeply and we like to think they would trust us with their lives. The Nduga and their land are such a beautiful part of the Lord's creation.'

This image of the Nduga as simple, lovable and, hence, harmless was somewhere in my mind, too. Perhaps western prejudices pre-vented me from believing that uneducated and seemingly primitive people could be anything more. But my preconceptions were more confused than that. The Nduga tribe had taken on a mythical status in my mind. I believed they would be wise. I believed their culture would hold a spirituality my own had lost. I wanted to feel it and come close to it.

THREE

MAPNDUMA

It was half past four in the morning. The air was cold and dry. I walked along the pot-holed streets towards the Wamena airfield and paused to check the sky. On the northern slopes of the Baliem valley it was clear, dark blue, a few fading stars signalling dawn's approach. But on the southern side, above the high mountain wall that separated Wamena from Mapnduma, there was a dense band of cloud. This morning the weather meant everything to me.

The door of the MAF cargo shed was half ajar. The Indonesian proprietor had just arrived and was standing wearily in the middle of the concrete floor. Around him were wooden shelves labelled with the names of airstrips. They were filled with sheets of corrugated iron, jerry cans of kerosene and bags of nails; materials for the resident missionaries or the local people, I wasn't sure. At the end of the shed our cargo was stacked up to the ceiling. It weighed more than a tonne.

I went out on to the airfield where a Cessna stood waiting. It had a single propellor at the nose, two large headlamps, a wing slung above the fuselage and two windows on each side. I looked in. It was about the size of a car: two seats in the front, two in the back with a tiny one in the tail where the boot would be.

I heard a distant whine. Staring up the valley I saw a small bright light growing steadily. A second one followed some way behind.

'From Bokodini airbase, coming to do your Mapnduma run,' said the proprietor, who had followed me out. 'If the weather's any good.'

The Cessna passed low over a small Dani compound about a mile away. As it neared it dropped further and skimmed the long grass at the end of the runway before bumping on to the concrete at about sixty miles an hour. It bounced twice and came to a halt within a hundred yards. It accelerated again and taxied over the grass towards the hangar like an aeronautical go-cart.

There was a crackle from the radio inside the shed.

'Wamena, Mapnduma. Wamena, Mapnduma.' More crackle. 'Wamena, Mapnduma.'

'Mapnduma, Wamena, come in Mapnduma,' said an American voice in Indonesian. There was more distorted noise from the radio and a short conversation. I went inside to find out the news.

'Hi there,' the man said, raising his hand. I had met him the day before. Like most of the pilots he was ex-Marines, Vietnam stock. It took that kind of experience to make it as a pilot in Irian Jaya. 'Mapnduma's closed, I'm afraid.' My heart sank and he could tell. 'Sorry. Clouds down, visibility down.' He cleared some papers on the desk and took off his cap. 'More likely tomorrow. Difficult to know. This time of year's usually pretty good. June to August now, that's different. Then Mapnduma is closed for weeks on end. It's a difficult airstrip.'

'What's the latest we could leave?' I asked.

'It's a morning strip. We don't go in after nine. The sun comes up, you see, warms the mountain and creates an upcurrent. Mapnduma's a south approach and only 180 metres long. With a tail wind it makes it difficult to stop in time. If you don't, it's down the cliff into the river.' His hand nose-dived off the end of the desk and he laughed. 'Not that I've ever not stopped, of course.'

The rest of the team arrived. Everyone was disappointed. We wondered how many days we might have to hang around in Wamena waiting for the weather to clear. The three aircraft were loaded just in case and we went to sit in the café next to the airport. I drank coffee with condensed milk, ate stale cake and stared up at the mountains, willing the clouds to lift. A few small stalls and shops began to open. A car drove past and I watched a dazed old Dani man wander along in his penis gourd and head dress. I went back to my little Indonesian dictionary and continued learning words half-heartedly.

Navy walked back into the cafe. 'OK, we're off,' he said calmly. 'Adinda, Bram and I are going now. Dan, Annette and Markus will follow.'

The propeller was already running and we leant forward into the slipstream as we climbed aboard. I was at the front, next to the pilot. I fastened the straps and stared at the wall of controls and knobs. Navy's plane taxied to the runway and straightened itself up. With the brakes locked it increased power. The air moved so fast over its body that its contours wavered and the tail twitched as if it were a cat about to pounce. The brakes were released, it hurtled down the runway and within a few seconds it was floating into the air.

We waited ten minutes then followed. The speed was modest but the plane made an almighty noise. Once airborne, we banked round to the left and began a steady climb out of the Baliem valley and into the mountains around. Within ten minutes the altimeter in the centre of the dashboard read 9,000 feet, and we were flying over a plateau: savannah scattered with tussocks and stands of giant tree fern. Next was the wide crystal expanse of Lake Habbema and ahead were the craggy grey cliffs of the mountain cordillera rising like ancient sentries from the green forest. We were still climbing and heading for the highest peak.

'Mount Trikora,' the pilot shouted above the din. I nodded enthusiastically. The land below was faulted with ridges and cut by ancient glaciation. Small streams disappeared into large sinkholes and cave systems in the limestone karst. The land began to rise again in a series of steep escarpments covered in layers of dense evergreen scrub. Trikora was a black wall looming ever closer. It was clear that we were not going to make it over the top.

'Mbuwa Pass,' the pilot wailed again, indicating with the flat of his hand that we would cut through the mountain wall. The altimeter was on 13,000 feet. There was patchy cloud around us and a freezing draught on my legs. The aircraft was being knocked and buffeted by the whistling turbulence. We were flying into a gaping hole in the mountain side, being swallowed on all sides by towering black rock. I peered up to the left to see the summit of Trikora, a jagged outline almost a thousand feet above me. The rock walls seemed only a wing's length away on either side of the aeroplane. The smooth lines of stratification were pitted with faults and cracks and in places icy water was flowing down, splattering on shattered boulders far below. We banked steeply to the right, and then the left, following the narrow passage, the pilot's face stiff with concentration. Then suddenly, we left the mountain and stretching out beneath the layer of high, patchy cloud was a vast expanse of tropical forest laid over a prehistoric landscape of deep valleys and soaring ridge tops. On the horizon, about a hundred miles away, the land shimmered in the low morning sun. It was the Arafura sea with Australia beyond. We had passed into southern New Guinea. This was Lorentz, as far as the eye could see.

As we kept our height the green land dropped away below. It was drained by gleaming, finger-like rivers and, in places, waterfalls that fell down the sheer valley sides. I spotted smoke rising from a point in the forest and nearby were small patches of a lighter green, probably where gardens had been made. I saw a series of hairline scars on the hillside. They were landslides. I had read all about them.

We lost height and dropped below the cloud, still at least two thousand feet above the forest. Ahead the mountain sun flashed on corrugated metal. Above the confluence of two rivers I could make out a few buildings perched on a improbable outcrop of flat land, just big enough for an airstrip.

'Mapnduma?' I yelled. He nodded and the plane banked as we began to descend in gentle circles, each revolution bringing more of the village into view: several buildings next to an airstrip; two waterfalls shimmering on the hillside above; large areas of garden in the valley; high ridges and peaks all around.

With one final turn we dropped low into the valley and straightened out for the approach. Our shadow chased us across the tree tops as we followed the line of the deep gorge several hundred feet below. As we reached the lip of the Mapnduma plateau we dropped abruptly and hit the ground with a jolt. Within one hundred metres we had stopped.

A huge crowd had gathered to meet the planes. I fumbled with my cameras, trying to put them back in the bags, not wanting the Papuans to see them and think how rich I must be. I climbed down, and kept behind the plane, hiding nervously from the crowd. I was suddenly ashamed by our flamboyant entrance and obvious wealth. The pilot and some local people were unloading and I watched them uselessly for a while before offering to help. Navy appeared and signalled for me to follow him. 'Leave it,' he said. 'I have arranged people to do that.'

I followed him and Annette towards the missionary house, a large two-storey structure with timber walls, a corrugated iron roof, a pretty porch and garden. The path was lined with brown bodies of all ages, standing motionless, staring expressionless at the new-comers. The children hid behind the legs of their mothers and the men whispered. I squinted in the harsh morning light. There were no smiles, no welcomes and although a few replied to my 'wa, wa' greetings I felt awkward and uneasy as they eyed us suspiciously. The house was just yards ahead and I quickened my step to reach it as the crowd broke up and followed us, talking excitedly among themselves. I jumped up the step, through the lobby and stood in the kitchen. Already ten, twenty, thirty faces were watching through the open door. I moved into a corner where they could not see me and leant against the sink.

A far-off whine signalled the arrival of the last plane. The house quietened as the crowds ran back to the airstrip. I sat in silence on the stairs in the main room. The sun streamed through the bay windows painting the polished floorboards with a golden glow, glinting off the frames of family photos that lined the bookshelf, basking my face in its warmth. I felt so foreign, but in the sanctuary of that room I could hide.

The crowd returned, excited and noisy, throwing down the boxes and bags they had brought from the airstrip. Navy was barking instructions and people were unpacking and sorting. I braced myself and went out to join them.

'Busy are you, Daniel?' Navy said sarcastically, raising his eyebrows at me. 'These men need paying for carrying the boxes.' I struggled to understand his Indonesian above the noise. Outside the open front door twenty men were fighting to get to the front line. They looked anxiously at us, holding out their hands. Some cowered under imaginary weights. 'Very heavy boxes, oh, so very heavy,' a few whined in Indonesian. A number of small boys had squeezed through their legs and were already inside, cautiously approaching, trying to catch a glimpse of the things we had brought.

'Paying?' I whispered to Navy in disbelief. I was angry that we had a pay dispute already.

'Yes, they want 2000 rupiah each. Go on. You're the project coordinator. I thought you were in charge of money,' he said pointedly.

'*Me* in charge? You're the field leader. Anyway, we can't pay them that,' I said in English. 'That's over a dollar. That's what the missionaries pay for half a day's work. Tell them we'll discuss it tomorrow when we've settled in.'

I spent the afternoon treading carefully. Navy and I had completely opposing ideas about how the bedrooms, workrooms and kit should be arranged. Each time we tried to talk to each other we stalled in increasing hostility. My Indonesian was poor and he resented having to use English. It was easier to let the people and kit diffuse silently and naturally along the path of least resistance and so the British and Indonesian groups ended up in opposite ends of the house.

By early afternoon I was dying to escape. I looked out of the window at the incredible land around me. Only a small crowd of children were left by the door and I felt I could brave the village.

'Dan, maybe it's best to leave it for today,' said Navy.

'Why?'

'Maybe just best, that's all.'

But my mind was made up, so I persuaded Anna to join me and we walked out towards the airstrip. The children talked excitedly and began to follow us, running circles behind us, jumping up and down on the spot.

'*Nea-wa*,' said Anna, fumbling in Nduga. 'Hello children.'

'*Nimbo-wa, nimbo-wa*,' they replied. 'Hello mama, hello mama.'

Anna and I talked and laughed. More children came running down from the huts and slopes around and began to follow us, chanting loudly. As we reached the airstrip I began to run as fast as I could and Anna galloped behind me, roaring like an aeroplane with her arms to the side, banking this way and that with a long stream of children screaming with delight in her wake. We careered to a stop at the airstrip's abrupt end and the land plummeted down to the turbulent river several hundred feet below. They pointed down to the water. '*Jima!*' they cried in Nduga. '*Jima* Gul, the river Gul.' Anna was talking to a young, bright-eyed girl who was weaving a string bag. The boys were motioning me to follow them down a steep, narrow path which wound between mixed plots of sugar cane, sweet potatoes, cassava and bananas. I scrambled over boulders and down muddy banks until we arrived at the heart of the deafening gorge, the valley towering a thousand feet above us on either side. I sat motionless for a while then I turned and began to climb. A gang of older boys had formed. They stood around me jabbing their arrows in the air, staring at me with wild eyes, and I was scared for a minute until I realized they were playing. For half an hour I laboured back up the slope as the boys mimicked my heavy breathing. As we neared the plateau the first drops of rain began to fall from the darkening sky. We ran back up the airstrip and our crowd scattered across the village to the tin-roofed huts and small buildings that stood among the grass. Only a few bedraggled boys remained to follow me back to my house and watch me peel off my wet clothes.

That evening as we finished dinner men began arriving at the house. One joined us at the table while others peered gingerly around the door.

'This is Philipus, the village preacher,' said Navy in Indonesian, getting up to introduce the gentle-faced man. 'And this is Daniel, the leader of the expedition.' I stood up, wiped my mouth and shook his hand. Philipus nodded meekly and stepped back. I smiled and looked to Navy, hoping for some explanation.

'Markus, you and I are meeting with the village heads tonight,' he said.

I was taken aback. I followed Navy into the kitchen area. 'I thought we agreed we were going to meet with the whole village first,' I whispered. Why had he gone ahead without me? Perhaps I shouldn't have wasted the afternoon playing with the children.

'It's easier this way. The other men are outside.'

In the lobby four elderly men were hunched over their tall penis gourds following our every move with lively eyes. Philipus introduced them reverently while the candlelight flickered on their wrinkled skin. There was the *Ap Nggok* of Mapnduma, literally the Big Man, the traditional leader of the village, chosen by the people for his charisma, generosity and wisdom. It was he who dealt with disputes and brought the village together. Next was another *Ap Nggok*, this time of Kurukmu, a village in the next valley. Next to him was the *Ap Noe Kwalmbo*, the Head of the Forest, responsible for choosing good places to make gardens, for blessing the sweet potatoes and for luring possums and other game meat close to the village with magic. *Ap Noe Wimbo*, the Head of War, was at the end. He was responsible for finding good opportunities for making war with other clans and coordinating the warriors. 'War is good,' Philipus translated. 'When there is war everyone is happy. But when a man is hurt or killed, then everyone is sad and the war is stopped.'

But none of these old men seemed to hold any real power. As they squabbled over who should hold the candle or have the last sip of orange squash, it was clear that it was Philipus and a small group of younger men who were more influential. Over the last thirty years the incredible new world of the missionaries and Indonesians had been creeping slowly through the mountains towards the Nduga. Its influence had already begun to alter the fabric of society and everybody knew more change was inevitable. It was just a matter of time before a road or a mine came to the Nduga as they had come to their Amungme neighbours. It was no longer enough to grow old, confident that knowledge and experience would bring status and respect. The Nduga men who were already a part of the encroaching world were the real leaders in their evolving society. Generally they were the church people or those with money.

It was Philipus, the priest, who led the meeting. He was honest, wise and widely respected. He wore T-shirt and shorts, spoke and wrote excellent Indonesian; had travelled to Wamena many times and had even visited Jayapura to attend a church conference. The health worker or *mantri* for Mapnduma was also there. For twenty years Elfrieda van der Bijl had run a barefoot doctor scheme whereby the most promising students of the church were trained in basic medicine and sent out to treat the people for malaria, pneumonia and dysentery. Lewi was pleasant enough, but knew full well that he was the only man in the village rich enough to afford not only trousers but trainers as well. 'It is difficult for me,' he explained. 'Often the people cannot afford to pay me because there is little possibility for them to earn money. I treat them anyway and every Sunday their debt is read before the church so they will not forget.' He explained that in his childhood they had slaughtered pigs to appease the spirits or made potions from magic plants. 'Only the old men believe in those things now,' he said. 'Now any illness can be cured by taking a pill.'

The village head appointed by the government was there as well. A local man, he sat apart from everyone else fiddling miserably with his Freeport watch. He asked to see our paperwork and checked it meticulously as we looked on. As the token symbol of Indonesian rule his job was to operate the short-wave radio that made daily contact with the other Protestant mission stations in the area and collect fees from people using the MAF planes. These came inter-mittently – less than once a week – and brought cooking oil, salt, matches and batteries from Wamena, for those who could afford them, and returned with pandana fruits or pigs to be sold at the market. Although everybody wanted to see the wonders of Wamena, few could afford the £10 passenger fare, so for most it was an arduous five-day trek across the mountains.

Navy talked with Philipus and the other men in Indonesian as I struggled to follow the conversation. The expedition needed to carry out fieldwork over a range of altitudes and Navy asked if we could visit different areas of forest around Mapnduma village.

'Every garden plot, every pandana tree, every acre of hunting forest is owned by somebody,' said Philipus. He looked kindly to me. 'Even the path that you took to the river this afternoon belonged to somebody. But they are not angry.' He described how Nduga classified themselves as hot or cold people depending on whether they lived in hot or cold forest and whether they ate *buah merah*, 'red fruit' or *buah pandana*, 'pandana nuts'. To the Nduga hot meant Mapnduma, at about 1000 metres altitude, while cold was nearer 2000 metres. The fruits I knew were from the *Pandanus* genus of palm which was common in New Guinea.

'If you want to go to cold forest then you will need to talk to the cold people who are a separate clan in another village,' continued Philipus. 'And to visit any forest, you will need to pay the owners. If you trespass you could start a war. Pigs and wives start many fights but nothing is as important as land.'

The following morning Yakobus, our Nduga colleague arrived, and the entire team introduced itself to a large group that had gathered in the centre of the village. When I returned to the house Annette took me aside.

'Dan, I think you should talk to Navy. He's organizing a trip to the forests in the south, leaving the day after tomorrow.' I looked at her furiously. Why on earth hadn't Navy talked to me first? It was the last straw. Annette held her hands up in defence. 'I only know because I'm meant to be going, too, to do the fish work with Adinda. Look, don't get mad with him, Dan. Just be cool.'

I walked over to the workrooms at the back of the house, breathing deeply and evenly as I went. Navy was packing up a rucksack. Tessy was lounging in the hammock he had strung up across the corner of the room. 'Hi, Navy,' I said innocently. 'Are you going somewhere?'

'We're going to lowlands,' he said slightly awkwardly. 'Me, Tessy, Adinda and Annette, maybe Bram.'

'Why didn't you discuss it with me first?'

'Look, Dan, we have a concept. We work in different sites, different forests. You know that.'

'Well, in my concept we were staying in Mapnduma for a week or so first. Just because you have a concept doesn't mean everyone else's is the same.'

'Certain things are agreed. In Indonesia, if you agree to something, then you stick by it.' We argued while he continued to collect bits and pieces from around the room. He was getting angry, too, pulling his fingers through his shock of silky black hair, stumbling over the English words, gesticulating to get his sense across. He tripped on a large sheet of paper on which a local man had made a sketch map of the lowlands in blue crayon. Piles of clothes were laid out on the floor. The desk was covered in books, papers, toiletries and biscuit wrappers.

'I thought we were going to ration biscuits?' I asked accusingly.

'I need biscuits to think,' he replied. 'So does Tessy.'

Tessy was smoking a clove cigarette, depositing his ash in a neat pile on the nearby window sill. He was pretending to read a magazine but he had been eyeing me all along. Now he put the magazine down and gave me a proper scowl. Defeated by numbers I left humiliated and stomped back to the main house.

'I just don't believe that man,' I hissed to Annette. 'And you know they've already eaten a packet of chocolate biscuits.' Annette put her arm around me and tried to calm me. 'Then he accused me of coming here for a holiday. He asked me if I just planned to hang out in Mapnduma for ten weeks. Can you believe it?' She sat me down on the bright orange sofa and patted my knee. 'And Tessy just sided with him automatically although I doubt that he understood a word of what we were saying.' I looked to her anxiously. 'You know he's going for two weeks, maybe longer. And he couldn't even be bothered to discuss it with me.' I shook my head forlornly. 'I want to go to the lowlands, too, you know. The whole point of the project is that we coordinate the studies around sites in which we can all work. That's why it's inter-disciplinary. What's the point of him marching off on his own?'

Annette made all the right noises and I was calm within a few minutes.

'I think Navy's plan is really good,' called Anna gaily. She had been listening from upstairs.

'Whether it's good or not has got nothing to do with it,' I said exasperated.

'Well, there's no point getting so cross.'

'I'm not cross,' I snapped.

Bill joined Annette and I from outside where he had been trying to fix up the antennae for our walkie-talkie base station. He was as disappointed by the news as I was. He had planned to collect flowering plant from the lowlands.

'Look, we can all go,' said Annette patiently. 'Let Navy, Tessy and Bram make a start with their birding work and then you can come and join us, next week sometime.'

When I saw Adinda head off the next day to check her water meter and fish nets in the Gul river I was glad she would have Annette with her. Adinda was a city dweller, brought up in Jakarta. She was standing outside the front door in a wide-brimmed hat, full waterproofs and jungle boots. A compass, whistle, water bottle and binoculars hung around her neck. She tucked her trousers into her socks and set off with a stick in hand.

'It's only fifteen minutes away,' I teased. 'You look like you're set for an expedition.'

'Dan, Dan,' she said, grabbing my forearm to steady herself. 'That river is a very long way down.' She threw her hands in the air and smiled. 'Maybe it take us the whole day!'

After the stress of arriving and settling in, it was an incredible relief when Navy, Tessy, Adinda, Annette and Bram finally seemed set to leave two mornings later. But although the guides and porters had been agreed in advance with Philipus a large crowd still formed, demanding to be employed. I watched Navy with admiration. Not only was he patient, he was charming *and* knew when to stop.

After four long hours, when there was still a large dissident crowd, he cancelled the trip and sent them away with no work at all. The next day the men were more reasonable and the group left within an hour. The rest of us settled down to enjoy some peaceful work in Mapnduma. But it was soon clear there would be no peace until the Nduga had squeezed every last penny from us. They began by placing a tight boundary around the house which we could cross only with fully paid guides. And there was no hope of sitting down and chatting casually with the people who hung around outside. They knew that we were interested in the forest and wildlife and so the moment the conversation moved in this direction they would nudge each other, go dumb and ask for money. Everywhere we went, everything we did, they tried to charge us.

Money had taken on a worth far beyond its face value. To have some, however little, was to own a share in the fabulous new world. They were ashamed of their old, outdated ways; ashamed of their poverty, their ignorance, even their nakedness. Ten, twenty years ago this shame had not existed. The forests had been rich, the old men had been wise and there was no other way. Now the women covered their breasts and looked to the ground when I passed them. Money was their ticket into the twentieth century.

It began to dawn on me how hopelessly naive my fantasy had been. How could I ever meet the real Nduga people while I flaunted everything they desired and while they were demeaned by my very presence? And how could I hope to see the traditional Nduga way of life by coming to Mapnduma? While most Nduga villages were just a handful of huts in remote forest, Mapnduma was a virtual metropolis. It had tin-roofed shacks, a small clinic, a missionary house, an airstrip and even a school with a proper yard, fence and Indonesian flagpole. There was little forest, most having been stripped for cultivation to feed almost a thousand people, over 15 per cent of the Nduga population, who had been attracted to the Gul valley in search of progress.

Deep down I was disappointed that one of the last places on earth had already been tainted by our western ways. However, the expedition had no wish to balk the aspirations of the Mapnduma people. We had money budgeted for community development projects. Some was given directly to the school and clinic in the form of books and medicine, but the bulk was used to pay teams of men, women and children to carry out essential maintenance work on the airstrip. As this project got underway we hoped that it would quench some of the money hunger that was proving so incapacitating to our work.

When Bill and I set off to join Navy and his group in the lowlands it seemed that our plan had failed. First we were held to ransom by two tenacious teenagers who blocked the Gul river rope bridge and demanded an extortionate toll. Then we were blackmailed by our own guides who refused to walk faster than a snail's pace unless we gave them a bonus. Finally, late in the day, after much negotiation, we arrived at the camp. Wading down the fast-flowing lowland river at dusk, catching the silver eyes of nocturnal tree kangaroos in our torch beams, we caught sight of Annette and Tessy laughing by a large fire on the riverside, smoke and sparks billowing up through the tall, thick forest around. For half an hour all was peaceful and then the guides starting arguing again. Navy dropped his head and Annette sighed: 'Just when we thought we had finally got away from it all, you bring half of Mapnduma with you.'

We stayed at that site for two weeks, working around the clock to squeeze as much data from the forest as possible. While Adinda and Annette netted many streams and rivers, Navy, Tessy and Bram cut and tagged several kilometres of transect paths and each day at dawn set off on these with binoculars and bird books. Bill generally left for the forest slightly later and would return mid-afternoon with a troop of men carrying armfuls of flowering plants which he then pressed and preserved in alcohol under the tarpaulins of our primitive jungle camp. Together the six of them collected some of the first specimens and data for that part of New Guinea.

My work was to classify the forest according to Nduga tree types and uses. Generally I worked with three or four men counting and naming trees in one-hundred-metre plots and collecting samples of

51

the most common types. The men and I would also talk and draw maps showing the forest's geology and ecology as they saw it. Their knowledge was remarkable. They could identify any tree or shrub within seconds. They knew the properties of the leaves, bark or roots and which birds or mammals might feed or nest in it. For trees alone I compiled a dictionary of over five hundred Nduga names and uses.

Once the men were receiving a regular daily wage they began to relax and we were able to have some fun together. One of the men, Nathaniel, became a good friend, although he spoke no Indonesian. One morning he spotted something on a tree way off in the distance. He threw me his red cap, chopped a piece of vine and bounded through the undergrowth. Holding his penis gourd in so that it didn't get caught in the creepers, he began to climb high into the canopy using the vine as a belt. The other men and I rushed after him and cheered him on from the safety of the ground. Clinging to the bark, high up among the colourful epiphytes, were two brown, fibrous pouches. He prized them off and threw them down. Inside were scores of fat caterpillars. '*Mino! Mino!* Let's eat!' he said patting his stomach proudly. I had some orange sherbet with me which I suggested would compliment them well so we baked them on a fire there and then and enjoyed delicious sugar-coated caterpillars for lunch.

Back in Mapnduma, away from the forest, Lita and Anna used interviews and group sessions to document the use of plants and animals in everyday Nduga life. Markus and Yakobus spent time with the older members of the village documenting traditional customs and beliefs. Of course Yakobus already knew many of these men from his childhood and this made the work much easier for them. Markus took to working and sleeping alone in the draughty attic above the workrooms. Up there he would write all night by the light of two flickering candles. His desk was piled high with notebooks, papers, pencil sharpenings, coffee cups, cigarette papers, tobacco and ash trays. Late one night when I couldn't sleep I crept up the stairs and found him hunched over his papers, his great, black curly beard twitching with the movement of his hand.

We sat on the bare plank floor while he rolled cigarettes and told me of his day's work. 'This is a land of spirits and taboos,' he began dramatically. Many mountains, lakes, rivers and forest were sacred and nobody was permitted to visit them. To trespass on spirit land could cause landslides, earthquakes or floods. 'But many of the young men have taken wood or hunted in the last remaining sacred forests,' said Marcus glumly. 'The old men think now there will be trouble.'

As November passed and December began everyone grew much more tolerant of the language difficulties and cultural differences within our mixed nationality group. Navy and I battled out several long-standing feuds in late-night confrontations and decided that we would probably never agree on some things. I resented him treating the British team as younger and less experienced, although undoubtedly we were. He was suspicious of foreigners and was sure that we would steal his results and claim them as our own. Through all the British–Indonesian conflicts it was Annette who held the group together. During her trips to the lowlands she had grown close to Adinda and also to Tessy with whom she smoked and sometimes flirted innocently. Somehow Annette's vivacious smiles and simple jokes could cut straight through Tessy's sulky moods and Adinda's shyness and bring fits of laughter to the tense dinner table.

'Tessy *sayang*, Tessy darling,' she would tease in Indonesian as she passed him the salt or chilli. He would blush and then Lita would begin poking him in his ribs, asking indignantly: 'Tessy? Are you really Annette's *sayang*?' and his mischievous smile would broaden and then break into gentle laughter.

I grew to love my work in the forests, although my first impressions of the wildlife had been disappointing. The mammals, mainly bats, possums and rats, tended to be nocturnal and, of course, there were no monkeys, tigers, elephants or suchlike. But in this absence of competition or predation it was the bird life of New Guinea that had evolved into the most spectacular forms. Bill and I hoped to catch some of the most remarkable species on video. On one occasion guides took us into deep forest in the next valley and there, one dawn, we found some Lesser birds of paradise calling distinctively in the canopy above. Several males, with yellow crowns and green chins, had spread their wings wide and puffed out their long plumes in a tall, cascading panache of white and yellow around them. Perhaps the females watching were unimpressed because the males left soon after, flying floppily through the air, trailing their bright tail feathers two feet behind them. Several weeks later we found a courtship display site of the Macgregor's bowerbird. The male bird had arranged a stack of twigs around the base of a slim sapling in a small palm grove on the hillside. Around this maypole a wide circle of forest floor had been cleared, laid with a delicate carpet of moss and adorned first with orange leaves and bark and then, as an outer ring, blue and indigo berries. The bird came to its 'bower' at the same time each morning, just as the first rays of light hit it. He would tidy the place up, removing old berries and bringing new ones and then, if females were watching, he would dance around the may-pole throwing his head forward to display a bright orange crest.

When we returned from our forest excursions Bill disappeared into the workroom for the afternoon to prepare the day's specimens. There he could usually enjoy several hours of solitude with just his plants and the BBC World Service for company. He was man of small pleasures and fixed habits and I knew he received enormous satisfaction from that part of the day.

On Sundays we went to church in the large tin-roofed hall with over a hundred Nduga who came to worship in Mapnduma. Some were wealthy families with smart shirts, Nduga Bibles and children dressed in frocks, but most were of more humble means and had come from the many small villages around. The men and women wore flowers in their hair and and everybody brought an offering of a few potatoes or some vegetables. The adults sang hymns in Nduga, the children ran amok and afterwards everybody would congregate to talk and exchange gossip. One Sunday the hushed and secretive gossip centred around a special guest whom we were soon to meet.

*   *   *

Mapnduma is not the type of place one expects to receive passing visitors, so there was some surprise when, one afternoon before Christmas, a bare-chested white man in his early thirties strolled into the house as if he owned it. 'G'day. Ben Bohane's the name.' It was Crocodile Dundee come out of the jungle. 'Mind if I use your shower, mate? It's been over a month.' He smiled from under his wide-brimmed hat and walked to the bathroom. He seemed to know the place. The shower ran, steam billowed from under the door and he began to sing. Navy came in furious. He had been sitting outside with Lita and Adinda and the man had walked straight past them as if they didn't exist. 'He didn't even bother to cover his chest,' he whispered furiously. 'Even though Adinda and Lita were there.' Anna, Bill, Annette and I were grudgingly prepared to forgive the newcomer for his infelicities and, as he had eaten nothing but sweet potatoes for a month, we invited him to dinner. It was not a diplomatic move and after ten minutes of angry silence and gobbled eating the Indonesians left in protest. Ben Bohane had brought his Papuan guide with him, a man in his thirties whom he introduced as Yudas. He wore a green beret, a puffed-out shiny bomber jacket and tight shorts over his long, slender, bare legs. He had refused to join us at the table and now he sat gloomily in a dark corner behind the fridge waiting for Ben to finish. With half the group gone, I tried again to tempt him to join us for coffee. He shook his head to that as well so we retired to the sitting room without him.

'So, where have you been, Ben?' Bill asked.

'Oh, all over really.'

'Like where?'

'To the west mainly.' I suggested a few places. 'Yeah, maybe, I'm no good with names. I'm a photographer.'

'What have you been photographing?'

'You know, plants, animals, mainly.'

'What animals have you got on film?'

'Oh, none really.'

It was clear he was no normal photographer. He had no permits and he spoke no Indonesian. He and Yudas had both spent time in Papua New Guinea and they communicated in Pidgin English. Finally he admitted that he was a journalist who had been on walkabout with the OPM. We were interested, although not particularly alarmed.

'So what do you know about them?' we asked.

'Well, nothing to concern you guys. There's quite a big group of them to the west, a hundred or so. They had a pig feast while I was with them in a village over there, three valleys away. Everyone knows about you for miles around, though. There's a fair bit of curiosity. Here, in Mapnduma and in the next valley, you're fine. But if you go too far west you'll find the atmosphere is much more tense. Likely you'd have no problems if it was just you and the Papuans, but don't take the Indonesians.'

Ben left the next day by plane but Yudas remained, hanging around the house looking for work as many men did. He was a Nduga, related to several people in the village and seemed well known and respected. He spoke good Indonesian so we decided to employ him for a while and he began working with Bill collecting plants from the forest, and then helped Anna and Lita record the Nduga names for different birds and mammals. He was quietly spoken and gently mannered but he knew his mind. He was happy to tell Bill that he found plant collecting deadly boring and was confident enough to dictate to Anna and Lita how he wished his interview sessions to proceed. He was a curious-looking man, with bushy sideburns, a frizzy moustache, and a wide army webbing strap around his waist. I was intrigued by him and his associations with the OPM but, like most of the villagers, he made a point of being pro-Indonesia and extra polite to Navy and his team.

Over the weeks I grew to know a number of the men well. I met their children and wives and they began to trust me with secrets and give me presents. They told me about special powders they gave to their dogs to make them run extra fast when hunting. I asked if they had anything for humans but they said it would turn a man crazy. Once I received a handful of traditional magic herbs which I was told could make any woman fall in love with me, although I was never sure if I or the woman should eat them.

With growing confidence, I asked some of the men about Ben, Yudas and the OPM and, when we were away from the village and alone, they talked openly. Some said that Ben, or Boss Ben as they called him, was their leader and would bring the Australian army to help them defeat the Indonesians. 'Around us, as we speak, there is a war,' they said. It had been going on for over thirty years and they claimed that Papuans had killed many thousands of Indonesian soldiers. From how they spoke it seemed almost everyone supported the OPM and I wondered if the real OPM was less a band of rebels and more a faith and conviction within every Papuan. We were already surrounded by OPM, it appeared, but this didn't scare me. Instead it made me feel safer. After all, many of the villagers were friends and had grown to understand how our work could help protect their land and gain recognition for the Nduga people.

It was prophesied that 1996 or 1997 would be the year of their freedom and that the Lord would send a sign. Victory, they said, was only a matter of time. Already people were gathering together to help them, like Ben Bohane and our Lorentz 95 team. .Then as the first days of 1996 dawned, the year of freedom, a small group of Dutch and German people arrived from WWF and Unesco. Never before had so many important foreign people congregated together in Nduga land.

FOUR

THE INQUEST

About thirty OPM warriors were sheltering from the rain in the main room of the house. Their body paints had been smudged and their greenery crumpled by the crowd. Yudas was shouting to be heard as the rain battered on the tin roof and there was knocking, scratching and rummaging from every part of the house as the men up-ended chests and rifled through cupboards in their search for guns. In the bathroom, adjacent to the drawing room, a small group were whispering in a huddle and on the coffee table Murip had collected two walkmans, a microphone holder and battery charger and was listing them in his book.

Standing in the kitchen with the others I felt numb, and strangely distant from what was going on around me. Through the bay window I watched the stream gushing past the house. In the driving rain it had swollen and was washing over the footbridge on the path to the airstrip. In the village beyond people were darting between houses, talking urgently through small doorways or gathering up their pigs and belongings.

Silas marched back in, shouting orders, waving his arms and demanding food. I tensed as he fixed his stare on me and prodded his barbed knife near my face. I pointed to the stove as I pressed myself flat against the fridge door. Markus had bought half a pig that morning and had been preparing his special pork and ginger dish for lunch. It was still bubbling away with a large vat of rice. I hoped Silas would take it and go, but he strode out, stopped, scratched his chin under his white balaclava, and stormed back in.

'Well, don't just look at it,' he shouted, this time glaring at Tessy.

'Eat it. You think you can afford to waste good food?' I had no appetite and my stomach was in cramps but I was relieved that this man was encouraging us to eat now, although an hour before he had seemed happy to see us killed.

We were officially unbound and Lita and Adinda brought out plates and cutlery and began to serve the food, passing the first portions towards the OPM crowd. Silas intercepted them angrily. 'I told you to eat. Eat first!' I carried some plates over to Mark, Martha and Frank who were sitting at the table in the main room and then cautiously joined them, watching carefully for Silas's reaction. We chewed together in silence for a moment.

'I told you that you were asking for trouble bringing Indonesians here,' hissed Frank, leaning across the table towards me. 'It's having them here that's caused all this.'

'I don't think you turning up has been altogether without effect either,' I retaliated. 'High-profile government people on an official visit to the area? It's bound to cause some reaction.'

Mark frowned, making furrows in his high forehead and eyeing us cynically as we spoke. His face was lean and angular and his short brown hair was ruffled into a tuft. He was the cautious Dutch man whom we had met at WWF in Jakarta several months before. Frank Momberg was his much less conservative German partner. We had met Martha in Jakarta as well. She had been working at the Unesco offices on the UN World Heritage Site proposal for Lorentz. Mark and Martha were partners and she was three months pregnant with his child. The three of them had been in Mapnduma for two days and had been holding a meeting that morning when the ambush had begun. They had been with the village heads discussing WWF's plans to map traditional land rights. Yudas had been present at the start, but I had watched him walk out later.

Bill, Anna and then Annette brought their plates over and joined us at the table. Silas allowed food to be passed out to the OPM men now and a calm settled as plates clanked and people ate. I looked around nervously. 'So what do you think these people are up to?' I asked Frank, raising my voice slightly to avoid sounding suspicious.

'Who knows?' he said, through a mouthful of rice. 'Presumably they're the OPM but it's difficult to be sure. That French guy said he had trouble with the OPM when he first came to Lorentz.'

Frank was talking about Manuel, a biologist who had been working near the Amungme–Nduga border to the west, much closer to the problems at Freeport. He was the only outsider to have visited Lorentz in the last few years and we had spoken to him in Wamena before flying to Mapnduma. He said he had bumped into the OPM but didn't seem too concerned about it.

'During his first few weeks he was raided by the OPM,' Frank continued. 'They tied him up, threatened to kill him, stole everything and then ran back into the forest.'

'So they're going to run off soon?' I asked hopefully.

'Let's hope so. Once they've eaten and the rain stops.'

'You scheduled a plane tomorrow to pick you up, didn't you?' I said, looking at Mark.

He nodded. 'But we didn't manage to confirm it. We were going to do that this afternoon on the radio.'

'That plane is going to be critical,' I said. 'If these men are still here in the morning and the plane comes in, it'll either take off again in a hurry or we'll have another white face with us. Either way the news should get back to the Wamena airfield on the pilot's radio. The military will find out pretty quickly after that, depending on how MAF handle it. Once the military know, I presume they'll come straight in, with choppers and things.'

I stopped, breathless. Adrenalin ran through me as I thought of us escaping deep into the jungle. Images of helicopter gunships, jungle hideouts, freedom fighters and rebellion were going through my head and they were glorious and exciting. Life was running full tilt around me and I was hungry for more adventure. I felt I needed to laugh manically, to shake someone or scream as loud as could.

I looked to the others and wondered what they were feeling or thinking but it seemed an idiotic thing to ask. They looked sombre and serious and I remembered how dangerous the situation was. I was meant to be the leader, I was meant to be rational. I tried to calm myself, to bring myself down to earth. I thought of responsible things, boring things. I tried to imagine my old headmaster sitting with me and pictured what he would be doing, how he would be acting. He would be calm, patient and quiet. I tried to eat my rice.

'What about the short-wave radio?' asked Bill. 'I suppose they smashed that?'

'It was one of the first things to go,' said Annette. 'They ripped it out of the wall. I heard them do it while we were upstairs.'

Suddenly I felt incredibly frightened. The radio was everything; the one vital link to the outside world. It was manned by mission headquarters almost twenty-four hours a day and was always there in an emergency. Now there could be a massacre in Mapnduma and nobody would find out. My mind began taunting me, throwing up fragments of OPM stories I had heard. I looked to Frank across the table. 'What do you know about those Indonesian mountain climbers murdered on Mount Jaya near Freeport?'

'That was in the late 1980s,' said Frank. He put his elbows on the table, his chin on his hands and stared straight at me. 'They were shot full of arrows and robbed. It was the OPM, but the Indonesian government said it was just bandits and robbers. Same thing depending on your viewpoint.'

'And what about that Swiss pilot . . . ?' I asked.

'Yes, a missionary pilot, near the Papua New Guinea border in 1984. He was only held for a few days and apparently he became an OPM supporter after that.'

'And his Indonesian passengers were killed immediately, if you remember,' Mark added. 'Dan, Frank, let's just forget it, okay?' He leant back against the wall again and took Martha's hand.

I finished my food and stared at the floor. Just how much danger had we been in out there in the garden, in the frenzy of the attack? Could they have killed the Indonesians, or even us? I looked at the men crouching on the floor and perched awkwardly on chairs, eating meekly with their fingers from a few shared plates. I watched a man cautiously examine an ornament from the window sill, discussing it with his friend. Would those men harm us now? In cold blood? I watched Daud come down the stairs, stand at the bottom and look slowly about the room with wide feverish eyes. He began smiling and hopping from leg to leg again, shaking his machete in the air. I didn't trust him, or Silas. But at least if they decided to beat us, or cut us, I knew I wouldn't be the first. I looked over to the kitchen area. There was Tessy talking quietly in Lita's ear. I watched the flicker of a smile cross her face and she turned and looked tenderly at him. They were almost like twins. And Adinda was with Navy, rubbing dried blood from the cut above his eye. I wondered what they must be feeling, how scared they must be, and I thanked the Lord I was not them.

Annette cleared the plates away and we sat silently for maybe half an hour. Anna sat with her head bowed, staring into her lap, fiddling with the material of her tie-dye dress. I saw her look up once with an expression of contentment and calm, as if nothing were wrong, but then she frowned to herself and stared down again. Bill's face became inanimate and strained and I could almost see his worries pass before his eyes. When I looked to Annette I caught her eye and realized she was watching me.

There was some more muffled rustling from upstairs and Frank broke the silence. 'They're still searching, you know,' he said flippantly, pointing up to the ceiling. He seemed relaxed and unafraid, leaning back in his chair and fiddling with his black curly hair. 'So, Bill, what do you keep up there? Kalashinikovs? Grenades?'

Bill started. 'Yes, all that,' he said, coming back into the real world. 'Loads of them.'

'Tanks, too,' I added, enjoying a chance for humour. 'He needs them for the botanical work; for getting fruits down from the canopy.'

Frank laughed and was about reply when I saw Silas approaching out of the corner of my eye. He slammed his hand down on the table. We sat back paralysed in fright. 'You think because you are white you are not part of this?' he snarled in Indonesian. 'That maybe you are in no danger? Do you know who we are?' He passed his knife under each of our noses in turn. 'We are the OPM.' He stepped back and began striding up and down as the whole room fell into silence. 'It was white people who sold the Papuan people to Indonesia. They had promised us freedom. They cheated us and left us for dead. And if you are spies for the Indonesians, if my troops find guns, or documents . . . we will kill you.'

Murip came down stairs and whispered with Silas. 'Who owns the baggage upstairs?' demanded Silas. All the women, except Martha, kept their things in the upstairs bedrooms. Annette explained to Frank, who spoke to Silas in Indonesian.

'All the women upstairs now,' ordered Silas. Annette and Anna looked nervously at each other and stood up slowly. Navy came over with Adinda whose hand clasped her mouth in fear. Lita followed and Navy asked to go with them but Murip told him to sit at the table. So he joined us, his head in his hands, and we sat in silence together, listening anxiously for signs of trouble. Ten minutes on there was more banging and rustling and Frank called over one of the warriors, demanding to know what was happening. He did not know.

Twenty minutes later the women came down the stairs seemingly unharmed.

'What happened?' we asked.

'They asked us to pack,' said Annette.

'Pack what?'

'Everything. Didn't they ask you to do the same?'

We shook our heads.

'Maybe they are taking us into the forest,' said Anna.

There was silence. 'Maybe they just want to steal your stuff,' I said. 'It's easier if you've packed it all up for them.' But no one believed that.

Our friends from the village came and went, talking with us and the OPM. They squeezed our hands and looked into our eyes, shaking their heads and muttering, trying to reassure us that everything would be all right. As the rain turned to dreary drizzle there was still no sign that the OPM would run back to the forest, and as the remains of the afternoon began to fade it seemed increasingly likely that our guests were expecting to stay the night. The mood had become too heavy for talk. Further speculation was disturbing and anything else seemed too trivial. It was tempting to reassure each other, but it was obvious now that the situation was evolving into something much more elaborate than mere robbery. I was exhausted by the uncertainty and anxious for news.

The dusk settled and the house grew dark around us. The twelve-volt lighting circuit had been smashed so candles were brought out and given to the groups of warriors seated quietly on the floor. Most of the people who had stormed the house were strangers to Mapnduma, from villages further to the west. They had nowhere to stay and many had been keenly marking their floor space. Yudas, Murip and Daud, absent for much of the afternoon, appeared from the twilight and talked with Silas. Murip ushered Bram, Markus, Tessy and Lita over from the kitchen and seated them around the table, watching over us carefully. We waited obediently in the candlelight. Finally it seemed there was going to be some form of explanation.

Yudas moved forward and the other leaders closed in behind. 'You will tell me your names, nationality and what you are doing here,' demanded Yudas. He still had his gun, now slung over his shoulder with a strap. Murip had one, too, but I had seen no others.

There was a pause then Frank began, making the point that he was working to support the land rights of the Papuan people. Mark went next and explained that Martha worked with the UN and was also pregnant. Yudas was surprised by this and conferred for a moment as the information spread in murmurs across the room.

Yudas nodded to Anna next. 'I'm Anna McIvor,' she said. 'I'm a university student, from Britain.' And so it went on, Bill, Annette and I speaking in turn and then Navy speaking for all the Indonesians, omitting the fact that Adinda's father was a high-ranking government official. The Papuans, Marcus and Bram, were very scared because they worked for Indonesian government departments but Yakobus, our Nduga colleague, was nowhere to be seen.

Yudas moved closer to us, placing his hands on the edge of the table. He was quite a young man and he was intelligent. 'I have lived on this land all my life and my ancestors have lived here before me. This is Papuan land and it belongs to Papuan people. Indonesia is a different land, with different trees, different animals.

Papuan people have different skin, different hair, a different culture. Anyone can see.' He stepped back and gestured towards the troops crouched behind him. 'So why have our lands been taken away from us and our sacred forests and mountains destroyed? Why have our children and wives been tortured? Why have the Indonesians sent bombs, fire and chemical weapons to destroy our gardens, houses, villages and people? Why are Indonesians everywhere, living on our land, tricking and cheating us? Why do we walk naked and have no money when they are rich? Why did the United Nations and Holland promise to give us back our freedom and then do nothing?' He had been counting the questions on his fingers and now stopped and looked to Mark. 'We have been waiting now for thirty years. Why are we still waiting?'

He spoke in fast, fluent Indonesian and I had got the gist. Now Frank and Mark, who spoke excellent Indonesian and English, filled in the blanks.

'We are a proud people and a fighting people. For thirty years we have asked Indonesia to return our nation but they have done nothing except steal from us, lie to us and beat us. I have prayed to the Lord every night and asked him how we can find salvation. Whole villages have prayed. And now the Lord has answered our prayers for freedom. Your countries promised our freedom, and now the Lord has sent you to deliver it. When we are free, you will go free. We are prisoners together. We are one.'

I thought I had misunderstood his rhetoric but Frank groaned very audibly, shaking his head in disbelief. The Indonesians had all dropped their heads and Mark was whispering to Martha. The audience of brown eyes and gleaming torsos was watching silently in the flickering darkness of the room. Bows and arrows were neatly lined along the wall. I could hear the stream running through the darkness outside. I closed my eyes and swallowed. All I could think of was a story about a hostage whose finger had been sent out in a box.

Philipus, the preacher, had recovered from his despair earlier in the day and I was sure he could help us now. He climbed on to a chair, defiant and furious, and shook his fist in the air. 'How dare you men come to our village and make our hearts heavy. The people of Mapnduma do not want you here. This is our village and our land, these people are here working with us. Why do you come from another place to steal from our guests and bring trouble to our people? Go back to your own villages and cause trouble there!'

'You are an Nduga man. We are Nduga men,' argued Yudas. 'We are all fighting for the Nduga cause. We all want to be free, to be rich, to fight the Indonesians. The Lord has promised us freedom, and this is our way.'

Philipus grew calmer but I willed him to keep going. 'I believe in our freedom as every man in Papua does. If you are here for the true cause of the OPM, where is the letter from your leader? Where is the official stamp, where are the official papers? If this is the beginning of the revolution that we have been promised, then convince me. Otherwise leave here with your men and take away the trouble you have brought to our community.'

'This is the year and these people are the sign,' said Yudas frankly. 'This is the chance. The Lord has promised. What more proof do we need?'

Silas was nodding along to Yudas's speech. 'And if the Lord see fit we will die together, for Papua,' he shouted out.

'Come on. This is ridiculous,' Frank burst out at last. 'If you take us prisoner no one will help you. Holland, Britain, Germany will not want to help you if you steal their people. Anyway, they cannot give you your freedom. The army will come tomorrow and they will bomb the village and kill everyone.' He turned and pointed his finger at Silas. 'Yes, you are right, we will all die together. And we will die for nothing. We are the first people in decades to come and help your people. Our work is to help protect your lands, your forests and your rights. If you take us, then no one will help you ever again. Then you will have only the Indonesians and their bombs for company.'

Silas was infuriated at the outburst but didn't seem to have the ability for further argument. 'Don't mock us,' he spluttered, 'and try to deceive us with your smart talk or you will die on the end

above From the Mapnduma plateau looking up the Gul valley to Mt Koro (4250 metres), one peak along the New Guinea central cordillera. The military and mines have never come to the Nduga mountains.

right Moving mountains: Mount Jaya (4884 metres) in the Amungme tribal area, the Freeport copper and gold mine is beneath. An entire mountain peak, rich in copper ore, used to stand in the foreground.

Those displaced by the mines were resettled to camps near Timika where they tried to adapt to life in the lowlands under strict military rule.

A typical highland village of five or six families.

above Making fire by rubbing bamboo cord against a wooden pole filled with kindling.

left While we were being marched through the forest, streams often cleared a path through the trees but in the highlands the terrain is rarely flat like this.

Crossing the river one at a time on a rattan bridge. Many bridges in more remote areas are just single rattans which the men and women climb along.

Opening up a cooking pit, filled with potatoes, greens, pig and hot stones.

above Morning mist fills the deep valleys.

left Some of our houses were in sunny clearings like this one. Others were in the depths of the dark forest.

These *buah merah* or red fruit are a delicacy found only in the low foothills between November and April. The fruit are cooked and mashed into an oily slop which tastes like a cross between dark chocolate and coffee.

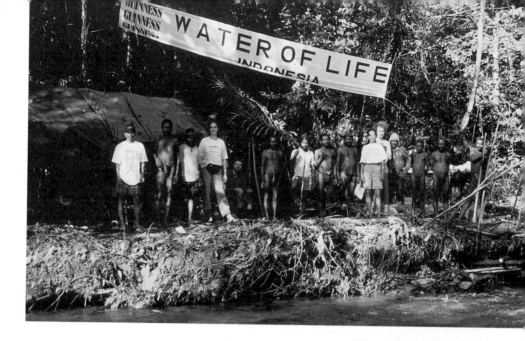

above Working in the lowland foothills on the Paro river south of Mapnduma during the expedition in mid–November 1995. The group includes (from left to right) Tessy, Annette, Adinda and myself.

right Bram and Annette fishing. This was a promotional shot for Guinness who sponsored our fish studies.

The metropolis of Mapnduma, the biggest village in the 3000 m² Nduga region. The missionary house is in the far left corner.

Our first camp 'on the run' in late January 1996.

Silas asked us to take pictures so that our parents would cry and come to get us.
Tessy, Navy, Adinda, Annette, Markus (in front), Bram (behind) and Silas.

On Sunday 25 February we received letters through the ICRC after being 'lost' for five weeks on the run and in the cold house. From left to right, Bill, Mark, Martha, Annette, Anna and me.

left Annette, Adinda, Lita and Bill wash in the sun near the third river house. Adinda has wounds on her ankles. Anna is reading a book sent in by the British Embassy.

below Navy, Mark and me in the pig village after meeting the ICRC. During the walk there from Daud's house, we had been convinced that Kwalik's men were kidnapping us again.

On the look-out for the ICRC helicopter, shouldering one of the three OPM guns.

A village elder leading the ICRC to a village where they hoped to make contact with the OPM and, eventually, us.

of my blade.' He waved his knife in the air, stepped backwards, stumbled over someone's stray leg and then stormed out of the door. The room fell to quiet whispering again.

'Be careful, Frank,' said Martha. 'That man could do something crazy.'

'They need to understand,' Frank said. He was exasperated. 'This is just a disaster, a disaster for everything we were going to do.'

'It's a disaster but let's get out of it alive,' said Annette. 'Did he actually say they were going to take us prisoner? I didn't understand.'

'*Tahanan bersama-sama*, wasn't it?' I asked. 'Prisoners together?'

Navy nodded sullenly in confirmation. He and the Indonesians had been staying well in the background. Anna suddenly looked exhausted and upset, almost on the brink of tears. Bill put his arm around her awkwardly.

'It's all talk,' said Frank. 'These people are just excited, that's all.'

'And what are the military going to do when they find out about this?' I asked.

'Bomb us into oblivion, knowing their record in these parts,' said Annette dryly, flicking her hand across the table in a series of small explosions. 'Just bomb, bomb, bomb.'

It felt like eight o'clock, although none of us had our watches any longer, and I was desperate to use the loo. With some encouragement from the rest of us, Anna and Annette had asked permission and gone together. Now I considered it, too. The bathroom was near the back door just ten metres away but the route was crowded with muscular men, standing tall, wearing penis gourds or tight shorts. As I approached they scowled and I was scared that they might hit me, but as I passed they flinched timidly, and I could feel their nervousness. It gave me confidence and I stood by the open back door for a moment and stared out at the cold, starlit sky above the mountains. The faint breeze brought in the smell of wet vegetation and smoke from the village. If I ran now could I hide or escape into the darkness? But escape to where? Wherever I ran they could track my footprints, wherever I hid their dogs could sniff me out. The forest was never empty. Always there would be watching eyes.

I wandered into the kitchen area where Anna and Annette were sitting in slumped silence on the floor. I put my arm around Anna, smiled stoically and sighed.

'Don't worry, Dan, maybe they'll run away,' she said simply. 'Some of the men are quite nice. Look what I've got.' She showed me a cold *ubi*, the local sweet potato, possibly the most disgusting brand of tuber in the world. She pulled off a bit and gave it to me.

'Thanks.' I was hungry and pleased to see it.

Opposite them Markus was telling one of his tales and two young OPM men were listening intently, exclaiming intermittently and smoking furiously. I craved the nicotine and I caught one of the men's eyes with a pleading expression. He smiled and handed me his smouldering, leafy construction. I gave it a good, noisy wheeze, as I had seen them do, then choked in a splutter of smoke. They were delighted and clicked their penis gourds as I sank back and closed my eyes in euphoric faintness.

'Where will you sleep tonight?' I asked Annette after I had come to.

'Upstairs,' she replied. 'They said that's OK.'

'Will you be all right?'

She nodded wearily.

I took a candle into the small bedroom I shared with Bill and shut the door. Our private room had been ransacked. I checked through the draws, then crouched on the floor, collecting the scattered clothes and piling them into the cupboard.

'They haven't found my binoculars yet,' I said to Bill as he came into the room. 'They can't have searched that well.'

'They found my wallet,' he said picking it up from the desk. 'And emptied it.'

I got up to look for mine. It was empty too. All the money I had saved for our post-expedition holiday had gone. I made my bed and decided to shave.

'What are you doing, Dan?'

I was spraying foam into my palm. 'Getting ready. They're going to take us into the forest, Bill, and it could be anytime, even tonight. I hate being unshaven.' Bill looked at me blankly. I started scraping the foam from my face. 'Bastards took my credit cards, too,' I realized.

'What are they going to do with those around here?' he asked. 'Put them through their noses, perhaps?'

The tension of the day seemed to be slipping away with the thought of sleep. 'Can I listen to your last message?' I asked as Bill reached down under his bed and brought out the tape recorder.

'No way.'

'Are you going to do another recording?' He was meant to be making a radio diary of the expedition for BBC Radio Four.

'Do you think I should? It might be useful if anyone comes searching for us.'

We discussed the options together and recorded them on to the tape. There was still the possibility that we would wake up in the morning and the OPM would be gone. If they weren't, there was a chance they would hold us in the house for another day, but that was unlikely given the military threat. Their most sensible option would be to take us into the jungle.

I got into my sleeping bag feeling remarkably relaxed and calm. I certainly wasn't worrying about how I should use the last days of the expedition any more. The decision was someone else's responsibility. All I had to think about now was obeying orders and not getting hurt.

Bill blew out the candle and I stared into the darkness waiting for the contours of the room to form.

'How violent do you think the Papuans really are, Bill?'

'You know about those mountain climbers, Dan.'

'Hmm. And Nlam killed his second wife with an arrow because he thought she was a witch,' I added.

'Go to sleep, Dan.'

'Goodnight, Bill.'

I lay there listening for while. Screams echoed across the valley as the people slaughtered their pigs in the night and I heard Philipus calling through the village like the death van, 'Flee to the forest. Run and hide'. Then I slept deeply, intoxicated by wild, hallucinatory dreams. I was woken only once. There were people in the room, around me, whispering, crawling and banging. A door closed, and there was silence. I lay still and breathless in the darkness until the scratching and clanking of the cockroaches' armoured bodies on the floor and walls signalled calm. Then I slept through until the first light of morning.

FIVE

OUT OF MAPNDUMA

I watched the room through the draped veil of the mosquito net. The orange curtains were fringed with light and I could already read the words on the children's games stacked on top of the cupboard opposite. I guessed it was about six, later than I usually woke. There was a muffled sound of movement from next door and I wondered who was up and what was happening. I remembered WWF's chartered aeroplane. On a clear day it might leave the airbase in Wamena this early and already be droning over the mountains towards us.

I thought of curling up and turning off, of facing this morning another time, but already I was too apprehensive to lie quietly. I crawled out from under the mosquito net and stood uselessly in the middle of the tiny room, shivering in the chill morning air, too drowsy and cold to think straight. I stared blankly at the heap of clothes in the bottom of the wardrobe. Today anything could happen so I should wear the best I could find. A shirt was most versatile, with long sleeves and a collar to give protection from the sun, forest and insects and a button front that could be opened for ventilation. I chose the coral one, my favourite. I found my thick cotton slacks and I fastened them with an expensive suede belt, a Christmas present from my brother. I felt smart and confident.

There was definitely movement in the house, but I didn't want to be involved for now. Bill was asleep and I decided not to wake him. I tiptoed to the window and eased back the curtain. The dawn light was cold and grey and I could still see the moon above the ridge. It would be several hours before the sun rose above the surrounding mountains and burnt out the mist and dank air from deep in the valley. I drew back quickly as I saw Silas and Yudas approaching across the garden, pointing and planning. I didn't want anything to disturb the peace and solitude of the room. It seemed very precious.

I began collecting some essential items together in a plastic bag: my sleeping bag, but not my camping mattress; my soap and tooth-brush, but no toothpaste or shaving material; a T-shirt, polo-neck and a pair of socks, but no boxer shorts. Finally I found my torch, medical bag, knife, pen, paper, lighter, compass and whistle. The kit was compact, simple and gave me a feeling of self-reliance. I felt no fear now, just a strong, stoic resolve. I no longer imagined that the OPM would harm me but I anticipated hardship, possibly severe. Strangely, there was even something about the thought of it that I relished.

Bill's bed creaked and I looked to him. He was lying very still, but through the mosquito net I could see his eyes staring wide at the ceiling.

'Bill, we should get up really,' I said softly. 'I think the rest of the house has been up for ages. I don't know what they're doing. I haven't dared go out yet.'

He rose slowly and sat on the edge of his bed. 'What's that?' he asked pointing to my plastic bag.

'Useful things. In case they decide to take us into the forest or something.'

'I should put some things together too.' He sounded very tired.

'Look, you get ready. I'll go out and see what's going on.'

I opened the door quietly, not wishing to draw attention to myself. Navy was hurrying towards the back door carrying pots and pans.

'Hi,' I said as he passed. He gave me a long, slow nod as he went by. Annette and Tessy followed close behind. Tessy was carrying a large box, and Annette had a tent under each arm.

'Annette?' I said.

'What?' she asked shortly

'Would you like a hand?'

72

'No.' She placed them outside in the garden and I stopped her as she came back in. 'What's happening? How long have you been up?'

'About an hour, maybe longer. You know we're leaving?' she said, irritated that I was so ill informed

'Are we? Where to?' I had expected this, but not so soon.

'Into the forest, presumably. They keep talking about the army.'

'When are we leaving?'

'Now. They want to clear Mapnduma and just leave OPM troops to fight when the army comes. Did you hear Philipus calling in the night?'

'Yes.'

'Well, the village is completely empty and so are all the villages on the other side of the valley. The people slaughtered all their pigs so the army wouldn't be able to take them. Now the OPM have told us to pack everything.'

'Everything?' I said in disbelief. 'But we've got about a tonne of equipment here.'

'Well, it's all going wherever we're going.'

She walked off just as Silas came.

'Where's Anna?' I called after her.

'Outside packing up with Navy and Tessy. Frank's there, too, I think. All the others are packing in the storerooms round the back.'

'What are you doing?' shouted Silas.

'Packing,' I said.

'Good. We leave now.' He stormed past and I heard him shouting outside in the garden.

I went straight back into the bedroom and closed the door behind me.

'Bill, we're going. Now, apparently.'

'What the hell?'

'Yes, pack up. Have you got everything?'

'No, what are you taking?' he asked. He sounded panicked.

'That,' I said, pointing to the plastic bag on the bed. 'They want us to take everything, but there's no way we'll be able to carry it. I'm taking the bare minimum.'

'What shall I do with my tapes, do you think? What are you going to do with your films?' I had twenty rolls of film and three hours of video footage, much of it unique.

'My films, I hadn't thought.' Now that I remembered my precious films I began to feel really worried. I didn't mind losing anything else, but not my films. 'It's stupid to take them with us; who knows where we'll end up. I'm going to leave them here and maybe we can recover them sometime.'

'I'll do the same with the tapes.'

'Okay.' Bill was frantically looking for things in the mess of the room. 'What shoes are you wearing?' I asked. I had no shoes on yet.

'My jungle boots, they're out the front.'

'So are mine. I'll get them.'

I went into the drawing room. There was no one about. In fact the whole house seemed very empty and bare now. I pulled out the bottom draw of the photographic cupboard in which my films were stored. They were still there. I opened the airtight boxes, took out the films and threw the canisters under the bottom of the stairs. Now they looked less important, scattered like rubbish. Next I went to find the shoes. In the lobby the benches had been broken and there was a gaping space in the wall where the radio should have been. I scanned the floor for the boots. Nothing. Even my big rucksack that I had hung there was gone.

'Bastards,' I said out loud. If there was one crucial thing in this forest it was good shoes. I went back into the house, through to the back door and down into the back garden. In front of me on the grass was a pile of boxes, bags and sacks almost as tall as me. I was horrified.

'Who's carrying all that?' I asked Frank who was busy with his rucksack.

'That's not our problem,' he said.

'Does anyone know where the boots in the hall have gone?' No one was very interested in the question. I went back to Bill. 'No boots,' I said. 'They've all been stolen.'

'Shit.'

'Exactly.'

I began rummaging around in the bottom of the cupboard. I had a pair of brogues which I used for church on Sundays. They had a good grip and seemed comfortable but I wasn't sure how long they would last on the steep forest paths. I put them on.

'This completes the outfit nicely,' I said standing up. 'Perhaps I should take a tie as well.'

'I'll have to wear my deck shoes,' said Bill, shaking his head. He continued packing his rucksack despondently.

'Can you leave space for my stuff?' I threw him my bag of things.

I didn't pack anything extra. I don't know why. Maybe it was because there was no room in Bill's bag and I didn't have my own. Perhaps I still thought I would have to carry it myself. Most probably, packing shaving foam and slippers didn't seem quite appropriate to the trip on which we were about to embark.

We congregated in the back garden. The fence was broken in many places and yesterday's feet had churned up the flower beds and lawn. The rain had turned the turf to sticky mud. Several boxes stood around the growing mound of baggage. We had carried our freight from Britain in them and my father's address was scrawled on each in Annette's compressed handwriting. I hadn't been in touch with home for months. It would be half past ten on Monday evening there now. I wondered when my parents would hear about us. I wondered if they would ever hear the real story, told by me in my own words. I had this feeling that if we left Mapnduma now we might just disappear off the edge of the world and never be seen again.

'Hi, Dan,' said Anna, coming up beside me. 'Are you okay?'

'You know, up and down.' I was still staring at the boxes. I turned to her. 'Do you have any idea where they're taking us?'

'No. But they came from up there.' She pointed to the west, to the ridge above the village. 'So presumably they'll take us back that way.'

'I know, but have you heard them say anything, heard any place names mentioned?' She was by far the best of all of us at the Nduga language.

'No. You?'

'Well, not recently. But you remember when I drew that map with Nathaniel, when we were down in Kurukmu last month?' Kurukmu was a tiny village near the Yugguru river in the next valley to the west, on the other side of the ridge. Anna and I had worked there with a small group of families for about a week. 'He marked the next river west of Yugguru; the Kilmid he called it.'

'The one where you said there were no villages?'

'That was it. Nathaniel called the whole area *hutan kosong*, empty forest. There were some villages there once, he said, but they had been abandoned because of bad spirits and nobody went there, except the OPM. He said they had secret gardens there and at the top of the river, nearer the mountains, he drew caves. He said they were for hiding. When they fought Indonesia he said they would hide in there, under the earth, and never be found.'

'What, you think we're going to Kilmid?' asked Anna, slightly alarmed.

'I wondered if you'd heard anyone mention it, that's all.'

I was perturbed. If we were being taken to Kilmid the army, or whoever, could search for a year without finding us. Not even the locals went there. I went back inside and found a piece of airmail paper. I began what I hoped would look like an innocent letter.

9th January 1996, 07.00

Dear Mother,

Having a difficult time here on the expedition. Have been taken west, probably to the second major valley to the west, or possibly the caves to the north of it.

Hope to see you soon,
With lots of love,
Daniel xxx

It was a fairly pathetic attempt but it made me feel better. I left it on my bed, half hidden by the pillow.

Back outside there was general commotion. About thirty OPM troops were standing in small groups looking cold and tired. They were talking among themselves and pointing at the pile of luggage. Silas was further away, shouting orders and motioning to the men. Silas's lieutenant was blowing his white whistle.

The normal carrying accessory in the highlands was the *nokin*, a string bag made from woven strands of fibrous bark, slung over the forehead and down the back. It was tiny when folded but could expand to carry a child, twenty pounds of potatoes or, in this instance, a large box. *Nokins* were natural brown or dyed in muted colours when new but quickly became black and smelly, stained by grime and sweat. Each man, woman and child possessed a *nokin*. For a Papuan man it was part of the essential kit, together with a bow and arrow, penis gourd, various necklaces, arm and leg bands, fire-lighting equipment, a spoon made from pig bone, a rain mat for sleeping on or sheltering from the rain, a bamboo tube for keeping things dry, tobacco wrapped in leaves, and a knife or machete, if they were lucky.

Eventually the troops came up one by one and begrudgingly took pieces of baggage, returning to their groups to argue about the weight and bulk. Some gear just wouldn't fit into the *nokins*, so rattan was used to make long carrying straps which hooked over the forehead and held the weight down the back. The men found the shoulder straps on the rucksacks peculiar so they carried them upside down placing the belt strap around their foreheads. Once they were loaded up there was no hanging about; they were off, hunched forward, striding across the village and up towards the ridge.

The village was almost empty but I saw Philipus in conversation with some other locals at the front of the house. He came up to our group and squeezed each of our hands in turn, and said softly, '*Puji Tuhan*, Praise the Lord.' He climbed on to the low wall, there was silence from the crowd and even those with loads stopped to listen.

'If you, the OPM, are taking our friends away I can do little to stop you. I ask only this: that you treat them as the guests that they are. You treat them with the friendship you would treat another Nduga.' He turned to us and tears were in his eyes. 'I ask God to bless you in the time ahead. You are with my brothers, Nduga men, good and peaceful men. No harm will come to you.'

The men began murmuring and sorting baggage again.

'Start walking,' Silas ordered. 'We must walk far today.'

We looked at each other, an uneasy and awkward group, unwilling to leave familiar territory. Even Philipus, the village head, could do nothing to help us now. We shuffled forward nervously, looking to each other for reassurance. Was this it? Did we really have no option? Massive feelings of anxiety and impotence welled up inside. Suddenly I had to do something, anything, if only to stop us being taken so far. Perhaps if we went slow enough the aeroplane would arrive before we were out of sight. Perhaps if we looked pitiful enough they would think Kilmid or the caves were just too far. I moved up to the front of our group towards Navy. 'Navy, we must go slow. Very slow. What do you think?' He nodded stiffly, staring straight ahead, almost willing me not to draw attention to him. He was the male Indonesian leader, the symbol of everything the OPM resented. He bore his fear with a courage and composure I could only look to.

I began to hobble and stumble like a pensioner and our convoy set off at a crawl, all of us trudging wearily with leaden limbs. We moved along the neat, paved paths lined with ditches; we crossed the grass kept trim by teams of women armed with wooden blades and we reached the water-logged ground at the edge of the village. The mud oozed up over the top of my brogues as we crossed the fence and entered the pig pasture that stretched far up the hillside.

The path zigzagged up through shrubland and low woodland. We were leaving Mapnduma behind, empty and cold in the morning shadow. Above me, the forest was already flushed with morning light. The glow was creeping down the hillside towards us. I stopped for a moment and sat down on a rock, pretending to be out of breath. To the east, on the opposite ridge of the valley, the sun was just rising, a blinding incandescent ball. Squinting, I turned my face away and held out my hands to warm my palms with its rays.

The rain-cleansed sky was a deep and brilliant blue, but flecks of white cloud were already beginning to collect along the jagged northern peaks. I strained to hear the whine of a Cessna aircraft approaching across the mountains, but there was nothing except the rumble of the river foaming through the gorge below.

Frank was climbing up the hill and out of the shadow below me. 'Do you think your plane will come?' I asked, still staring out across the valley.

'No, I don't think so,' he said glumly, his hands on his hips and his silhouette black against the sun.

'Frank, I don't think we should let them take us away from here. I get the feeling that once we're over this ridge and into the forest, then things might get really bad.'

'So what do you suggest?'

'We don't know what's waiting in the forest and once we're there it's too late. We need to do something now, while we still have an advantage. Even if we could just delay a few hours the plane might come. Can't you and Mark talk to them again; your Indonesian is so much better than ours. Explain they're making a big mistake.'

He thought for a moment. If anyone had the nerve to try and talk the leaders round, it was Frank. 'Okay, I'll try,' he said as he started back down.

'Even if we just sit here and refuse to move,' I called down after him. 'It's worth a try, isn't it?' I wondered what would happen if we did. How far would they go to make us move? How long would our group hold out for?

Frank was in discussion with Silas and Yudas. I could hear the faint voices. I heard Mark and Martha join in, too. Up ahead the others had stopped so I climbed up to join them.

'What's going on down there?' asked Bill.

'Frank and Mark are trying to persuade them not to take us into the forest.'

'They'll be lucky,' said Annette.

'We could be in Wamena tomorrow buying Frank a beer,' I said, tormenting myself. We sat on the rocky path waiting in tense

One of the OPM men swung his head signalling we should
n. 'Jalan! Walk!' he urged in Indonesian.

a minute,' I said forcefully. 'We're waiting for our friends.'
stood there, watching over us impatiently. 'It's late,' he said.
'The rain will come early today. We must move quickly. We have
far to go.'

Far to go. The words filled me with dread. We had to stay close
to Mapnduma or everything was lost.

'Just a minute,' I said again, angrily this time, pointing down the
hill at the distant figures negotiating our fate. I was damned if I
was going to move when it looked as if Frank and Mark were
having some success.

Navy, Tessy, Lita and Adinda were sitting silently on a stone
above. 'Where are Markus, Bram and Yakobus?' I asked them in
English.

'Maybe they're ahead,' said Anna. 'I think because they're
Papuans they can't get away with walking slowly.'

'No, they were definitely behind us when we left the village,'
said Annette.

Their whereabouts concerned me but then Frank, Mark and
Martha started to come up the path with Silas behind them. Yudas
stood below with his gun over his shoulder, looking agitated. 'Walk,
walk,' he shouted up at us and so we moved slowly on again.

I pulled my shirt up and on to my head to protect me from the
sun. The air was still cold but I could feel it burning into the back
of my neck. I dropped back to speak to Frank.

'What happened?' I whispered.

'We got close. They agreed with everything we said. They agreed
it was wrong to take prisoners. They said that all they really wanted
was the money and baggage.'

'Did Yudas agree as well?' I asked.

'Yes, he was the one who was talking the most. He was almost
apologetic.'

'Really? So why won't they let us go?'

'They said they can't. They talked about a big leader who's
already on the way with more troops.'

My hope turned to fear. Again I began thinking of the empty forests and caves of the Kilmid valley, the dense expanse of jungle and mountains that lay to the west, all crawling with OPM.

'What did they say about this big leader?' I asked.

'He's from the Amungme tribe to the west. He lost some of his family to the military a while back. Did you ever hear of Kelly Kwalik?'

SIX

INTO THE FOREST

The morning wore on as we laboured along the steep path whispering news and ideas back and forth. OPM were nearby but we were
sure they could not understand English. The man with the white
whistle was helping us navigate the path, positioning himself ready
with a hand and encouraging smile to steady us along the more
difficult sections. Silas had become suddenly helpful and considerate
with no hint of the violent streak we had seen the day before.

The walking charade I had begun in the village began to take
me over. By building up a mental picture of an old man with very
poor balance, unable to see many steps in front of him and with a
severe fear of falling, I succeeded in tottering precariously with
every step. Sections of the path which I would have normally
enjoyed for the sporting challenge were terrifying in my new condition. The OPM men looked at me with sympathy, shaking their
head as they helped me across slippery logs and up steep mud banks.
They mumbled about me being an *anak kota*, a child of the city:
unable to walk or run, crippled by a sedentary lifestyle. They, of
course, were naturally strong. Posing, they stood on the path flexing
the muscles in their arms and legs. They could walk for many
weeks, they said, sometimes eating only leaves and insects.

As I staggered along, Anna giggled sporadically behind me.

'You look hysterical,' she said. 'You're making my day.'

'Oh, shut up,' I snapped. I was beginning to feel like a fool. 'At
least they'll think twice about walking us all over the place if we
look this bad.'

I wondered if I had started something I would later regret. Now they believed I was this slow, how could I ever return to being a normal walker, nimble and fast? Was I destined to hobble through the jungle like a cripple for the rest of my time here?

'Does it look as if I'm faking?' I asked, turning around and quite unconsciously reaching out to grab a branch for support.

'No, no, you look quite real, just funny, that's all.'

'Anyway, it might be part of a plan.'

'What kind of plan?'

'Anna, I'm really scared what might happen once we get into the forest,' I began apologetically. 'I mean, I don't want to be alarming but there is this big leader and his troops. It could be a re-run of yesterday, but worse. If things look bad and we have to do something then I could run back to Mapnduma in the night and wait for the army. They would never suspect me because I look so pathetic.'

'Do you think it'll get that bad?'

We had been going for over two hours and were out of the open bush of the pig gardens below and into degraded, secondary forest which clung precariously to the steep slope. It was thick and impenetrable in parts, a tangle of tall thin saplings, spiky vines and ground vegetation. For many years the village had used the original forest as a source of firewood and building material and had removed all the mature timber. We were shaded from the sun, but the humidity was rising. I opened my shirt and the gnats began sticking themselves to my clammy skin.

The path was gradually ascending the steep hillside while crossing to the left, moving us into the fold of a wide gully; a deep groove that had been eroded from the flank of the ridge. After perhaps a kilometre we reached the main stream which cascaded down over large boulders towards the Gul river and I realized it was the same valley that fed a waterfall and pool below Mapnduma in which the local children and I used to swim. We followed the shallow river using the open course as a route up through the forest to reach the ridge. Some way along I saw Yakobus resting in a patch of sun on the bank. I hadn't seen him since we had been in the kitchen together the previous day and I thought they had let him go. It seemed strange that they should kidnap one of their own people. His Dani wife, Ola, and their baby daughter were with him now as well. They had flown into Mapnduma to join him for Christmas. Yakobus was washing out his child's nappy sending swirling yellow debris into the clear drinking water below.

'Yakobus, Ola, how are you?' I asked in English, too surprised to use Indonesian.

'I'm okay, Dan,' he said in his husky American accent. Yakobus had learnt English at university and always sounded very cool. He was short but had a wonderful smile and all the women fancied him.

'I thought maybe they had let you go?'

'Dan, you think I am not in this, too? You think because I have black skin there is no danger?' He raised his voice and threw his arms out in some despair. 'I work for the government, you know. I'm in trouble, too. Because I work for the government maybe they want to kill me.' I remembered he had worked distributing government aid to the surrounding villages in the form of pigs.

'Sorry, I didn't think.' I knelt down and cooed at the baby who stared at me wide-eyed and began to cry. Ola came quickly and picked her up and I carried on up the stream embarrassed and uneasy. He sounded sincere but I was not sure. He had once told me he was related to Yudas and I wondered just how much he had known in advance about the raid. I decided that it was even possible that with his good English he was not a prisoner at all but a spy. The thought of it filled me with anger and fuelled my paranoia. Bill was waiting ahead for me to catch up and we carried on walking together.

'Where are Bram and Markus?' I asked.

'I haven't seen them since this morning.'

'Bill, do you think they might have run?'

'What?' Bill looked surprised. 'You think that's possible?'

I looked around. There was no one in sight. To the left and right there was thick forest. Ten metres in and you would be hidden.

'Or maybe they've let them go,' I said. 'Come on, what use are Papuans to them?'

'They wouldn't leave us?'

'Want a bet?'

I felt deceived and humiliated. I remembered an old army maxim: escape as soon as possible. The longer one waits the more difficult it becomes. Like lemmings we were walking deeper and deeper into the unknown, into the hands of their big leader, whoever he was. I felt emasculated and as helpless as if I were in a sack whose narrow opening was tightening above me. Our options were shrinking away with every step we took and now was the time to get out. But while it was possible for one or two people to run, the whole team could never escape. I would never leave the others. If I did I would die of shame.

By late morning the stream bed had shrivelled and dried. The new path was also worn but steeper and rockier as we neared the top of the ridge. The trees became smaller in stature and their branches were clad in moss which fell in green tentacles towards the ground. I had travelled this path before with Philipus. It took him to his gardens, over the ridge and down into the next valley and to the Yugguru river. From a small natural clearing Mapnduma came into view again, shrunken to a few small dots on a tiny green plateau below. The two-hundred-metre airstrip was just a thin line running right along the edge. From this height I could see right over our valley towards the parallel ridges that stretched to the eastern horizon like a row of buttresses supporting the mountain chain. Each crest marked the watershed between the rivers which drained the high cordillera. Cumulus cloud had heaped up obscuring the mountain peaks but the sun was still bright and hot. We stopped frequently at the small streams that crossed the path, drinking from our water bottles and hands.

It was about midday when we reached the top; a small flat clearing with steep forested paths leading down on either side. Some of the OPM men were there with our baggage, smoking tobacco next to a small fire made from bark shavings and twigs.

Markus was sprawled on his back, his body stiff with pain, his pink sweater filthy and his right hand on his lower abdomen. He was groaning gently and inhaling deeply from the leafy cigarettes which the OPM men were carefully administering to him. Bram was several feet away sitting motionless against a tree, staring sorrowfully down at his tightly clasped hands. I touched him to say hello, and realized he had been crying. Markus was only able to moan '*hati*, liver'. He was suffering from a recurring complaint. It seemed absurd that a few hours before I had felt so sure they had escaped.

Mark and Martha, Navy and Adinda finally arrived and so did Silas who was bringing up the rear. The sky was clouding up quickly above us. We rested for a while before Silas became impatient. 'Soon it will rain,' he said looking up. 'We will make a shelter in the forest nearby. Start walking.'

'Now this is what I call a path,' Anna said as we began to descend. There was a flight of wooden steps built into the slope and she plonked gracelessly down them in her heavy army boots and baggy jungle fatigues. 'Does this by any chance go down to Kurukmu?'

Kurukmu and the path we had taken to it were further to the south. From the maps I had made with locals I was sure that this path went down to Aptam which, like Kurukmu, was near the Yugguru river. There was bound to be a path linking the villages, which meant that if we ended up in Aptam I would know two routes back to Mapnduma, should I have to return.

I caught up with Martha along the path. She was tall and slim, in her early thirties, with short, light brown hair. She had draped a green sarong over her head to keep out the muck and mop up the sweat. I had talked to her only briefly since her arrival in Mapnduma a few days before and she was still a virtual stranger. I wondered how to begin. 'How are your feet after your walk here?' I asked.

'You know, they really are very sore. All of us got really bad blisters. Frank, he has a horrible one under his toe. Have you had much problem from skin infections in Mapnduma?' She spoke sincerely with a lively, intonated Dutch accent.

'Yes, we've all had problems. I got a really nasty boil on my foot when we arrived. It just blew up from nothing and within a few hours my whole foot was inflamed. Really painful. I had to take antibiotics, erythromycin.'

'It's okay now?'

'Better, but still a little infected. The antibiotics stopped the infection spreading, and I managed to get most of the pus out, but now there's a wound that just won't heal. Seven weeks now and every time I go into the forest and my foot gets wet it opens up again. Have you been in tropical forests before?'

'Oh yes, I did my masters' study in Guinea Bissau, west Africa before I joined Unesco.'

'Guinea Bissau, sounds interesting. Did you enjoy it?'

I cringed at the banality of the conversation, so inappropriate to the situation.

'Oh yes, it was a very fun time.' But she was more concerned about skin infections. 'You have much medicine with you?'

'I think so. I think we brought the big medical kit.' In fact I had no idea. I hadn't checked and I was embarrassed that I had forgotten something so crucial. 'We've got lots of insect repellent. I grabbed a whole lot of that this morning.' I had seen all the bottles lined up on the shelf and put all eight in Bill's bag. I hated being bitten by mosquitoes and, there was a serious danger of malaria, of course, but now it struck me how ridiculous it was that I had brought so much my yet left behind my toothpaste and even spare underwear.

We were both quite cheerful. The group still together; I knew more or less where we were; I knew they weren't taking us for miles that afternoon; Silas was being reasonable; Frank had almost persuaded Yudas to let us go. My anxiety had lifted. It was probably not as serious a situation as I had thought and the big leader might well be a rational man. We were likely to be released within a few days and I felt quite foolish for having worried earlier on.

'So what do you think of all this?' I asked Martha. It was the question I had wanted to ask originally.

'Oh, it's so stupid, so stupid,' she replied emphatically. 'I don't know what they think they can achieve by doing this.'

'Well. let's hope they get bored soon.'

'Surely it will be just a few days.'

I tried to imagine the news reaching Britain and wondered how it would be interpreted. We were just some researchers who had been walked a few miles away from their home by some over-excited men. It didn't seem particularly consequential. I hoped my parents would see it that way and not worry too much. With a bit of luck we might be in Wamena before anyone found out.

The clouds were darkening above and the air was heavy. It was two hours since we had left the ridge and still there was no sign that we would stop and make a shelter. The path had become less clear; I was unsure if I would remember it if I had to return. We had joined a mountain stream that flowed down the course of an old landslide, a scar of grey rubble that stretched below us like lava winding down the steep hillside. It was fairly solid with new vegetation growing up between the broken rock and shale, but careless feet still sent a cascade of debris on to those below.

A new stream joined from the right and I made a mental note of the junction. Further down more tributaries converged and I stopped to drink. I was tired, dizzy and dehydrated. As we dropped lower, the land grew flatter and the river deeper. We followed the course closely, crossing back and forth between the banks, wet up to our knees in the cold water. A mist had descended, coating us in a fine film of moisture. The pace quickened, and our OPM chaperons goaded us on with false promises. 'It's not far, you're almost there.' They had been saying this for hours.

The river crossed a belt of harder sandstone rock. The land rose but the river cut through via a narrow gorge. With no banks to follow we waded into the tunnel, keeping close to the outer wall as the course curved round to the left. The eddies had bored neat circular patterns in the stone and fifteen feet above us a jammed tree trunk marked the highest flood water.

The path moved back into the forest and then emerged where

the river had spread to a wide flat open bed of rounded rocks and stones. There was a small central island of grasses around which the river had split into two streams.

'Look at this,' I said excitedly, turning to Bill as we came out of the forest. We had been walking together, talking about the army. The flat bed of the river had just come into view.

'Shit,' he said in amazement.

'It's perfect isn't it. How big do you reckon it is?'

'I don't know. I'll pace it out as we walk.'

'I bet its at least sixty by a hundred metres, maybe more.'

'And no overhanging trees, just gardens on either side.' It was extremely rare to find such a large piece of open ground. 'You could easily get a helicopter in here, maybe two.' It was another place to remember.

The mist had lifted and for a while the sun appeared again, but the clouds were black and vengeful. Up ahead two women were kneeling by the river. They had the same wide eyes and pleasant faces and both wore grass skirts, ankle rings and beads. One was young, a teenager and the other was older, perhaps her mother. The young girl's breasts were full, while her mother's sagged like empty skins to her wrinkled navel. It was likely we were drawing close to a village. Two *nokins* lay next to the women, spilling earthy potatoes by their side and they scrubbed them in the current with a handful of scrunched leaves. The women bit their fingers and giggled with embarrassment as we approached.

'*Wa, wa,*' I said, smiling as I passed them.

The daughter hesitated then replied, '*Nord wa,*' throwing her head forward with gleaming, almost flirtatious eyes. She turned immediately and buried her head behind her mother's shoulder, giggling uncontrollably. Further round the corner there were more people. Two young brothers with slightly bloated stomachs were sitting on a large rock by the river. One I knew. He was the son of Nathaniel, the local man with whom I had worked for much of the expedition. He was about eight years old and wore a small penis gourd to show that he was not yet a man. His little brother was naked and throwing stones into the river.

Nathaniel's eldest son was very bright. He had joined us in the forest most days and knew almost as much about the trees and wildlife as his father. We had stumbled across a bees' nest hanging in a tree and I had been stung. He had set out to steal the honeycomb using smoking sticks to stun the bees. He returned sporting huge weals and the hexagonal comb. He had offered me the delicacy, but there was no honey, just tiny baby bees and the translucent larvae were disappointingly tasteless. The next day I had paid him to collect lizards for me and he had returned with eight different kinds. One was almost four foot long and still alive. He had tied a leash around its neck and had tried to muzzle it with rattan but the muzzle had slipped off and it had started lashing about on the end of the lead, snapping its razor-sharp jaws in every direction. The boy's most impressive skill was his archery. From a sapling and some vine he had constructed a tiny bow and arrow. Within a few minutes a tiny brown bird, about the size of a sparrow, had fallen from high in the canopy to his feet, an arrow straight through it.

He was playing with his bow now, aiming crude arrows at a rotten tree stump. Many were clustered around the same point. I looked at his aim and put my thumb up, nodding in appreciation.

'*Bagus*. Very good,' I said in Indonesian as we approached him.

'*Ba-gus*,' he repeated back to me. He knew little Indonesian, I remembered. He seemed unusually reserved, as if he didn't quite know how to treat me. I wondered what he had been told and how much he understood. Nathaniel and his family liked and trusted me, I thought, but if the OPM had spread stories that we were bad people maybe it had turned them against us.

'Aptam?' I asked, pointing down the river.

He raised his eyebrows. It was an Nduga peculiarity; an expression that did not show surprise but an unwillingness to answer. I tried again, using the Nduga words for yes and no to make the question more emphatic.

'Aptam? *Ya*? *Lak*?'

He thought for a moment, smiled and then nodded. I was relieved that he had decided to talk to me. His family and village might be crucial support if our lives were in danger.

Some of the others in the group caught up with us and we continued walking along the river, Nathaniel's sons following at a distance. The leaves above swished as a light breeze stirred the air. Rain was rolling down from the ridge and I felt the first few drops on the wind. We hurried on, leaving the river and entering woodland but the approaching patter reached us and rose rapidly to a din. Within seconds the rain was streaming down through the leafy canopy. Nathaniel's two sons were ahead of me, jumping around, signalling that I should follow them quickly. I took off my shirt to save it from getting wet and rushed past Martha who was wrestling to pull on a red anorak. I followed the boys through a small clearing and up a short slope. I could see smoke ahead through the now driving rain. A hut appeared, and several others beyond as I climbed over a fence. Sliding along the muddy path we reached the nearest house. I heaved myself up, kicked off my shoes, climbed inside and sat there panting in the darkness.

SEVEN

APTAM

The hut was warm and dry, empty except for the scent of wood ash. Sheets of tree bark tiled the floor and thin streaks of light glowed up through the cracks. The hut was raised about three feet above the ground on stilts just like those in Mapnduma. I put my eye to one of the small gaps. The ground below was arid and dusty, scattered with vegetable skins and other kitchen rubbish in stages of slow decomposition. At the periphery of my vision two shivering piglets stood close together, wet and waiting, like me, for the rest of their family to arrive out of the rain.

It seemed impossible we would stay here that night. It was too open and obvious, bang in the middle of the village. I slid myself down the wall and stretched out flat, first across the hut, then along its length. It was about ten foot each way, but the corners were rounded and the central fire place took up a large portion. If fourteen of us were to sleep in here it would need some arranging.

My trousers were cold and clinging. My shirt, scrunched into a ball in my hand, had been saved from the rain but was damp with sweat. I put it back on. I was beginning to shiver.

I got up and stepped back through the door on to the porch. The palm roof and floor extended forward about two feet, forming a sheltered platform along the front of the house. I crouched against the wall and my cold toes clung to the knobbled floor poles.

'Is this where we stay tonight?' shouted Martha through the rain, glowing like a beacon in her red waterproof. She had climbed over the fence and was negotiating the mud rink in front of the house.

One of our OPM guides was standing supporting her, ox-like and unflinching as the rain pelted on his skin.

'I think so. I just followed those boys. It's empty.'

She arrived and leant against the porch for a moment, steaming and puffing. I gave her my hand, she climbed up and peeled off her muddy boots and socks.

'It looks good, eh?' she said, nodding approvingly.

'Not bad.' It was warm and dry and we were in a normal village, not some guerrilla hideout in the middle of the jungle.

I hadn't seen Anna for a while. Now she came out of the forest and through the storm. Her hair was matted and her clothes sodden. She used a long staff to pick her way barefoot along the track, wincing occasionally as she stepped on roots or thorns. The sloppy mud had painted her feet with brown socks and clotted up her shins.

She stopped to stare a few paces from the hut.

'Wow. Are we staying here?' she asked, glad to have arrived. The rain poured down her face but she was beyond caring.

'Looks like it,' I replied.

'A real Nduga hut. I've been wanting to see inside one of these ever since we arrived.'

I had only seen inside a few huts myself, and then only by peering nosily through the door. People around Mapnduma were too ashamed to show us their homes and we had been shy of asking, given that we lived in such splendour.

'Anna, where are your boots?'

'One of the men has them. The dratted things make me fall over. Bare feet are much easier.'

'But what if you cut them? They'll get infected and won't heal.'

'Oh, stop worrying about me.'

'I'm not. I'm worrying about the rest of us. Look, are you going to stand in the rain all afternoon?'

'You're right. I'm not, I suppose. Although I'm so wet it wouldn't make any difference.' She laughed and flapped her arms. 'Now how do I get up into these things?'

A slimy ramp led down to the ground from the ledge on which

I was sitting. 'You could try that,' I said, teasing her. 'Try gripping the notches with your toes.'

She looked at it and back at me, wide-eyed with disbelief. She put her hands on her hips. 'Now can you really see *me* getting up *that?*'

Soon Navy arrived, leading Adinda by the hand, then Tessy with Lita and Ola sheltering her baby. They all squeezed together on the narrow platform, shivering and wet. Footwear piled up around the doorway; socks fell through the floor of the porch onto the ground and soggy boxes arrived and were stacked up around. Inside the walls bumped with the congestion. People undressed, unpacked, pulled bags inside, stood on each other, swapped clothes, dressed again. There were questions, accusations and exclamations in various languages. The pigs were squealing too, below the house. I sat outside, listening to the commotion, hanging wet socks and stacking boots until finally I found the impetus to enter and search for my own dry clothes.

Mark and Martha were claiming space with their inflatable sleeping mattresses, Yakobus was using boxes to build a partition for his family and Navy was hanging rucksacks from the ceiling. In the dim light, with bags swinging from the roof and limbs lining the floor, it was impossible to navigate.

The hearth was a square pit made from dried mud. Posts at each corner held up a firewood rack and above that was a layer of large logs, black from the smoke, which protected the palm roof from burning. An OPM man was squatting nearby, peeling small strips from the stack of firewood and blowing on the embers. Soon flames were consuming the dry kindling and licking up through a stack of timber piled on top. Acrid smoke puffed out of the wood and raced up into the apex of the sloping roof. It eddied, then clung and slowly began to descend bringing a veil of diffuse, toxic fumes to ground level.

As there was nowhere to sit I stood with my back to the fire, trying to dry my trousers. My head was high in the smoke zone and I held my eyes tightly shut, opening them momentarily when I dropped down to ground level to gasp for fresh air. I stood with my legs apart to increase the drying area and to allow more heat through to Bill, Anna and Annette who were crouching in front of me in a row against the back wall of the hut. Annette was holding her socks up to the fire between my legs and Bill was holding out his shirt to the side.

'Don't do that, Daniel,' said Navy. 'Your clothes will turn yellow.'

'I don't care,' I replied. 'My limbs will turn feverish if I don't dry out.'

My buttocks and legs were steaming as the searing heat expelled the water. When the back of my legs were stinging and the trousers were stiff I turned to grill the front. Finally my eyes and throat could no longer hold out and I stumbled with streaming eyes towards the door and porch.

The rain had levelled to a steady, pounding onslaught. Mother pig and piglets poked about under the eaves and floor. A small stream had formed by the side of the house. Men ran backwards and forwards through the village and Silas appeared with a gun which looked liked the one Murip had been holding in the house the day before. He gave it to a young man with a blacked-out face and then inspected the hut, telling us to arrange everything neatly. Silas left, but the young man remained stationed outside our door, clutching the gun and scowling at us if we dared to look at him. He seemed to be our guard.

The rain had begun to ease. Towards the north I watched the sun break through the higher cloud, illuminating the thick mist that rolled among the trees. OPM men arrived out of the forest carrying long straight lengths of timber on their shoulders and threw them down into a neat pile. Nearby there were several squalid pits filled with rotting leaves and water and around them the ground was littered with pieces of rock and charcoal. Twenty minutes later the men were back with more wood and other men were gathering too.

They began to scoop water from the pits and collect the stones into a large, broad pile. The long lengths of timber were laid on top of the stones to make a rectangular stack which was crowned with leaves. One of the men shouted to our guard, who shouted into the hut. There was a mumbled reply from the interior and then a man came running out, whooping with pain and excitement and throwing red hot embers from hand to hand. He placed them inside the stack and tended them for several minutes.

Smoke and steam filled the damp pyre. The fire began to reach up to the leaves which ignited and withered in balls of yellow flames. Soon the blaze took hold and the construction began to buckle. The stones began to crack, and then explode into hot splinters which landed on those around.

About ten men were standing behind the curtain of hot smoke and wavering air. Most of them wore penis gourds but they had all adorned themselves in different ways. They wore headgear: a cowboy hat, a plastic bag, a hair-net made from *nokin* material, a red cap, even a white Freeport hard hat, stolen from the mine site one hundred miles to the west. Many of the natural accessories I had seen the day before, such as pig bones, feather and beads, had already been replaced by synthetic items from our house in Mapnduma. One had a large hoop around his neck, made with thick coaxial cable from our radio system. Plastic noodle bags and tin-can labels were popular; stuck in arm bands, under penis gourd straps or rolled up and inserted through the nose.

I watched them in their strange uniforms, their faces set into mean and nervous expressions, their machetes and bows close to hand in the grass behind. I wondered what they were doing with the fire and pits. I thought they might be cooking but I couldn't be sure. I felt as if I couldn't be sure of anything any more. Twenty-four hours before these very same men had been transformed into an altered, almost ritualistic state. They had seemed uncontrollable and murderous. Nlam who I had thought was a pleasant, straight-forward man had aimed arrows at me with frenzied eyes. Would they turn on us again? And what might they do to us? For an instant my mind taunted me with gruesome images. I was being tied up and burnt on their pyre as part of some terrifying ceremony. I shook myself awake but I felt scared. I wanted to know they were just normal people whom I could talk to like anyone else. I rolled up my trousers and tiptoed carefully down the ramp towards the most imposing man I could find.

'What's this for?' I asked pointing at the fire. He stood with his arms folded and his chin up. His massive biceps were bulging out of his T-shirt.

'Food,' he replied. I relaxed slightly.

'Lots of food?' I queried, patting my stomach. I remembered we had not eaten that day.

He laughed and gave me a friendly punch. '*Ubi, buah merah*, vegetables,' he said listing the food on his fingers. 'Delicious.' He smacked his lips. 'And tomorrow, maybe, we will eat pig.' I smiled at him and he winked.

Three women appeared, trudging along the path towards the village, bent forward under the weight of their *nokins*. They emptied the *ubi* from their string bags on to the grass nearby. Two village men came over; one with a baby in his arms, another with toddlers around his feet. I knew them both from my work in Kurukmu and was relieved that they greeted me so warmly. Nathaniel himself appeared with his two sons. He cupped his hands to his mouth and whispered, '*buah merah*' into my ear.

'*Buah merah, bagus.*' I replied, trying to look enthusiastic. To the Nduga it was a revered pandana fruit. It looked like a huge, red suppository and was over a yard long, several stone in weight and coated in a layer of hard seeds. After two hours cooking the seed came loose and a bitter oil could be extracted that tasted like rancid margarine. Nathaniel squeezed my arm, laughed and walked off shaking his head.

The wooden inferno was burning itself out leaving a large rectangle of glowing charcoal and stones. The pits had been emptied, lined with fresh leaves and were now re-lined with the hot stones, using split lengths of wood as tongs. *Ubi*, vegetables and *buah merah* were placed inside, covered with more leaves and rocks and left to steam.

There was a strange calm to the afternoon. The Indonesians stayed in the hut, happier to be out of sight and mind. I felt the opposite and tried to make contact with each of the OPM men in turn. I needed to make them laugh and see their faces soften before I could feel safe with them. I was sure that if they grew to like me they would not hurt me. So I sat on the porch, and by the cooking pits, talking and joking and only our young guard with the gun refused to smile. I went in once when Navy cooked a meal of rice and sardines and I ate gratefully but when I went out again I felt ashamed that I had not shared my food. Nonetheless, when the pits were opened the men brought us generous portions of potatoes, and when we had taken those the women brought us a gift of a chicken.

The sun came out for half an hour before dusk and I sat with Annette listening to the birdsong from the forest and talking quietly about the day. The peace was shattered as we spotted Silas striding purposefully across the village with two henchmen in tow. I climbed into the house after Annette; already everyone was sitting up straight and whispering anxiously. He stood outside a moment, took the gun from our sentry, then came in and crouched down. Everybody fell silent.

'You stay in the house this evening,' he ordered, propping the gun against the wall. 'If you need to leave, you ask permission from the guards. You take a torch. We shoot anyone who moves in the dark. Understand?' He sniffed and looked about the room, scratching his chest through his T-shirt. 'Take care of your baggage. If you leave it out I can't be responsible for my men. Maybe they will steal it.' He picked up Martha's penknife lying on the floor. 'Who's is this?'

'Mine,' she said.

He pushed it across to her. There was silence again as he followed a cockroach across the floor and squashed it angrily with his finger. It bled and he wiped the juice on his leg.

'Who knows what will happen now,' he shouted. 'Now it is begun, who can say how it will end? Maybe the army will come. Maybe they will shoot you. Maybe they will take my family. If I die, you will die. We will all die. If it is the Lord's will, so be it. You should pray to the Lord for a good end. Pray every night and every day.' He stared at us all around the room, although many of us looked away. 'So? Didn't you hear me? You're all Christians, aren't you?' We nodded. 'Well, pray! Bram, you pray for us.' I watched him as he closed his eyes and clenched his hands together. Silas was as afraid to die as the next man. That evening he was scared and had come to find solace with us.

There was little talk after Silas left. Markus, Bram and the Indonesian team had placed themselves and their sleeping mats longitudinally down one side of the hut. Martha, Mark, Yakobus and family were down the other. Bill, Anna, Annette and Frank were sitting along the back wall with nowhere to put their legs because of the fireplace. I found my torch and sleeping bag from Bill's rucksack and with Frank outside brushing his teeth prepared to take my position between him and Annette,

'You're not seriously considering going here, are you?' asked Annette as I sat down.

'Where else do you suggest?' I realized she was now in the middle with even less leg space than before.

Annette looked about her in disbelief. 'Where am I going to put my legs now?'

'Oh, come on, you'll sort it out. What about over there by Bill's.'

'I'm not moving,' said Bill. 'My legs are already cramped. You know how long they are.'

'Well, put them on top of mine,' I said. 'At least it won't be cold.'

Frank came back inside. 'Hey, what are you doing here?' he demanded indignantly. 'You are leaning against my sleeping bag. That was my space.'

'Not any more.' I threw his sleeping bag at him playfully. 'So now you lose your land rights.'

He sat down next to me and started pinching and poking me. 'I will never give in to a stinky Brit!' He tickled my ribs as I squealed and flipped around like a fish, my eyes watering with the pain and laughter.

'Hey, careful,' said Mark seriously. 'What if Silas sees you.'

Frank turned to him clucking like a chicken, wagging his elbows up and down and blowing raspberries.

'Yeah, Frank,' I said pointing my finger at him, 'act like the filthy prisoner you are and move over.'

He launched into my ribs again. 'If I catch you touching my sleeping bag, you will be punished.'

'Help, mercy, help,' I pleaded as quietly as I could, wriggling about on the floor in hysterics again.

'Frank!' reprimanded Mark, but Martha was already chuckling, covering her mouth with her hand. The tension sparked by Silas's entrance was jumping about the room like static, igniting everyone into excited laughter.

'Oh, have a sense of humour. This whole thing is so bloody ridiculous,' Frank said to Mark. 'Hey, Mark!' He nudged him.

'What?'

'We had a really good idea coming here to Lorentz, yes? WWF wants to set up a nice management team for conservation. But how silly we are.' He started laughing again and gave himself a camp slap on the wrist. 'Because we forget Lorentz already has its own management team, all fully trained in the art of land protection! Don't call WWF. Just call the OPM!' His head fell between his knees in gasping laughter. He came up for air and wiped his eyes. Annette was in hysterics, too, totally incapacitated and holding on to my arm for dear life. She threw her sleeping bag over her face and started banging her head against the wall.

'And this lovely house will make an excellent field office when you've got the email and telephone lines installed,' I added, coughing and choking on my own laughter 'And such a good place to lock up all those nice European consultants when they come to visit. Lorentz: where the locals are so friendly they won't let you go home!'

My eyes were streaming and I felt high. Even Mark had begun laughing and Anna and Bill were smiling. Then as suddenly as the mood had come up, it fell away. I felt empty, needy and incredibly homesick. And then from outside there was the screech of a whistle.

We stared at each other in deadly silence. About twenty men were chanting loud and aggressively nearby.

Mist was swirling outside the door in the half light. We sat stock still, listening with all our might. The voices broke into discordant whooping.

'What the *hell* is that?' asked Bill slowly and quietly. He looked as frightened as I felt.

'That's the OPM troops,' whispered Frank. The whistle blew and they started chanting again and stamping their feet.

'What the fuck are they about to do?' I asked. 'What can you see through the cracks, Bill?'

Bill jumped up and peered through the wall. It was made of interlocking flat wood. 'I can't get a clear view.' He moved his head along. 'Okay, I can see them now.'

'What are they planning to do with us at this time of night?' asked Annette.

Navy's head was bent down, his eyes were closed and he was murmuring to himself in prayer. Adinda was holding on to his hand.

'They're all lined up, like a parade. They're standing to attention,' Bill called. 'That man with the white whistle, he's in front.'

'Maybe it's just a practice,' said Martha, 'like, how do you say, a drill.' Martha's explanation sounded feasible. Bill sat down again.

'These OPM guys, they're crazy. They could do anything,' Frank said. He looked around him at the floors and walls. 'I don't like being cooped up in a hut like this. We could all die in here. What if there's a fire?'

It was a well-constructed hut. One couldn't just break through the wall.

'That's a bit unlikely isn't it?' said Annette scornfully.

'What if the army come in helicopters tomorrow?' said Frank. 'What if the OPM get shot up, panic and torch this place? What if the army don't know we're in here and throw in a grenade? You think that's unlikely?' I looked around the packed hut with its tiny door and shuddered at the thought. 'I tell you, it's much easier for the army to come in, kill everyone, do a nice cover-up and say the OPM did it, right? And if the army don't get us in the shoot-out, the OPM will.' He dropped his voice and looked at those close around him. 'If not us, our Javanese friends for sure.'

'He has a point,' said Martha quietly. She had worked in Jakarta for the UN for three years and she knew what she was talking about. Any plans I had to run back to Mapnduma and get the army were evaporating fast.

We sat in silence watching the bright flames of our fire. The Indonesians were on the other side of the hut listening quietly. Between them and us sat Bill, his long legs folded close to his body like a concertina and held in place with his clasped hands. He was wearing his black sarong and flexing his toes nervously. Anna was next to him, her nose in her knees watching her fingers pick mud from her caked feet while Annette swept the bits away.

'How loose are those boards beneath you, Frank?' I asked, leaning over him. He subtly moved the mats, peeled back the bark floor and began to wiggle the poles struts. I looked around. There were no OPM men in the hut or near the door.

'Pass me your penknife,' Frank said to Martha. 'I need to cut the rattan ties.'

'Careful, Frank,' she warned, but passed it over and he began to cut and move back the poles until there was a hole big enough for a man to jump down through.

'Look, say the army come in or the OPM go crazy or whatever,' I said, 'and we're forced to split up and run for our lives. What should we do? I mean, where would we go?'

'I would say head south for the lowlands,' said Frank. 'It's a few days' walk down to the beginning of the plains, yes? The Asmat people sometimes come that far north in their canoes and they could take you down to the coast. If you go north and get into the mountains, you could die of exposure.'

I thought about Frank's plan. It was madness. It was at least a week to the lowland plains, assuming you had a guide, a path and bridges to cross the major rivers. The chances of meeting a wandering Asmat with a canoe were minuscule. To the south it was just tens of thousands of square kilometres of forest and swamp, and crocodiles, some of the largest species in the world.

'Look,' I said checking around to see who was listening. '*if* we have to get away from the area, stay in pairs and follow the Yugguru river south to until it meets the Gul, the next big river. It's about two miles. I think there are some gardens there and we have a chance of meeting some of the people who fled Mapnduma.'

'Well, I can tell you, if this farce goes on for more than a fortnight,' said Frank, 'I'm out of here.'

'And what about the rest of us?' I asked.

'You can run, too.' Frank stopped and his words hung heavily in the air. We all looked at him suspiciously.

'Look, just stop worrying about it anyway.' He was irritated. 'It'll be over long before then.'

Outside it began to rain again, a steady patter on the palm roof. It seemed as if it might settle in for the evening. The door was just a black gaping hole. The fire had died to embers but a candle had been placed on the hearth sending long wobbling shadows across the walls. Yakobus was kneeling over his baby, singing softly while conducting with his fingers in front of her face. She gurgled and smiled at his buffoonery and he knelt to kiss her on the lips. Lita was reading from her bible and Tessy was fidgeting moodily, missing his evening cigarette. Annette unrolled her sleeping bag and got in and we all began to claim our spaces for the night. Frank began to poke me again but this time I was in no mood for fun.

I lay looking at the tar-coated roof, listening to the rain, drinking in the surreal sensations of the hut. I couldn't relate to any of it but the apprehension and fear in us all felt very real. If the army came in and the OPM panicked, we would be lucky to get out alive. I began to think of how I might die, what it might be like to have my throat slit or my body blown apart by a grenade. I realized that I was frightened not just of death but of my fear of death. It was that fear which would imprison me and take away my liberty, not the OPM. I knew I had to try to face it. I closed my eyes hard and began to imagine the scene.

We were all lined up and a man was shooting us in the stomach, one by one. I watched Tessy slump to the floor. I felt the blood splatter on my face, I saw the guts spill on the ground and I listened to the terrible screams as he died. I was waiting. It was my turn next. Lying in my sleeping bag I was cold and clammy, trembling and delirious.

I didn't want to be like that, stripped of any dignity or pride, before I died.

I turned over on the hard floor and fell asleep in the darkness.

EIGHT

THE PIG'S HEART

I was the first of us to wake. The fire had been re-lit in the night and had blazed heat at me until I was forced to crawl out of my bag and take off my clothes. Now the fire was dead and I was cold. In the dim first light a shivering man was blowing at the embers. I sat up and surveyed the sea of sleeping bags across the floor and the two Papuan bodies curled tightly by the door. It had been an uncomfortable night, wrestling against Frank's knees and Annette's elbows. I put on my shirt and trousers as quietly as I could and with two carefully placed steps negotiated the sleeping limbs and was through the door: the first to claim the morning.

A naked man walked briskly by, his arms clasped to his chest to keep out the chill. There was smoke drifting up from the nearby huts and a cock was crowing with all its might from the top of a rotten tree stump. Below the village, deep in the crease of the valley, shreds of cloud clung to the treetops and the Yugguru river rumbled on. To the north were the mountains: a flat, grey wall, topped with jagged teeth. There were no great peaks, like Dobo Koro that stood at the head of the Mapnduma valley, but the rock was high and wild, uncharted and unknown. On the other side was the giant Baliem river system that flowed down through the mountains to Wamena and the military base. What was happening there on this cold, clear morning?

I decided to make the most of the privacy that my early rising afforded me. I pulled on my mud-encrusted socks and shoes, took some loo paper from a nearby box and jumped down from the house. Mother pig was rooting with her piglets near a trellis of gourd plants along the side of the house. Each gourd-to-be had a small weight attached to pull it long and straight. There were several tobacco plants as well, deformed with the constant pruning. I walked between them, crossed a fence and followed an old, slimy log to a swampy clearing. A fragile wooden platform with a small opening was positioned above a shallow, wet pit. I prepared the area, folding back the spiky plants and scooping away the drying faeces from the rim with a stick.

As I waited, flicking away the insects that landed on me and humming gently, I heard a low whirr in the silent sky. I froze. It was the sound of a helicopter, maybe several, coming from the north. Everything I had thought of the night before came flooding back to me. Suddenly the forest seemed alive. A vivid green palm towered over my head from the left; a red-bodied spider hung in its fragile web; mosquitoes buzzed around my cold bottom and the air reeked of shit. Then ideas screamed through my head. Was this the big chance? I must try to escape. Do they know we are here? I could wave or signal. I fumbled with my trousers and belt. The whirr came nearer like a swarm of killer bees. Someone in the village was panicking, shouting, 'ABRI, ABRI,' the acronym of the Indonesian military. What would they do if they found me missing? I rushed back along the slippery log, jumped over the fence and shouldered my way through the tobacco plants. The OPM men were frantically heaving bags and boxes inside and tearing down the clothes that had been hung to dry.

'*Masuk! Masuk!* Get in!' they shouted at me pulling me up into the house by my elbows. No one was asleep now. Adinda and Lita were praying. Mark was pulling on his trousers. I went over and crouched by Bill.

'What do we do if it lands here?' I whispered to him urgently. 'What do we do if its the army?'

'Stay in the hut,' he said. 'Lie flat.'

'But what if they bomb or shoot the huts first, to clear the area? What then? Should we try and get out of the huts and into the bush around?'

The two of us crouched there trying to follow the sound of the helicopter with our eyes. It was moving to the east, possibly to Mapnduma. A few seconds more and the sound had gone.

We waited silently for a few minutes to see if it returned. If the army had taken Mapnduma it wouldn't be long before they found Aptam. The OPM men began to whisper outside, and then we also began to speak.

'When will your group first be missed,' Mark asked, turning to the Indonesian and British teams.

'By MAF in Wamena, today,' I said.

Navy moved closer to join the conversation. 'Yes. Some of us planned to fly out this morning. We already booked the mission plane.'

'The authorities can keep MAF quiet easily enough,' Frank said. 'When would you be missed by anyone else, like your embassy?'

'Two weeks?' Annette said, looking to the rest of us.

'Maybe less,' Bill said 'What about you lot?'

'There's nobody in the WWF office in Jayapura, is there?' Mark asked Frank. He shook his head. 'And Martha just came with me on holiday. It's not an official Unesco trip.'

'So what are you suggesting?' I said. 'That no one knows this has happened?'

'Well it seems *someone* knows,' Martha said pointing to the sky. 'And they own a big helicopter.'

'I bet ABRI are trying to keep the lid on this one as tightly as they can,' said Frank.

'I am really worried if ABRI come here,' said Navy, raising his arms in the air. 'Like Silas says, maybe we all die.'

'See, even Navy's worried,' Frank continued. 'It's in the interest of everyone here, OPM and us, to get the news out quickly so that our embassies can stop ABRI wading in with guns blazing.'

'Presumably the OPM have some demands as well,' Bill said. 'They'll need to get the news out if they want to communicate those.'

'Was the radio in Mapnduma definitely broken?' asked Mark.

'It must have been,' I said. 'They left the battery in the lobby.'

'Why did they break it anyway?' Martha asked. 'Such a stupid thing to do!'

'I don't think they were thinking very clearly when they attacked the house,' I said.

'Someone needs to talk to Silas,' Bill said. 'Make him understand we've got to get the news out.'

Silas was outside, holding the gun again, looking in the sky and talking to the other men. As Frank and Mark were debating which of them would approach him, he climbed up, poked his head through the door and then came in and crouched down with us. His rough, bare feet were splayed on the bark and his blue and white shorts were tight about his groin. We squeezed up as two more men followed him in while others crowded around the entrance.

'This is Indonesia in the air, looking for us, yes?' Silas asked pointing up. We shrugged or nodded. Silas's face was furrowed with concentration and concern. 'If you hear aircraft you go into the house or under a tree. Otherwise, we will shoot you. Understand?' I wondered if they had precious ammunition to waste shooting prisoners. 'When Indonesia come they kill everyone of us. Black people, white people, men, women, babies. Everyone.' His cheek twitched and he picked up a spoon lying on the floor and began to caress and examine it intently. We waited but he seemed to have finished.

'We do not want the army to come,' Mark said. 'We do not want anyone to die: OPM, local people or us. I think our countries can help stop the army.'

'Yes. Your countries must help,' Silas said, shaking the spoon. 'You should make a letter to the headman in your country, demanding he help us. Write that if he does not help the OPM, he will never see you again. We have had enough of Indonesia. We have given up asking them to return our land. And the OPM is sick of bloodshed, sick of killings. That is wrong. Now we fight with letters. Now we fight a paper war.'

We all watched Silas and his angry eyes. No bow and arrow army could hope to fight the massive Indonesian military machine, but Silas had a vision of a new way that was potentially far more powerful.

'So what are you waiting for?' shouted Silas, getting up to go. 'You can read and write, can't you? You have been to school? Write a letter telling your leaders we have taken you and they must help.'

Once Silas had gone Navy began sorting through the boxes and found pens, a clipboard, carbon paper and a pad of paper. Adinda put her glasses on and waited for someone to dictate. Frank suggested we should address the letter to Bishop Muninghoff in Jayapura. He and the Catholic church had been pivotal in releasing news of the massacres that had occurred in Hoea, near Freeport, six months before. We had read a short article about them in the papers before we left but Frank knew a lot more. Apparently Bishop Munninghoff knew the big leader, Kelly Kwalik, as well. He had taught him at a seminary in Jayapura.

We made and signed two copies of our letter and placed them in plastic bags. One was to go to Yigi, the nearest village with an SB (Short Band) radio, about three valleys to the east. However, it was possible that even if a message was read over the radio from Yigi the military could still stop it getting to the outside world. So the second letter was to be taken to the church and missionary offices in Wamena. We included some cash and fax numbers with this one, so the church could try to fax the letter from the post office directly to our embassies in Jakarta. It all seemed pretty hopeless given that Wamena was more than five days' walk away, for even the fastest man. By then the military might already have launched an attack.

(ENGLISH TRANSLATION)

10 January 1996

To: British, German and Dutch Ambassadors; Unesco-UN; WWF; Indonesian Government, Indonesian Human Rights Commission, BScC, Environmental Organisations.

We, 16 people, including 6 females, one pregnant and one six-month baby, from UK, Holland, Germany and Indonesia, have been taken hostage by OPM on the 8th January 1996 at 13.10 in Mapnduma village. We are from various organisations such as WWF, Unesco, BScC, Cenderawasih University, Cambridge University. Some of us were part of the Lorentz 95 expedition. When we were taken the community in Mapnduma tried to free us but they did not succeed as the OPM group was too big. We are in good condition but are afraid if the requests of the OPM are not carried out. We ask that the individual government try to co-operate with the demands of the OPM. Please do not send in the military as it is dangerous for us and for the Nduga communities and is not necessary. We hope that the individual governments can seek a diplomatic solution. It would be best if the church could act as negotiator.

Signed: Adinda Saraswati, Navy Panekenam, Annette van der Kolk, Daniel Start, Anna McIvor, William Oates, Abraham Wanggai, Markus Warip, Mark van der Wal, Family Yakobus Wandikbo, Martha Klein, Matheis Lasembu, Jualita Tanasale, Frank Momberg.

The village had little shade and by late morning the ubiquitous mud began to pale, dry and then crack under the hot sun. I was longing to wash so two OPM men agreed to accompany Frank, Bill and me to a small river near the village. We followed long logs between tall reeds and deep mud until we reached a small grove of banana palms shading two huts. Two young children were playing outside with a huge stick insect, at least a foot long with purple, knobbly legs. They began fighting over it, pulling off its legs in the process. When they looked up and saw us their faces paled, the crippled creature fell to the floor and they ran crying to their mother who took them inside the house. A third child ran round from the back of the house. He was older and braver and pretended to throw a large beetle at us from his clenched fist. The bug came flying towards us but bounced back. It was secured to his wrist with a long piece of rattan and buzzed in circles around his head, tugging at the leash, as he snatched the air trying to catch it again. We walked on past several more huts, empty with their doors boarded up while their owners worked in the gardens. We climbed down a steep earthy slope and there was a small river, about fifteen feet across and about one foot deep, flowing briskly between stones and over small waterfalls.

Our guards sat and watched us. Ironically Nduga men were very shy of complete nakedness and never took off their penis gourds while washing in groups. I wondered if it was taboo to undress completely in public so decided to go down river a little way to avoid any embarrassment. I lowered myself into the stream and the cool, clear water gurgled noisily around my navel. I peeled off my grimy shorts, submerged my head into the tumult and sat up, shaking my hair. It was cool and refreshing and the sun beat down on my tropical spa. Birds were singing from the forest and yellow butterflies were drinking at the bank, but still a sinister feeling lingered. Three black helicopters were in my mind. Each time they rose in slow formation above the horizon and ignited the sleepy village into an explosion of mud, fire and bodies.

I scrubbed my pants, socks and shirt on a rock with soap. I rinsed them, wrung them out and laid them down to bake on the hot, flat rocks. Then I washed my hair and body and sat dripping naked in the heat watching the clothes dry before my eyes. I began thinking of my childhood faith. When I was eight, I believed my spirit would go on living after death and journey on through the heavens and universe. I had imagined a part of me floating up and away when I died. It had seemed beautiful and blissful. When I thought of dying now there was nothing but a cold, dark loneliness. Living a good life in the real world was all I thought about these days. After all, I was a young man with things to prove and people to meet. I felt had let something precious slip away. I had neglected my faith and now I wanted it back more than anything.

Bill and Frank were still washing by the time my clothes were dry, so I returned alone. Anna was outside the hut on a large rock. She put her hand to her forehead, and squinted at me through the glare.

'Was it nice?' she asked, smiling.

'Yes. It's good to get away. You should go.'

'I will, later. You know we have visitors?'

'No. Who?'

'Yudas and Naftali. They came over from Mapnduma this morning.' Naftali was one of the village *mantris*, trained by the missionaries in health care.

'I thought Naftali was on our side. What's he doing with Yudas?'

'I haven't quite worked it out, but he's got a radio hidden in the forest.'

'Really? What kind of radio?'

'A proper one, a big one. You know: come in, over and out.' Anna was talking about an SB radio. 'There was always one in the clinic in Mapnduma, apparently, but we didn't know. Naftali was in the clinic when we were attacked and he got the news out to the government post in Wamena as it happened. He thinks there's a chance the news has already got out to other countries.'

Naftali was standing alone by the side of the hut wearing a red-and-white striped T-shirt. I shook his hand and put my hand on his arm. 'How is everything, Naftali?'

He shook his head gravely. 'There has been much fighting between the Mapnduma people and the OPM outsiders,' he said miserably.

'Are your family safe?'

'They ran into the forest.'

'And you think the news is out?' I asked, but before Naftali could reply Yudas and Mark came out of the hut.

'Leave it, Dan,' Mark said quietly. 'They're sensitive about him.'

Yudas was friendly and shook my hand and greeted me by name. Mark began to explain the situation in Indonesian: 'Naftali has taken the radio into the forest with the solar panels and battery and Yudas has used it to speak to ABRI. ABRI want to speak to one of the hostages before they will believe that the OPM have taken us. Yakobus has agreed to go because he can speak Nduga but we need one more, preferably a European. I can't go because I don't want to leave Martha.'

Yudas nodded and spoke: 'Mark must take care of his wife. How about Bill. He has strong legs.'

I looked at Mark. 'He's pretty hopeless at Indonesian and I'm not a lot better.'

'You'd better get Frank from the river then.'

As the afternoon drew on the sky filled with cloud and the chance of a military operation passed for another day: we were certain that aircraft could only cross the mountain range from Wamena if it was clear. Frank and Yakobus left for the radio which was somewhere high up on the ridge. They took sleeping bags, torches, rice and coffee in case they had to spend a day or two away. The women returned from the gardens with potatoes and vegetables and the men returned with firewood and *buah merah* fruits. We sat and watched them prepare the fire and the pits again, but this time they rounded up their pigs as well and tied them by their hind legs to stakes. The village and OPM collected together near our hut and Nathaniel stood on a large grassy mound and made a speech in Nduga while Silas translated.

'These five pigs were given to our village by the government two years ago,' he began. 'We have kept them and fed them and they have grown large. In peaceful times we would sell them and use the money to buy more pigs and send our children to school in Mapnduma. But bad times are upon us, so instead we kill our pigs today. There is danger everywhere. Maybe Indonesia will come in the night. Maybe they will take our homes, maybe our women or our lives. But today we are still free and can eat together and with the meat grow strong for the unknown times ahead. It is better to eat than to risk leaving our pigs to the army.'

Some pigs were squealing and straining from their stakes, others were happily chewing, oblivious of their fate. Nathaniel stood down and the young men began to prepare their bows and arrows.

'In our tradition,' Silas explained to us in a low voice, 'if we take prisoners in war time, the pigs are a sign. If a pig tries to run as it is shot then our prisoners will run. If a pig drops quietly then we know our prisoners will not try to escape. This is our belief.'

He turned back to the proceedings and watched with concentration.

The first man selected his arrow carefully from his sheath. He chose one tipped with a long sharp bamboo blade stained brown with blood. He placed it ready in his bow, stretching and aiming a few times to feel its weight, and then began to tiptoe with great stealth towards a large pig feeding quietly about twelve feet away. As he got nearer the pig looked up casually. He froze to the spot. It began grazing again and he approached closer. When he had reached point-blank range, with the tip of his arrow almost touching the hairy black skin, he took aim.

In deadly silence he stretched the bow right back, held it for an instant and then released. The arrow pierced deep into the bloated flank. The terrified animal let out a mammoth squeal, jumped into the air, broke its tether and went hurtling across the village trailing the arrow and spilling blood along its path. Every single man and boy went dashing after it while every woman and child ran screaming for the safety of the nearest hut. The pig bucked and snorted and then began to slow. The men cautiously surrounded it. Its eyeballs rolled and it tottered from one leg to the other, dizzy and faint. A second arrow struck into the body and there was another more pathetic squeal. It fell, grunting, on the floor and closed its eyes. They cut its throat with a machete, and with one last squirm, it died.

'Well, that'll be Frank escaping to the lowlands,' said Annette dryly. 'Lets hope the rest of us are better behaved.' Silas was still watching the proceedings intently.

A second man approached another pig in the same manner. This time the shot went straight through the heart. Blood gushed out in a jet a foot long and an inch thick. The pig stood silent and still, rooted to the spot, staring at the village with a wilting gaze. After five seconds the flow slowed, and the blood began to spurt and then dribble from the hole. The pig wobbled, its legs crumpled, and it fell in a heap upon the floor.

The four remaining pigs had worked out what was going on by this point. They grew anxious and pulled at their stakes but the archers moved in. Silas seemed happy with the overall result. The bodies were drained and cut and the meat wrapped in large leaves and placed in the pits. As well as the pig and potatoes we ate sugar cane and *kopi*, a pear-shaped green vegetable that tasted of cucumber. I even tried a little *buah merah*. With all this good food inside me I lay dozing inside the hut as the afternoon rains soaked the village.

About an hour after dusk, as we were prepared for our second night in Aptam, Naftali appeared from the darkness with Silas and three of his men. We had expected Naftali to be in the forest by his radio but it seemed he had returned. The men stood in the doorway watching us and then came and sat around the fire. To our surprise it was Naftali who began to speak.

'What I have come to say is very important for your safety.' He moved closer to the fire and then laid his *nokin* out on the floor in front of him. With two hands he carefully picked out a dark piece of flesh wrapped in leaves. He held it up in front of him and in the flickering light of the fire I could see tubes sticking out from it. 'This is the fresh heart of a pig,' he continued. I felt sick at the thought. I didn't like meat much and had been a strict vegetarian until some years before. 'In our culture, to share a pig's heart is to be joined as a family. It is a very powerful sign to the spirits and there is nothing more binding. Those who eat from the heart tonight make a solemn oath to protect one another.' Silas nodded in agreement, but I wasn't sure why he was there and if he would be part of the ceremony. I could understand Naftali and the villagers promising to protect us but why would Silas when he was the one who had kidnapped us in the first place?

'Everyone, including the OPM, will eat from the heart,' Naftali continued. 'This is their guarantee to treat you well and do you no harm.' Naftali put the heart to his lips, tore off a tube and some flesh and began to chew. He handed it to Silas who held it delicately in his fingertips as if it were a sacred object. He bit into it gently and passed it to his companions and then to Navy, who looked it over hungrily searching for a good piece of meat. The organ was passed round until it reached me. It was cold and rubbery and smelt foul, like kidneys. I made a shallow bite into the flesh, avoiding the cartilage of the arteries and veins, and began to chew on my small morsel.

Anna was next to me. She was a strict vegetarian and I knew she would hate it. She shook her hands at it and hunched her shoulders up in dread.

'You've got to eat it, Anna,' said Bill firmly.

'No, I can't, I'll be sick,' she moaned.

'Go on, just do it,' I whispered. 'It is cooked.' I tried to put it in her hands. She shook her head again almost crying at the hideous sight of it.

'Eat it!' Mark said furiously. 'Don't you understand the significance of this?' And closing her eyes, trembling with the horror and shame of it, she brought it to her mouth and bit.

I didn't know what effect the ceremony would have on Silas. I was unsure how superstitious he or the Nduga were. It was their Christian beliefs they talked of most. Both days we had been in Aptam Silas had come and prayed with us and told us that only the Lord could decide what would happen now. Almost all the men with us claimed to be Christians and many spoke of Adriaan van der Bijl as if he were the father figure of the Nduga. 'We place our hope in Father van der Bijl,' some of the OPM men had said to me. 'Maybe he will come and help us find a solution to this problem.' It was clear that many men were frightened of what they had started. Some said they wanted to release us but they were waiting for their big leader. Few of the men knew who the big leader was and many had no idea when he would arrive or if he had even been called. I was sceptical and remained hopeful that the OPM would give up with the increasing military threat.

On Thursday, our third day in Aptam, we heard some news that made us realize that the OPM were more resolved and determined than we had thought. A friend of ours from Mapnduma arrived to tell us that the OPM had burnt down the van der Bijls' house. This shocked me. I did not believe it was to spite us or the missionaries. Instead it seemed to be another show of defiance and rebellion, just like the kidnapping itself had been. It was a desperate action by an angry people which said to the outside world: it's time you took us seriously and listened.

On that very afternoon it appeared that the world was listening. Yudas brought a wireless with him on a visit from Mapnduma and suddenly the words 'Indonesia', 'Lorentz', 'Mapnduma', 'Organisasi Papua Merdeka – OPM' and 'Frank Momberg' were being spoken on the Papua New Guinea Pidgin English news service. The OPM men jumped about in celebration and the rest of us sighed in relief that finally the news was out.

'My mum knows then,' said Annette, staring into the distance. 'God almighty, my mum knows.'

I worried about my parents for a while, too, but there were so many other worries that I quickly gave up. Suddenly everything was beginning to sink in. Hearing the news on international radio moved the event into a neat pigeon hole that I could relate to. Images of Beirut and Kashmir came to me and suddenly I wondered if we might be here a whole lot longer than a few days. I wondered if it was sinking in for the OPM as well. Now that the whole world had seen what they could do, would they not have to see it through to an honourable end?

NINE

THE EMPTY CHURCH

It was almost dawn. Five o'clock, I decided. My mind wandered to England as I worked out the time difference. Nine p.m. on a Friday night. At this very moment, ten thousand miles away, my friends would be sitting in the pub drinking beer. Meanwhile, I was in my sleeping bag waking to my fourth morning in Aptam and the same worries were going through my head. Would this be the day the military attacked? Would we be taken away by the big leader? I felt the cold air with my hand, turned over and tried to doze against Annette's elbow.

There was a sound from outside. Men were talking and then someone was climbing into the hut.

'*Bangun*! Get up!,' a voice shouted. I lay still, pretending to be asleep. Whatever it was, it was all happening far too early.

'*Bangun*!' he shouted again and I felt people begin to stir. I sat up in my sleeping bag. Silas was standing in the doorway, an indigo sky behind him.

'Pack up. Quickly. We are moving.'

We pulled on our clothes and collected our possessions, moving tightly among each other and passing items back and forth across the hut. I went outside to collect the pots and pans and checked the boxes which were damp and crumpled on the porch. Silas was watching with his hands clasped tightly behind his back.

'Where are we going?' I asked him meekly, looking as busy as I could.

'Just across the river. We have built a house in the forest. Hurry up.'

I went back inside and helped pack Frank's bag ready for his return from the radio. Within twenty minutes we were outside waiting next to our luggage.

'Okay, we go. The bags will come later,' said Silas and we trudged off, over the fence and away from the village. We descended a steep slope, crawled across a large tree that bridged a gully and climbed up the opposite bank.

Suddenly there was the deep, guttural whirr of helicopter blades moving slowly over the forest behind us. It was low, much lower than the last one we had heard three mornings before.

'Get down, behind a tree,' I shouted to Anna. There was little chance that we would be seen through the thick canopy, but if this was to be the beginning of an operation I was worried about stray gunfire or shrapnel. I pressed myself between a pair of thick buttress roots and closed my eyes. The sound was gone for a moment and then back again, reverberating through the trees behind me. Had it come down in Aptam? If we had left just ten minutes later . . . But then the sound faded further away until there was nothing. I waited and then one by one our group began to creep out from their hiding places in the forest.

Silas was standing on the path brandishing his machete. 'Don't run!' he shouted threateningly. 'Never run.' He looked us up and down suspiciously. 'You will regret it if you try.'

I walked on depressed. However much I feared a military attack I also longed to be rescued. Every time it seemed close it came to nothing. We cleared the brow of the hill and the valley of the Yugguru opened up before us. In Mapnduma the Gul river had run in a deep, narrow crease but here the river curved its way more gently across fertile flatland covered in garden and islands of forest. On the left and right were steep valley walls, and about three miles to the north a series of alternate interlocking spurs climbed up to the base of the black mountain wall which I had seen from Aptam. As we dropped, the river's distant rumble fell away. We walked through the mixed shrub, palms and grassland of old garden plots for twenty minutes and then, as we climbed a small incline on to the lip of the bank, the full body of the Yugguru appeared fifty feet below.

Anna and I stopped abruptly, staring down at the dizzy sight. It was a violent, undulating river of foam one hundred and fifty feet across smashing between house-sized boulders.

'You don't want to fall in there,' I shouted to Anna above the roar. I was awe-struck. It was like watching the power of a wild, stormy sea. For an impulsive moment I wanted to throw myself into its heaving currents and become a part of it.

Down on the bank about twenty men were working frantically to build a bridge across it. Five pieces of rattan, each about two hundred feet long, had been tied around the trunk of huge red-barked trees on each bank. Nathaniel was among the men and came over.

'*Mbik*,' I said, pointing to the trees. While working in the forest he had taught me about the red *mbik* and the strength of their roots. He nodded and patted his chest proudly.

'When Nathaniel was a boy he planted them with his father,' an Indonesian-speaking man explained, 'so that the bridge would be strong. There has been a single rattan here for many years but now they're making this big bridge for you.'

The rattan on which our lives depended was a genus of palm found through out south-east Asia which grew high into the canopy on a slim stem of incredible strength. I bent down to feel a section of it that lay coiled on the ground. It had a hard, shiny exterior but was fibrous inside. The men around me laughed as I examined it. I pointed to the water below and made a frightened face.

'Don't worry,' they said, pretending to heave on it. 'Not even fifty men can break this.'

Anna and I sat watching in the long wet grass of the steep banks as the construction team proceeded. The path up the bank was busy with men bringing freshly cut timber or rattan from the forest. The short muddy approach to the bridge was crowded with people cutting the wood into planks and poles of different widths and splitting the rattan into twines of various thickness. The materials were passed along to four boys balancing precariously above the waters at the construction front. They bound the flatter timber into the lower rattans to form a firm walkway and they used the short, straight poles and the upper rattans to build side rails.

I had been watching, totally absorbed, for about an hour. There was a second team on the other side working toward us and the boys were now close enough to shout to each other above the din of the river.

'Look at those people,' said Anna, pointing away from the bridge. A long line of more than fifty men were trotting along the near bank each carrying a heavy *nokin* of *ubi*. I did not recognize any of the faces, but they looked fierce and purposeful, trooping towards us. As they reached the congestion by the bridge the front man halted abruptly and the others piled up behind him.

'*Wa, wa,*' I said to him, making the most of his confusion. He was clearly surprised to see one of the prisoners smiling at him. '*Wa, wa,*' I said again.

'*Wa-o,*' he called back, trying to remain serious as the man behind him nudged him and chuckled. The men moved on a few feet, but then there was another jam further along and the line of men ground to a halt again.

'What's going on?' asked Anna quietly.

'That's a lot of *ubi* going somewhere,' I answered. 'Enough to feed an army.'

'More sweet potatoes than I'd ever want to eat in my life,' she said, making a face.

'Maybe they're taking food for the troops in Mapnduma?' I suggested. 'You're carrying a lot of potatoes,' I said to the nearest man. 'You must be very strong.' He shook his head dismissively but looked proud. 'Have you come far?'

'We come to bring food for the OPM,' he said in Indonesian.

'The OPM have a big appetite.'

'Yes.' He nodded. 'Eat lot, fight strong.' He clenched his fists and I tried to click my mouth in appreciation as I had heard the Papuans do. He squeezed my hand and the column were off and trotting past us again.

Two hours later, the bridge was declared ready and safe. We queued up and they pushed us forward, one at a time, as if sending parachutists out of a plane. The bridge bounced alarmingly just feet above the surface of the thundering river. A film of spray covered us. It was exhilarating to feel so close to death yet so confident in one's security. The OPM men were worried about how exposed we were and checked the sky constantly for helicopters. Once we had collected together on the opposite bank they marched us into the forest along a path parallel to the river. We turned right up a wide, rocky stream and half an hour later we arrived at a large shelter built beneath the trees on the bank of the river. There was a large sunny area of flat stones and several good pools for bathing.

A group of men were sitting around smoking and talking as we arrived, but they jumped up and began smoothing the leaf roof and brushing the earth floor with their feet. Silas was not impressed. He strode up and down, shouting and pointing, picking at the roof and pacing out what seemed to be his ideal dimensions for the house. Some of the men looked forlorn, others began to snarl and sulk behind his back. I just sat, skimming pebbles and drinking the clear, clean water. It seemed fine to me.

'Okay, let's walk,' said Silas, turning to us. We climbed through thick forest which eventually flattened into open, peaty heath. Rusty water seeped from detritus-filled sores in the ground and trees which dripped candlewax dotted the path. The woodland thickened and steepened again and we climbed along a series of slimy logs laid end to end up the hillside.

'Dan!' Annette shouted some way ahead. She sounded angry.

'What?' I shouted back through the trees.

'Come here, now! I need a husband. Quickly!'

I was off like a shot, storming through the vegetation and by-passing those in front. A few seconds later I crawled out from under a bush in front of Annette.

'Hello,' I said, panting and red faced. 'Can I help you, my dear?'

'Yes, you bloody can.' She was fuming. 'Get behind me and guard my bum.'

Two of the men were standing nearby looking slightly sheepish. One was the lieutenant with the white whistle.

'Those men have been taking liberties and asking if I am married.

Anna said she was married to Bill and I am now officially married to you.'

I gave each man a good, long stare and they looked to the ground, shuffling awkwardly. In fact, I was feeling equally ashamed. While Navy and Tessy had been looking after their female companions tirelessly; holding their hands and guiding their way, I had been inattentive. I hadn't thought Anna or Annette needed that kind of overbearing treatment.

'I'll be right behind you,' I said. 'Shout if you need a hand.' We started walking again, and the two men filed in behind me.

'What were they actually doing, Annette?' I asked quietly.

'Their hands kept slipping when they helped me. They're disgusting.'

'Bastards. Look, try not to worry too much, it might just be their way of flirting.'

'Oh, I'm not worried. I just don't want to be forced to knee one of them.'

We carried on up the path with Bill helping Anna and me helping Annette. I had given up trying to look like an old man now and none of the men commented on my transformation. After about an hour we reached the brow of a hill and the forest opened up to scrub. Silas said that it was the site of an old village. It had been abandoned many years before when people started dying unexpectedly. There were bad spirits here, he said, but we would take our chances that night. As we trudged through the marsh and standing water, I suspected malaria was a contributing factor.

Nearby a derelict church stood on an exposed plateau overlooking the Yugguru valley. It was about twice the size of the hut in Aptam but was constructed from wooden beams and planks. The missionaries had brought a saw mill from Mapnduma by helicopter and made the planks and beams from locally cut timber. Corrugated iron formed the roof and two square holes in the side walls acted as windows. Although some planks had been pulled down and burnt it was in good condition, presumably well guarded by the spirits.

Inside it was a bare and musty. The corners were clogged with spider silk and the iron ceiling was streaked orange by the rain; a ragged, decomposing *nokin* lay furled up near the far wall. I strolled purposefully across the floor listening to the boards creak.

'There's something quite eerie about this place, isn't there?' I said to Bill who was looking out of one of the windows. 'An old, cursed church high on the mountainside.' I went over, jumped up and hung my legs out of the window almost kicking him as I swung my feet round. He looked at me irritated. 'I can't work out if it's good to be this exposed or not,' I said.

'It's not a clever place to hide a group of hostages,' he said. 'I bet you can see the sun reflect off this tin roof for miles.'

'And there's room to land at least two helicopters. This will mean no daytime fires, which means no food; and no going outside. And there'll be no decent streams up this high.'

'Nice and big and waterproof, though,' said Anna coming up behind us.

Nice and big meant that the OPM would be sleeping with us. As our baggage arrived we arranged our mats and personal belongings along the end wall to make it clear where our territory was. Markus, Ola and child wanted to be in the bulk of the room with the other Papuans. As everybody settled down, both the prisoners and OPM began eyeing the food boxes that had been stacked neatly by the door. We would have to share our food as well as space.

I began to think of noodles. We still had about a hundred packets and although they were meant to be cooked they were equally palatable raw. With their chilli flavourings they made a spicy, crunchy snack. The temptation was all the more real because I had pocketed a packet while waiting at the bridge. I chuckled to myself and felt gloriously selfish and mean. I considered opening the bag in my pocket and nibbling small bits at a time but it would be much more satisfying to go outside and eat them all at once. People were coming and going, making loo trips into the surrounding bush so I waited patiently for an hour until I was sure I would be alone.

Out of the church, I was free. I crept through the marsh grass and shrub until I reached the edge of the plateau and could view the entire valley below me. It was like a giant green crater, over a mile across and a thousand feet deep, shimmering in the haze. Hundreds of rivers and gullies drained the steep valley sides and fed the glinting Yugguru. The ridge that we had crossed from Mapnduma was a forested knife-edge along the undulating eastern rim. To the north white cloud had piled up over the mountains like bales of fleece.

I stood in the warm sun, breathing in the pristine land below me. For an moment my spirit had wings and I was gliding forward and away, soaring high on the mid-day thermals above the winding river and forests below.

'Hey, what are you doing?' It was the voice of Silas. He was coming out of the bushes, fastening his belt and scowling. 'Were you watching me?' he demanded. 'Why were you watching me?'

'No, no, I was just thinking,' I replied innocently. 'And eating.' I took the noodles from my pocket and handed them to him in a desperate peace offering.

'No, I don't eat factory food,' he said sternly. 'It makes you weak. Potatoes and leaves and pig. Natural food. That will make you strong. And don't think too much. You'll get sick.' He started wandering back to the church. 'And don't hang around here too long either,' he shouted, turning to point his finger at me. I tore open the packet, poured in the sachet of flavours and began wolfing down the noodles, chewing and swallowing manically. I couldn't believe I'd been caught out so easily.

By nightfall the wind and rain were blowing in through the open windows. Navy placed a candle in the cross beams of the roof which sent a weak light through the room, illuminating the tops of our heads but casting deep shadows on our faces. There were about fifty of us crammed into the church and like the first night in Mapnduma the men sat quietly watching us in the flickering light. The young man with the blacked-out face and gun had gone and the rest looked so meek and innocent now that I wondered how they could ever have scared me.

There had been a subtle change in Navy over the week. When

we had arrived in Aptam he had been too scared to talk to any of the men but now he was cautiously civil. I watched him unwrap the tents so that the men could use them as blankets. Then he began to boil water and make coffee, giving to the men before the rest of us. We had spoken only a few times since being taken, usually when I asked him to translate Indonesian I did not understand. I had talked even less with Adinda and Lita, although I felt more relaxed with them than Navy. We always smiled and said good morning to each other and sometimes I helped them on the path. Very occasionally I would smile or share a joke with Tessy but he was very shy and still much of a stranger to me.

I spent most of my time with Bill, Anna and Annette. Although Mark and Martha spoke fluent English and were generally cheerful and upbeat, they kept them themselves to themselves. Bram was easier to approach because he spent much of his time alone. He was beset by thoughts of his new baby daughter in Jayapura. 'I only knew her for a week and then I came to Mapnduma with the expedition,' he lamented. 'How long will it be before I see her again?' Markus's children were older and he showed less concern. He kept an obvious distance from all of us and I wondered if he was trying to infiltrate the OPM ranks.

He and Silas were smoking earnestly, deep in conversation by the open doorway. Outside some men had made a fire in the porch and the wet wind was blowing smoke and sparks into the church. Ola had begun to sing traditional Dani songs as she cradled her baby. She was trying to clap and was encouraging the Nduga men nearby to join her. Bram had found Yudas's wireless again and was searching for channels against a background of crackle, hiss and intermittent Chino-pop.

A sudden hush fell over the church.

'The news tonight: ABRI has now released the names of the sixteen remaining hostages taken from Mapnduma, Irian Jaya by the OPM on Monday 8 January. From Britain . . .' And then all our names and ages were listed in the darkness like a litany of those lost at sea. Bram had found the Radio Australia Indonesian language service. According to the official Indonesian news agency, Antara, twenty-six hostages had been taken but twelve had been released, all of them members of the local community. The military were ready to move in if necessary but had asked Bishop Munninghoff and Adriaan van der Bijl to mediate a peaceful solution. The authorities were in radio communication with Frank Momberg and Yudas and hoping to arrange a meeting within days.

We talked and nodded enthusiastically. Martha was alarmed because she hadn't told her parents she was pregnant, and now everyone would find out from the news. Navy came over and whispered with Mark in Indonesian. The OPM looked blank at first and then the news began to filter through. Silas stood up and proclaimed that the Lord would give the OPM a good name. I was sure our release could only be a matter of time.

That night my head was spinning with the news. Everything was in place now for a prompt and peaceful resolution. I thought of home and wriggled impatiently in my sleeping bag trying to find a comfortable position. The men had curled up on top of my feet, making it difficult to stretch, and we were packed so tightly together that it was impossible to lie flat. It must have been about midnight when Anna started kicking and cursing next to me. At first I thought she was fighting in her sleep, but it went on and on.

'Are you okay, Anna?' I whispered to her.

'No, I am not,' she said with another kick. 'Some pesky, horrible man is trying to touch me.'

'Do you want me to talk to him? Or we could swap places?'

'Can we swap? Do you mind?'

'Of course I don't.' We swapped over. 'Wake me if you have any more problems. Don't think about it, just wake me.'

I drifted back to sleep worrying. At the outset I had assumed that the Nduga OPM were just like other Nduga men: friendly, polite and respectful. I was unsettled by the events of the day. It could be the prelude to more serious abuse of the women and then what could we do to stop it?

I came out of my shallow slumber to feel my toe being squeezed so hard that I almost yelped. It must have been an accident, I thought, but it came again, on another toe, precise and hard like a doctor feeling a joint for injury. It was so strange that it frightened me and I lay in the darkness wondering what I should do. When it came again I realized that this was what had been happening to Anna. I was the recipient of misplaced erotic affection. Somehow the man had not noticed us swap, either that or he didn't care who he went for. I cautiously felt for my torch while the pinching moved up to my ankles. Then in a sudden bolt of action I sat up and shone the torch into the nearest face.

'What are you doing?' I whispered angrily. The man's eyes were wide with surprise. Other men looked up, shielding their eyes from the flashlight.

'Nothing, nothing,' he whimpered, sitting up.

'Why are you touching me and Anna?'

'No, Mr Daniel, I just, I just want to know,' he paused and gulped for breath. 'I just need to know.' He leant forward and took my arm. 'How can I know if she wants me? What is the way?'

I sighed. 'She does not want you.' He sat there with his head cocked, looking love-struck. He looked so mournful, I wondered if Anna would reconsider.

'But how do I know?' he pleaded.

I considered how I could make it clear. 'Because she is married to me,' I burst out.

'Already married?' he said surprised.

'Not to you, to *Bill*,' Anna whispered behind me.

'Anna is married to me, *and* to Bill,' I said.

At that he shrank back, even more humbled, bowing and begging forgiveness.

'It's okay, it's okay,' I said trying to comfort the poor man. In Nduga custom a husband can kill a man who tries to take his wife. 'You made a mistake, that's all.'

'Yes, thank you, Mr Daniel, thank you.'

I turned off the torch and lay down again.

'Thanks, Dan,' whispered Anna.

'No problem, he was pinching my toes as well. It's hardly sexy is it? Is that okay, to have two husbands?'

'It's quite normal around here, I think. Or maybe that's having many wives.'

'Anyway I'll check that Annette doesn't mind in the morning.'

But the morning was still a long way off. It was only a few hours later when I was woken again by someone shaking my shoulder and whispering: 'Mr Daniel, Mr Daniel, wake up, wake up. ABRI have come!'

I sat up, dizzy, confused and scared. The candle had burnt out, but the rain had passed leaving a starlit sky with tall clouds sailing fast across a full moon. The room was filled with stark, silvery light and the smell of fresh, damp air. I fumbled about for my torch. Everyone else seemed to be asleep.

'Don't use the torch. Danger!' the voice whispered. The man stood among the sleeping torsos, rigid with fear. He had primed his bow with an arrow and stood aiming out of the window into woodland and shadows. He turned his head slowly towards me. 'I saw a man, moving,' he stammered. 'What if ABRI come in the night?' I stood with him and looked out but there was nothing but moonlit thicket.

'Maybe a tree kangaroo?' I suggested.

'No!' he cried. 'ABRI come to kill us!' He flinched again, and pulled his bow up about to shoot. 'There!' He nodded his head forward. Again there was nothing to my eyes. All around us the room lay sleeping. Why had he woken only me? What did it mean? I laid my hand on his shoulder for a moment and then left him.

Despite the radio news, fear had taken everyone that night in that haunted, moonlit church. A few hours later Silas woke us by stamping and shouting. The moon was still strong and there was no sign of dawn. We sat shivering in our sleeping bags as the fire burned brightly outside cooking *ubi* for our breakfast.

'Pack up, pack up,' he cried.

'Where are we going?' asked Mark.

'Nowhere. But always we must be ready.'

Their paranoia and anxiety was contagious. I worried into the afternoon. When would the meeting be? What would the bishop say? I began sorting through the eight or so boxes that we had brought with us from Mapnduma. Among the formaldehyde, dried-out felt-tip pens, dead batteries and fish nets I found several copies of our field guides. I took out *Birds of New Guinea* and browsed through the illustrations and descriptions of the seven hundred or so species. One by one the men gathered around me until a huge crowd was fighting to see the pictures. Like boys around a car magazine they called out the names, argued over the model and boasted about how many they had seen. They knew where each species could be found, what it ate and how it mated. Some of the men rummaged in their *nokins* for precious feathers which proved their claims. One of the more elderly men jostled to the front of our group and began to tell tales of lowlands birds while the younger men sat around enthralled. There was the cassowary with the kick that could kill. It looked to me like an emu with a shaggy coat of long black feathers. Then there were 'forest chickens' or megapods, which built large mounds of rotting, fermenting vegetation in which they left their eggs to incubate.

The man moved on to the Asmat people and their canoes and how they ate fish and sago palm. Then he talked about the great sea which the younger men had never seen. However, most of the men had travelled to the west, to Freeport where the Amungme tribe lived. They were a highland people like the Nduga but many had been moved to resettlement camps in the lowlands when the mine was expanded in the 1970s. There had been schools for their children and clinics when they were ill, but they were not used to the hot climate and many had died of malaria or tried to run back home to the mountains. I tentatively asked the men about Freeport. A few had worked there and said it was good to be able to earn some money. They said that the white bosses were good to them but drank a potion called 'beer' which made them sick. They said Freeport had come like a thief to the Amungme's land and brought only trouble.

They asked me about my home and I impressed them with pictures of cars, boats and computers from a magazine I found in the boxes. Most of all they wanted to know about wives and marriage. How much did it cost in England for a good wife like Anna or Annette? They were shocked when I told them that actually the wife's family paid for the marriage. It cost the Nduga men up to six pigs or £200 in cash, and how could they afford that? Many of the younger men were single, still looking and still saving. Some were hoping to study at school in Wamena but had to find money for the fees. Maybe another team like ours would come to the area, they said, or maybe they would walk to Freeport and look for work there. I asked how old they were, but few knew. One said nineteen, although he looked much older. It dawned on me that many of the OPM troops in the church with me were of my own age. Usually they lived a normal life with their families in the surrounding villages, but when there was OPM action they would join the leaders for some excitement and a few weeks away with the other men in the forest.

Late in the afternoon a messenger arrived out of the rain with a note. It was from Frank and Yakobus, who were well but had run out of coffee. Yudas was meeting the church people the next day in Mapnduma and wanted notes from us to show that we were alive and well. Silas agreed. 'Tell your families that the OPM are giving you lots to eat,' he said. 'Then the world will understand that we are good people and mean you no harm.'

> Dear Mother, John and family,
>
> Please don't worry too much – we also have a radio and heard the news yesterday. We are being treated very well – lots of food and the local community is being brilliant. This may all take some time to negotiate but now no weapons are involved I am confident of our safety. See you soon, at home. (I might need a holiday in Bali after this!)
>   Lots of love to everyone, Daniel

I wrote 'PS Happy New Year and belated Merry Christmas' at the bottom and then added a smiling face. We swapped notes. Anna and Annette had drawn happy faces, too. It was a brave symbol, shining out from the pathetic scraps of paper. I imagined myself sitting at home reading a note from my own child and without any warning I was crying. When I looked up Anna and Annette were in tears, too.

In the church we were so high up that there was nowhere to wash and my trousers became marbled with corned beef and coffee stains and contoured with thick daubs of dried marsh mud. The chilli flavouring from the noodles was there too, in reddish streaks. For Ola, with all her dirty nappies, the situation quickly became unbearable. By the third day Silas and his men had had enough of kidnapping stinking babies and sent them back to Mapnduma to be released. They were not the only ones. That evening Radio Australia announced that Frank had been conditionally released during the meeting with the Bishop and Adriaan van der Bijl. He had promised to return when the situation had been explained to ABRI and the world.

'I wonder when we'll see him again,' said Bill.

'Hopefully we won't,' said Mark. 'That big mouth of his was bound to get one of us killed.'

I had rather missed Frank's joviality. The mood had been sombre since he left and I hoped that he would be back soon.

TEN

THE RIVER HOUSE

On the fourth day, we moved down to the river house which had been upgraded to Silas's specifications. It had grown into a large, low, leafy shelter about the size of the church. The ridged roof area was covered with a mesh of sticks and a pot pourri of fresh leaves and had open gable ends. I took off my shoes and went inside, padding up and down the soft fern floor admiring the size and space. It was much larger than any camp I had ever built as a boy, and it was bounded by a sparkling stream and hidden within the trees.

At about midday, Nathaniel and the other men, women and children from the village came with food. The men prepared the hot rocks and pits while the older women came to the back of the house and sat among us, tucking their legs to their sides and arranging the straw of their skirts neatly about them. They squeezed our arms and smiled through wrinkled faces, *wa-wa*ing and tutting, saying the word 'ABRI' and biting their fingers in worry. They felt Martha's stomach, then touched each of the women's faces and then one of the Nduga women began to cry. So much was said through their bright eyes and sympathetic gestures that language seemed quite obsolete, even if we had known some. As they were getting up to leave they gave us a bundle of fresh chillies, eight ripe tomatoes and ten small, sweet bananas. Anna offered them one of her T-shirts in return and they were delighted.

I sat with our Aptam visitors that afternoon on the wide, sunny river bank next to the house. The boys were chasing each other, the men were preparing and cooking the food while the women

and girls talked among themselves. Nathaniel came up and offered
me a hand-rolled cigarette. I was overwhelmed by their generosity
when they had so many of their own worries. I thanked him for
everything his village was doing for us. He cocked his head, looked
a bit embarrassed and muttered something back.

'He says you are his guests. It is his pleasure,' replied his friend,
who was translating.

I wanted to be able to do something for them. When we were
in Mapnduma it would have been easy with everything I had to
offer. But now I was helpless and totally dependent on others. I
had nothing and could do nothing. 'When we are free we will do
everything we can to help the village,' I said. 'With new pigs and
money for schooling.' Nathaniel held my hand tightly. Then, to
my embarrassment, he stood up and announced the news to the
all people gathered.

Nathaniel was a man I had instantly warmed to when I had first
worked with him on my trip to the lowlands. Like many of the
Nduga he had innocence and charm as well as presence and dignity.
Sadly, we did not see Nathaniel or our other village friends again.
Silas was twitchy that afternoon, unsure how loyal they were to
him and his OPM men. Maybe he was worried that they would
tell the army where our camp was or that they would help us to
escape. He rounded them up and spoke angrily to them, telling
them they should only come to the camp if they had food to give.
As the afternoon's downpour began they hurriedly opened the pits
and brought the potatoes and vegetables to us on large leaves,
steaming in the rain. Then they packed up their own share and
returned to the village.

I ate the hot potatoes hungrily, sheltering just inside the house,
watching the rain and thinking of Nathaniel. The earth turned to
mud and the river swelled, creeping slowly up the bank. At the
back of the house water began dribbling through the roof and we
worked hurriedly to layer the worst areas with plastic bags and
leaves. As the daylight faded, some of us gathered around the warm
fire and the OPM men smoked, happy with their bulging bellies.
Silas sat there too, but he was anxious.

'I don't want visitors here,' he said abruptly. 'I don't want the village people coming here and talking to the prisoners.' The crowd hushed as he sat transfixed by the flames. 'They will trick and betray us, especially those ones from Mapnduma.'

He paused for a moment, broke his gaze and looked up at us. 'Give presents to the ones who bring you food. Then they will go home and their friends will say: Where did you get those new clothes? or Who gave you this soap? and the friends will be jealous and they will bring food too.' He grabbed the battered gun from the young guard and looked around at us. 'But if you speak to them then I will shoot Bill!' He pointed the gun towards him and Bill's face paled. 'And then everyone else. I have cut down many men. Yudas has shot down many helicopters. We are the OPM.'

He got up suddenly and handed the gun back. 'But we are not bad people and the world will see that we treat you well.' He began unbuttoning his belt. He pulled his blue shorts down to his knees and opened the white ones beneath to reveal a third pair below. 'See, I wear three shorts around my groin. This is how I know that the OPM men will not violate your women. But if ABRI come, they will drag the woman to the forest.' He pointed to Annette, who was by the fire. 'They will fuck you and the others.'

'They have raped our women. They have murdered our men. They come to our land with guns and bombs when they know we have nothing. We could keep on fighting them, but we don't want more blood. We want peace. We want freedom. Now we will fight together and, if it is the Lord's way, we will die together.

'We have waited many years and put our faith in the Lord to send a saviour to the people of West Papua. Now he has sent the second Messiah, as it is written in the Bible. Martha's baby will be born on Papuan soil, and it will be called Papuani, for a girl, or Papuana for a boy. The Messiah will come and West Papua will be free!'

He began to stride up and down the dark, cramped camp. 'And if our freedom doesn't come you will be here a very, very long time. You better start learning how to make your gardens, how to build your houses. Maybe you should start looking for a wife or husband. You better get ready to wear your penis gourds and grass skirts and you can throw away your clothes and fancy things. You can forget about ever seeing home.'

He glared at us. He had wound himself into a fury. 'Forget it!' he wailed again. 'Until we get a free Papua.' He sat down. 'Pass me potatoes,' he said, wiping his brow. 'I want to eat potatoes.'

The men whispered among themselves, clenched their fists and looked triumphant. One of them dug out a potato that was baking deep in the ashes of the fire. He rolled and slapped away the ash, crushing the hard skin gently between his fingers until he felt the soft potato flesh beneath. He nodded to Silas, and passed it to him.

'Tomorrow, you start writing letters,' Silas said to us. 'You write and tell the world about the OPM. You tell them to give us back our freedom, if they ever want to see you again. Now we are fighting a paper war.'

There was a long silence and the men began to talk again. Silas ate his potato and I went to the back of the house with Bill and Annette.

'I'm sorry,' I said. 'I feel like I started all that by talking to Nathaniel. Can you believe Silas wants us to pay for our food with presents? We're hostages for God's sake. You would have thought that food would have been provided free of charge.'

'At least it's the local people who will get the presents,' said Annette.

Mark walked past us and sat down next to Martha at the end of the house.

'They can't really believe that Martha's child is the new Messiah?' Annette asked in a whisper.

'I wouldn't be surprised by anything they say any more,' I said. 'It's not due for *six months* and Silas said it had to be born on Papuan soil.'

We sat quietly and Bill looked shaken. 'Why did Silas pick on me?' he asked.

'It's because you're a tall, strapping lad. You're obviously our headman,' I said, trying to defuse the tension. 'Look, you were just

the nearest. Maybe he thought you were me because I was talking
to Nathaniel earlier on.'

'But he did say he was going to shoot me, didn't he?'

'For God's sake don't listen to him,' said Annette. 'He's an idiot.
Anyone can see that. He probably doesn't even know how to use
that gun.'

'You heard what he said about showing the world that they can
treat us well,' I said. 'Hurting us isn't going to help them. They
know that. Look, everything is in the air at the moment. If the
Bishop managed to get Frank out, it's likely he talked a lot of sense
into Yudas in the process. Let's wait and see what Yudas has to say
for himself. We could be free in a few days for all we know.'

I had a disturbed first night in our new house. The women of our
group were sleeping well to the back of the house to keep away
from the OPM men. I had drawn the short straw and had ended
up on the front line. Sleeping Nduga bodies had a habit of gravitat-
ing towards other soft warm bodies and it was an on-going battle
to keep them away. Just as I was falling into a deep slumber I was
woken by shouts and laughter. I looked up to see a man jumping
around in the darkness with one hand over his groin and the other
hand holding the bits of a penis gourd which he had snapped in
his sleep. Then I looked down and saw that it was Silas who was
next to me and trying to roll towards me in his sleep.

I lay down again but images of Silas's face loomed large and
distorted in my mind and his crazy ranting filled my head. I began
thinking back to one of my late-night talks with Markus in Mapnduma when we he had told me about the Nduga's ancestors.
Apparently they had lived in a network of caves beneath Mount
Trikora. At that time there had been white men, too, but an
earthquake had come and the white men had been killed and their
bones buried under the mountain as an offering to the angry spirits.
The earthquakes stopped, but soon there were arguments among
the remaining men over pigs and women and the men had fought
and split, spreading out across new land, speaking new languages
so their enemy brothers would not understand them. The Nduga

and Amungme were forced over the mountains but the Dani remained in the Baliem valley, where the soils were flat and fertile and life was easy. Markus had said that the Nduga believed that the white ancestors would return to help them and some believed they had already come in the form of the missionaries. The Christian faith must have seemed quite plausible with its prophecy of a new Messiah. Could it really be they believed Martha's child was that new saviour? Did they really believe that the birth of this special baby would bring their freedom?

I awoke with a start the next morning to the patter of rain, surprised that I'd slept at all. It slowly dawned on me that my sleeping bag was soggy and cold. I looked up to the roof and it was dripping. Silas was already awake and he watched me get up and peel off my trousers.

'Why are you wet?' he asked crossly.

I pointed to the puddle that had collected in the lining of the ground sheet I was sleeping on.

'You shouldn't sleep in puddles, you'll get ill. You're a fool.'

Silas told the men to make a more sensible roof and later that morning they came back down the river loaded with piles of large, fat leaves which they arranged on the roof like tiles, beginning at the bottom and working upwards. I began looking for leaves as well; ones which were neither too smooth or too prickly. Our loo roll supply had already run out so it was back to nature for all of us. Our food was running low as well so we were eating mainly sweet potatoes, which were doing our insides no good. The starch was heavy and indigestible and we were all bloated with wind. I was also irked by my beard, which was beginning to itch furiously. And then there were the mosquitoes which were active in the cool shade, and the giant red and blue biting flies which came to life in the hot sun. I decided that the stream made up for all the discomforts so I walked down it a little way and had a dip in one of the foaming pools.

At about midday Yudas appeared, walking briskly up the river with some other men. Trotting up to me with his gun over his shoulder, he gave me a friendly salute and smile. He put his hands in the pockets of his shiny, black blouson and looked distinctly pleased with himself. I shook hands with his men and followed the group up to the house. Yudas and Silas talked for a while and we waited expectantly hoping for hints of what might have gone on. He left Silas and strolled about the house, shaking our hands and being charming. He passed on greetings from Yakobus who was still with the radio, and shared out a packet of cigarettes.

'How is the house?' he asked, inspecting the structure.

'It leaks,' I joked.

'This floor is no good either,' he said, crouching down to feel it. His lean thighs bulged out of the tight denim shorts. He sprang up again. 'There are worms in these forests that can crawl out of the ground and into your eyeball at night. This house is just a temporary arrangement. We will make you a good house soon where you can live without fear of worms.' My heart sank. Why were they were thinking of building new houses when they should be thinking about getting us home?

'There is not enough room for you all to live comfortably,' he continued. 'When Frank comes back maybe we will split you up. Then you will have more space and it will make it more difficult for the army to find you.' He laughed, as if it was all a big game, and my heart fell another notch. Being split up was my biggest dread. At least now we had one another for company and support. If we were split we would lose the power of our solidarity and I was worried about how the Indonesians would be treated in a group by themselves.

'Perhaps better to resolve the hostage problem *before* the army come in, yes?' Mark asked.

'Yes, yes. That is what we want. I am meeting the Bishop again on Friday, the day after tomorrow, and maybe they will have the answer about the free country by then.'

A free country? By Friday? I had thought Yudas was more realistic than that. Did he understand what he was asking for? The Indonesians would go to war with America and Europe before relinquishing Irian Jaya.

'But what if they cannot give you a free country?' asked Mark.

'We will go step by step, slowly and surely.' He placed his hands one in front of the other and looked up at us, nodding. 'I am waiting to speak with Kelly Kwalik who will be here within a week. He is a hard man, but also a wise leader.'

'The Bishop and van der Bijl, are they good people?'

'They talk of God too much,' he said dismissively. 'They say: Where is Christ in your actions? I said: This is not about Christ. This is about our rights. When their helicopter came I was hiding in the grass with my gun and I made them lie on the ground. Then what good was their preaching to them? They knew I was the boss.' He looked like a boasting child with his green soldier's cap, chubby cheeks and mischievous smile. 'When I was a young boy and Indonesia was bombing the land, thousands of us fled for Papua New Guinea, travelling for months through the forest with women and children. When I returned to my homeland I joined the Indonesian army but then I went back to the forest. When I heard about your team and the WWF I knew this was the chance the OPM had been waiting for. I came to Mapnduma, I worked for you, I spied on you. I worked with you, Bill, didn't I?'

Yudas was leaning casually against a pile of boxes at the edge of the hut. He put his hand into his pocket and pulled out a pair of garden secateurs, the ones that Bill had used to cut his botanical specimens.

'Remember these, Bill?'

Bill glared at him.

He began to snap them open and shut, watching the sharp metal blades grind against each other. 'When I saw you use those I thought to myself, they could cut off a finger, just like this.' He closed them in a laboured manner, cocked his head and smiled slyly at us. 'That could be useful.'

'I said they should make a letter,' said Silas, intervening.

'Yes, you should make a letter,' said Yudas. 'Send it to the big man in your countries. Tell him that if he ever wants to see you again he should start working on getting us a free country.

'We want Indonesia to give us our freedom and we want them to do it in front of the eyes of the world, in front of journalists, in front of presidents. Then they cannot trick us. Remember: the sooner we are free, the sooner you can go home.'

Yudas went outside and we sat around sullenly for a while, all the optimism crushed out of us. Adinda broke the mood by pulling out some paper and pens, and Annette got out her notebook and began scribbling.

'Our big man. Who's that then?' I asked. I felt exhausted.

'Whoever it is, they better be good,' said Annette. She began dictating to herself:

'Dear Ambassador . . . The intention of the OPM is to hold the group hostage until a Free Papua is declared before the eyes of the world . . . otherwise we will never be released . . . please do everything in your power to advance their cause by pressuring the Indonesian government . . . please pass this letter on to other important people and ask them to help the OPM secure a free West Papua . . . we are very grateful for anything you can do . . .'

When the letters had been taken and Yudas was gone, there was little place for talk or humour. Anna sat cross-legged in a corner busily making a pack of cards from tiny squares of paper. Annette curled up in her sleeping bag and shut out the world. Bill stared blankly at the *Birds of New Guinea* book, deep in anxious contemplation. I left quietly and wandered out to the river.

Now that I could see no possible way out, my body was welling up with an overwhelming sense of despair. All along I had kidded myself; putting my hope in Yudas, in Frank, the church, the community. I felt like a fool who had been deceived.

A new fear had crept in. It was different from that which I had felt during the ambush in Mapnduma or while waiting for the army in Aptam. There was none of the adrenalin or exhilarating immediacy of life running full tilt around me. There could be no sense of relief when we knew the danger was over. Yudas had shown us a side of him that worried me deeply. We would never know when or if he would decide that a few white fingers might bring the freedom of Papua one step closer.

My surroundings were beautiful, and that lifted me a little. I walked aimlessly up the river bank and sat cross-legged by the edge of the water. Toying with the pebbles, I picked up a small grey rock. A knot of red spiralled from its centre and I held its cold curves tightly in my hand.

I sat for a while feeling hopeless and miserable, allowing myself to wallow in my feelings. Why did this have to happen to me? Why had everything we had worked for gone so wrong? But soon I was angry. Angry that it was making me weak and beating me already. Angry that I was even questioning why.

I thought back to what had made me come to Irian Jaya; what had driven me and given me that unrelenting energy and commitment. I had yearned for a still place, away from the buzz of the world. I had wanted to feel the silence and power of the forests and mountains.

I watched the water flow by. It moved through calm waters and white waters, trusting and unquestioning of its natural course. I felt better. Here and now, events were unfolding. They were a part of my life and in time I would see their place in it.

A pair of red and black honeyeater birds were busy in the sun, singing discordantly and stitching in and out of the tall grass on the opposite bank. The trees brushed overhead, stirring in the gently shifting tropical air. The sun glinted on the stream. I dipped my hand into a pool of light, and drank. I closed my eyes and I could feel the hot sun touch my skin.

I began to breathe deeply, drawing in air from the forest and breathing it out over the mountains. The stream became distant and I could no longer hear the birdsong. All I could feel was the light breath entering my body and burning out the tension. It filled me with a glow that was spreading down into my abdomen and up through my chest. It was cleansing and emptying my mind, leaving stillness and confidence. The leaves were protecting me. The stream was flowing through me. The red–centred stone was deep inside me.

I was woken some time later by a soft voice calling from a long way away. I felt someone gently touch my hand and I opened my eyes slowly, not wanting to leave my place. Feeling dizzy and euphoric I looked up into open, honest, beautiful eyes. A man was crouching next to me, holding my arm and smiling.

'Are you praying?' he asked.

'Yes,' I stammered. 'Maybe, I was praying.' I nodded slowly.

'Praying is a good thing. We must all pray to Jesus. He will take care of us.' He spoke with a high, childlike voice and laughed sweetly. He wore a penis gourd and held a pile of plates and pots in his hand. I had seen him before with the OPM men.

'You're washing pots?' I said.

'Yes, I take care of you. That is my job. I am with the OPM.' His voice was mumbled and I strained to understand the words. 'Are you happy?' he asked.

'Yes. Very happy.' It seemed such a strange answer. 'What is your name?' I asked.

'Petrus.' He picked up a small stone and scratched the letters on to a flat grey rock.

'Petrus, why are we prisoners? The Lord did not take prisoners.'

'Because everybody should be free.'

'And what is freedom?'

He thought for a moment. I was beginning to feel more normal but everything seemed very bizarre.

'Indonesia keeps the doors shut and we have no freedom. We want the doors to be open so the white men can bring us clothes.' He smiled, and touched my hand again.

I looked at him, unsure if he was some enlightened guru or a fool.

'But if you take white people hostage, white people will not like you,' I explained.

'Oh, they will.' He nodded confidently. 'We will not hurt them. We only want clothes because we are cold at night.'

I was too confused to continue the conversation. I smiled and thanked him before walking back to the house.

Over the next few days I spent most of my time by the river, sitting out of sight of the camp, making collages on the rocks from leaves, stones and grasses. During the expedition I had been too busy to spend any time by myself or with the forest but now I had all the time in the world. Suddenly everything seemed to make sense to me and I felt incredibly satisfied and happy. I wanted to share my experience with Anna, Bill and Annette, but we were too distant and closed off from each other. I did talk with Anna a number of times and she told me that she had strong sense of fate about the kidnapping, too. She believed that there was something fundamental for her to learn from the experience and that it would end only when she had found it. Although she had no idea what it might be, it gave her a purpose which helped her to keep strong.

Navy, Adinda, Lita and Tessy were much closer than us. They had known each other for many years and, of course, Navy and Adinda were engaged and Lita and Tessy were best friends. They spent much of the day talking quietly or praying, and everyone but Navy tried to keep in the background as much as possible, well aware of the contempt that the OPM had for Indonesians. Navy worked selflessly to turn the Papuans' prejudices around. He shared his food, gave away presents, and treated wounds.

A few days after Yudas's visit Silas became very ill. He was sure that a spell had been cast on him by the women of Mapnduma and he lamented having taken us prisoner. 'It is not in our culture to take women prisoners. I have sinned and will be punished by the spirits,' he cried out as he lay sweating and delirious with fever. While the rest of us secretly hoped that he might die, and we might be released, Navy tended for him night and day. He rubbed Javanese balms into his body every hour and gave him anti-malarial drugs. When Silas recovered a few days later he was sure it was Navy who had saved his life.

If Navy was not caring for someone, Petrus was. He made us washing lines, paths and steps; he baked our potatoes and washed our plates. He had a special concern for Martha because she was pregnant, and when her feet became infected and sore he stood over her, stroking her arm and praying. The OPM men bossed and teased Petrus constantly. 'Don't listen to him,' they said laughing. 'Petrus fell out a tree when he was a boy and hit his head on a stone. He has never been the same since!' Undoubtedly, Petrus was slightly simple, forgetful and difficult to understand, but his devotion to us brought us great comfort and security.

It was a week before Yudas returned. He had held further negotiations with Bishop Munninghoff and Adriaan van der Bijl in the house in Mapnduma, which was apparently still intact, and brought back rice, condensed milk, tinned meat, noodles and cigarettes. Much more exciting was a thick the pile of letters and newspaper clippings. Murip and Daud, the other OPM leaders, arrived too. It had been a fortnight since we had seen them in Mapnduma. Daud was still grinning and dancing around with his plume of cassowary feathers but this time he was also waving letters from our Ambassadors. They stated that van der Bijl had been appointed as the representative of the embassies, but the documents looked highly official with their wax seals and embossed letterheads and he was very excited.

There were letters from our families as well.

'Oh my God, it's from Mum and Dad,' cried Annette. She had found them and was already streaming with tears. I tore open my envelopes. There was one letter from my mother and another one from my father and stepmother written three days before and faxed.

16th January 1996

My very dear Daniel,

We are all thinking of you and sending you love and light at this time. You are in my thoughts, and everyone's, all of the time.

I have had much information: this is a part of your journey and you will come through it. It is about growing beyond diminishment which is why you are a prisoner and hostage.

Everybody is telephoning and lighting candles for you – all of your friends – Jack, Julian, Diana, Will, Harry, Ted, the list goes on.

I am kept well informed by the Foreign Office.

I am renting from the 7th February the dearest little

cottage: a converted barn with a river running outside the kitchen window. It is a dream place waiting for your return, right in the countryside between Penzance and St Ives.

Remember the angels around you,

My love, your mother, xxx

I was in tears now as I fumbled to light a cigarette which had already gone soggy in my wet hands. I could see my mother writing at the table, being calm and clear. I could see everybody's worry and fear at home. Candles, friends and relatives phoning, the Foreign Office. With the letters in front of us, plain to see, the *reality* came flooding over us all. We were hostages. Would we ever go home? My father and stepmother had rented a cottage in Dartmouth in the summer and wanted me to be there. I wanted that too, and I imagined summer in England. Where would I be then?

'All the parents have met up in London at the Foreign Office,' said Bill.

'Oh my God, they're having a service in the college chapel to pray for us,' shouted Annette.

'We made the Six O'clock News,' said Anna.

Bill opened a letter from the embassy which was addressed to the Lorentz 95 team. 'It's dated this morning, 19 January. It's from Ivar Helberg, the Defence Attaché, the man who gave the party for us. He's in Wamena. He says everything is being done that can be done, that everyone thinks it should come to a speedy conclusion once the OPM have achieved their main aim, which is to raise awareness for their cause . . .'

'I wish someone would tell the OPM that,' I said.

'. . . so we should keep smiling and keep writing. He says his owl is well, and so is his family and he's looking forward to seeing us in Wamena in the not too distant future.'

'Well, it's good to know he's in Wamena, so close by,' said Annette. 'If there could be anyone trying to get us out, he's the one I would want.'

'He's not the only one,' said Bill. He had opened the other big envelope which was crammed with press cuttings and was holding a copy of a column from *The Times*: 'Jungle Hunt for British Hostages'. 'According to this, two Scotland Yard detectives have arrived to assist in negotiations.'

'Sherlock Holmes to the rescue,' joked Mark. He and Martha had letters from their family and embassy as well and were in good spirits, but the Indonesians had received nothing and were sitting stoically. We read them our letters and shared our news but it only served to make them feel more neglected. It was as if their families had already given up hope of seeing them again.

The kidnapping had created a good deal of media coverage in Europe and Indonesia and some newspapers had begun to explore the deeper issues. Even the editorials in patriotic Indonesian newspapers tentatively suggested that policies in Irian Jaya should be reassessed.

Jakarta Post

TUESDAY 16TH JANUARY 1996

Anyone with a sensible mind might say that the OPM is fighting a lost cause because the idea of establishing a separate nation in Irian Jaya would certainly be rejected by almost all Indonesians including the Irianese themselves.

The Forum of the Irian Jaya Younger Generation said the abduction should be seen as an expression of 'accumulated disappointment' towards the current development in their region, particularly in the highlands, and the kidnappings should not be seen as an effort to undermine the sovereignty of Indonesia because it was carried out by a small group who don't understand the concept of one nation and one people.

One could wonder: is the situation in the region bad enough to push a group of people to stage a publicity stunt such as last week's kidnappings in order to draw media attention? One cannot but condemn the action for putting so many people in danger while putting our reputation as a nation in the balance.

We have heard grumbles and complaints from many Irianese on issues ranging from transmigration to the 'exploitation' of Irian Jaya ... In fairness we believe that these complaints should be closely examined and if mistakes have really occurred it is not too late to amend the nation's policy on Irian Jaya.

'This is really good stuff,' said Mark flicking through the many articles on Irian Jaya and the OPM. He leant over to Yudas. 'These are from newspapers all over the world, talking about the OPM and the Papuan people. Have you seen?'

For a moment Yudas showed a glimmer of pride. Then he recovered himself and stared at us with wide, pathetic eyes. 'Yes,' he sighed. 'The eyes of the world are on us. But what does that achieve? We are still waiting for our freedom.'

He took out a crumpled plastic bag from his *nokin*, inside which were some pieces of paper. He unfolded them very carefully. The first was writing paper, with an emblem at the top.

'Look, this is the flag of West Papua, our country.' He pointed tenderly to the blue and white stripes as a child might touch a delicate flower. Beneath it in English was a motto: 'One People, One Soul'. He delved in to the bag again and brought out two plastic flags on black sticks. We passed them to the crowd gathered around us, who handled them like precious relics.

'These are from thirty years ago when our country was free and Papuan men were running our government. Why did the Indonesians take our country away from us? Why do the churchmen bring nothing when we have fought all our lives for this one cause?'

Mark drew attention to a statement from an OPM representative in Australia calling for our release. 'It says that hostage taking is an abuse of human rights and is prohibited by international law,' Mark explained, translating from the English. 'The OPM will reduce foreign support if it does not release the hostages.'

Murip was standing nearby and said he had never heard of that OPM man. 'Anyway, what does he know with his easy city living.'

He grabbed the sheet of paper from Mark's hand and stared at the words. 'Just because we do not understand English does not mean you can trick us. Already the missionaries have tricked us by not returning the German man. We will only believe you when we have a free country before the eyes of the world!'

Yudas had walked to the front of the shelter and now returned with a red bag and sat down. 'We are nobody but you are important people,' he said. He placed the bag on his lap and pulled out a battered old typewriter that had been taken from the house in Mapnduma. 'So you better start writing letters and using your influence. Unless you get us a free Papua you will never be released.'

Bill was a man of gritty common sense who always had a realistic and considered opinion. I talked to him that afternoon by the river but even he was unsure how we should proceed. 'So what are you two going to do?' I asked Mark and Martha as they walked by with their towels to wash upstream. 'Write real letters or just make up a whole load of rubbish?'

'You want to die here, Dan?' Mark said crouching down next to me. 'These men are fanatics so I suggest we take their orders seriously.' He walked off, throwing a handful of stones into the stream as he went, and I looked to Bill again.

'Do you think there's a chance we can actually do anything, if we write serious letters?'

He shrugged morosely. 'I suppose there *are* lots of things we can do. We could get folk back home writing letters, petitioning, protesting. It won't get a free Papua but it might at least make the Indonesian government compromise a bit. Mark's right. The OPM aren't going to let us out for nothing.'

Already my head was filling with ideas. Maybe there was a chance that the hostage crisis could actually do some good, maybe even effect policy change in Irian Jaya as the *Jakarta Post* editorial had suggested. 'I mean, Bill, we could really go for it. There's even the video camera and tape recorder back at the house. We could do an appeal from the forest. That would get on TV. Make the whole thing more powerful.'

Bill was slightly bewildered by my enthusiasm. 'I was thinking of a few letters to my family. It could get the OPM's hopes up otherwise. We still have to break it to them that we can't get them a free Papua, even if I was Bill Clinton and you were Boutros Boutros-Ghali.'

The OPM leaders were convinced they would be successful if they just pushed hard enough.

'I want to talk to you in secret,' Silas said one afternoon, rounding up the Europeans and talking to us in a hushed voice by the river. 'I know those Indonesians will never help us. But we know you white people are good people, and if you help us you will be rich. Our country has gold, oil, forests, many things, and if your countries give us our freedom we will share our land with you.'

No one was prepared to tell Yudas or Silas that their life-long dream for a free country was unrealistic. Instead Bill, Mark and I tried to persuade the younger OPM troops to set their sights lower while we all wrote letters urging our families and various dignitaries to push the Indonesian government towards a compromise. Daud and Yudas returned to Mapnduma with the first letters to hold more meetings with the church while Silas and Murip remained to take care of us. Our jungle camp became a hive of activity and it seemed that we had taken over the running of the entire OPM campaign. As the broken typewriter clattered and our pens scribbled, Silas paced back and forth like the editor on a busy news desk, nodding his head in approval and shouting commands.

'Write quicker! Write neater! Write a letter saying that the German man must come back. Write to the UN, to the USA, to Ireland! And order more noodles. Noodles and . . . cigarettes and . . . guns. We need guns to fight the Indonesians.'

Meanwhile Murip seemed more concerned with what he could steal from us. He already had my binoculars around his neck and I was furious. They were a beautiful pair that my father had given to me especially for the trip. I had hidden them behind the back of the wardrobe in Mapnduma, determined that they would not be found. With a little hesitation I went up to him and explained to him how much they meant to me. To my surprise he gave me a syrupy smile, said how sorry he was, and returned them. But the next morning he had taken them again and that night my torch disappeared as well. Keeping hold of my remaining possessions became a matter of honour. I had been humiliated enough and I was determined that he should not take anything else. For several days I worried and fussed over my belongings until I became so exhausted that I wished I had none at all.

I suspected Murip was not only after our inanimate objects. He seemed particularly fond of Anna as well.

'I think Murip's really nice,' she said. 'Better than Silas. At least you can talk to him'

'Anna, he's an unctuous, two-faced, lecherous cheat. And he fancies you.'

'Give the man a chance. I *like* talking to him. Anyway, I've told him that I'm married to you.'

'You mean Bill?'

'Wasn't it you?'

'Well, whatever, just be careful.'

As we began our second week in the river camp there were signs that Silas's single-minded determination for a free country was faltering. His illness had unnerved him and there was talk on Radio Australia that ABRI was planning a military operation unless the church negotiations moved quickly. In preparation they had moved into all the airstrips around Mapnduma, though none were fewer than thirty miles away. All the leaders, Silas and Daud especially, had described a large pig feast with lots of important people that would accompany their independence ceremony in Mapnduma. Quite suddenly, Silas dropped the word independence from his rhetoric as if a pig feast would do just as well.

We were learning that Silas's ideas came and went as clouds pass the moon. A few days on and he had forgotten the pig feast altogether and was preoccupied with the big leader and our valuables. 'Kelly Kwalik and his troops will be here soon,' he said. 'They are Amungme men and have seen many bad things. They will search your luggage and might beat you if they find valuable things, so I will look after all your valuables for you.' The next morning the OPM troops began frantically clearing up the house. Boxes were packed neatly and Silas did a last check to make sure we had nothing of worth. 'Kwalik is not allowed to bring his troops here,' Silas said forcefully. 'You are Nduga hostages and I don't want those Amungme men coming here, causing trouble.'

At mid-day the big leader was spotted, strolling leisurely up the river bank talking with Yudas on one side and a stranger on the other. Silas ushered us into the back of the house and we sat there willing this Kelly Kwalik character to be a kind, reasonable man. Yudas used both arms to guide him into the house and then tended to him obsequiously. Silas signalled for us to stand and Yudas smoothed out the leaf floor with his hand and laid down a mat for Kwalik to sit on.

He was a short man with stout, strong legs and thick wrists. He wore a clean red and blue striped T-shirt, black canvas shorts and a massive brown possum skin balaclava that looked a little like a furry motorbike helmet. He lifted his hand just slightly and Yudas stopped his busy activity. He nodded his head slowly as he gazed proudly at us and then touched his chest. 'I,' he said, with a peculiar emphasis, 'am Kelly Kwalik.' He smiled approvingly and then spread his arms out. 'Please. Sit down.' We all sat and so did he, carefully positioning his bottom and crossing his legs one by one. He placed his hands on his knees, straightened his back and spoke again, in Indonesian but with a very pompous tone. 'Maybe, you can tell me your names, and where you come from?' We introduced ourselves as we had done eighteen days before in Mapnduma and as each of us spoke he made glaring, but not unfriendly, eye contact.

And that was it. He didn't say another word. From this point on his companion did all the talking, speaking fast enough for both of them, spluttering, throwing his arms wildly in the air while a huge black cross swung violently from his neck. He paused for breath, gasping and wheezing for a moment. He was a tall, skinny man with a long chin and hollow eyes. His T-shirt was bright purple and his Bermuda shorts were orange. It was clear that he had been shopping in the mining town of Timika recently. He was obviously a Catholic, as were all the Amungme, and it was clear he was a fanatic. He pulled a brochure from his *nokin*. There was a large Red Cross sign on it.

'These are the only people we trust, the only people who will help us. They came to us after the killings at Freeport, they came to us after Hoea.' He opened up the brochure. There were picture of battlefields, helicopters and guns. 'See, they can help us fight our war.'

He talked for at least half an hour, full of enthusiasm for how we would be the key to their free country. It would be a simple exchange, he explained. Kelly Kwalik nodded along to all this and I felt myself filling with despair. We had been making progress with Silas and now it seemed that our fate was being passed from hand to hand.

As they were preparing to leave Kwalik's companion asked us to type copies of various documents which he pulled from an old brown envelope. There were about ten sheets, listing human rights abuses and reasons why West Papua should be given independence. He passed them around; many were signed and dated by Kelly Kwalik himself. Beneath the signature was always the same place name: Bethlehem.

'Where is Bethlehem?' asked Mark. 'Is it an Amungme village name?'

'Why, have you never read the Bible?' the man snapped indignantly. 'Bethlehem was the birth place of Jesus Christ. He was born here in Papua and now the Lord has sent his successor. Martha will bear the child and Papua will be free.' He straightened his heavy cross and he and Kwalik stood up. They walked out into the bright sunshine and disappeared down the river again with Yudas, presumably towards Mapnduma or where ever their Amungme troops were camped.

I sat silently for a while in the cool shade of the house, trying to find some reserves of optimism. Eventually, I got up and walked out to the river. Annette was sitting alone on a rock, her legs crossed, crying in fury. I passed silently by. We all had to work through our own pain and anger. Some distance away, I stopped and looked back. Already Navy had found her and was soothing her, stroking her hair and speaking gently.

'Why are they doing this?' she sobbed throwing her hands in the air. 'What right do they have to do this to us?'

It was through anger that she found her strength and resilience.

ELEVEN

ON THE RUN

Events moved quickly over the following days. There was another missionary meeting and we heard on the radio that Yakobus had been released. Sion, the man who had beaten Navy and Adinda on the porch in Mapnduma, arrived with other new men. They watched us with scorn and Bill spotted a hand grenade wrapped in cloth in one of their *nokins*. There was more talk of the army. Then one day we saw a plane circling high above us. The next morning five Amungme men arrived with freshly sooted faces and large cassowary feather head dresses. They were jittery, pointing all over the place as they talked with Silas.

'They look like they're panicking about the army,' Annette said nibbling on the end of her sweet potato. It was watery and bad. She grimaced and pushed it over to me. I took the potato and sat back behind a pile of boxes. Silas and the men were glancing at our group and I began to fidget uncomfortably. I wondered if they were talking about splitting us. Maybe Kwalik had made the decision. I prodded an old wound on my foot. It twinged slightly with pain. It was getting infected again and would need antibiotic cream. There was only a tiny scrap left and there definitely wouldn't be enough if we had to be split up. I prodded it harder. If it got really septic, I would get gangrene.

I sniffed the bad potato and felt sick. I wrapped it in an old envelope and placed the package carefully in my plastic bag for later. Everyone was apprehensive. Adinda was close to Navy, her cheek alongside his ear. She was murmuring gently; her lips only just moving. When they talked it was so silent that nothing stirred.

It had to be like that because they had no private language. Navy nodded softly. He touched her cheek and brushed her hair from her eyes in a quick and gentle action.

Silas came over and the new men postured behind him. 'Pack up, we're leaving,' Silas said. None of us moved.

'*Now!*' one of the men shouted, yanking the tarpaulin from the roof. We were startled into activity and my bag was packed within seconds. I started folding the tents and shifting boxes. I was good at packing and organizing and it felt good to be helping the team. Silas was walking back and forth between us. 'The army is coming,' he said tensely. We carried on packing and I wondered if it was true. 'The army is coming,' he said again with more urgency. Maybe they were very near, I thought. Maybe they were coming up the stream with machine guns and I looked behind me to check.

The forest and sky were silent except for birdsong and the babble of the river. We were led up towards the old church, passing a family from Aptam. They were herding their pigs and children along the path, moving into the forest to hide. The rest of their possessions were in their *nokins*: a pot, two rags, some potatoes and a tiny baby. We passed through the abandoned village and climbed further up the ridge. The path died and we were in thick forest on a steep slope. A small, lopsided shelter was made and we stayed there that night.

Early the next morning Yudas and Murip arrived. Apparently the army were about to attack Mapnduma and Kwalik had ordered that we should move further into the forest. Murip showed us a letter from the Secretary General of the UN calling for our release but he said it was probably forged by ABRI. Yudas had found Navy's camera in the house in Mapnduma and wanted to take some photographs as a souvenir.

'Good,' said Silas. 'We will send these to their parents. They will cry when they see their poor children and come to Papua to get them back.' We took photos of the men as well. They lined up in a row and made various poses with their bows, machetes and one gun. Then Kwalik arrived in his huge hat and posed too, sticking his chin up and chest out. Another twenty troops arrived but the film was finished. Some of the men tried to open the camera back to see the pictures but Kwalik told them that they were fools.

Bill spotted his jungle boots in a *nokin* and reclaimed them, thankful to have some decent footwear at last. By the time we had packed up even more men had congregated among the trees. It seemed that the entire OPM was with us, all nervous and excited.

'The army have taken Mapnduma,' said Yudas. 'We are moving west.'

We climbed through dense forest for the next two hours, up and away from the Yugguru. The top of the ridge arrived unexpectedly and Navy was already there with sugar cane that he had saved. He shared it around and we sat and sucked the sweet juices. There was a small clearing, a cool breeze and a breathtaking view. The Kilmid river was far below buried deep within the folds and contours of the valley. The opposite ridge was a mile away and beyond that were further ridges, fading into the distance. There were no patches of garden or columns of smoke. As Nathaniel had said, Kilmid was empty forest where no men went.

For a moment I looked out on the green expanse with joy, like Abraham casting his gaze on the promised land. But as the vibrant first senses passed, its vastness began to drown me. What was one tiny human being, one tiny life in this scene? I thought of myself stumbling for days through the undergrowth and spiky vines, turning in circles amongst the trees, falling in fever, rotting to bare bones, without a whisper or a trace.

The path dropped from the ridge crest down an eight-foot vertical bank of mud and rock on to a steep, slippery slab of rock.

'I can't do it. I can't do it,' cried Anna. She had lowered herself backwards off the edge but at the point of no return had panicked. She was desperately trying to cling on with her hands while her legs kicked in the air finding no grip. 'I'm slipping!' she pleaded. Navy was below trying to reach her waggling legs.

'Drop down, Anna!' he called, but she was disabled by her fear. I climbed down next to her, pressed myself between two trees and stuck my foot in the mud near her feet.

'I'm going to place your left foot on mine. It's secure,' I said. Navy placed her right foot into a second foothold and she was down, but crying from the shock. She wiped her eyes with the cuff of her baggy green sweatshirt. 'It's okay,' I said touching her hair, but the path was like this the whole way now, tortuous and dangerous.

By early afternoon we had dropped deep into the fold of the valley. It had begun to rain lightly. 'Quickly!' shouted Silas. 'The river will be rising.'

I didn't hear the whoosh of the water ahead, but I saw it through the trees as the ground flattened and became marshy. It was wider and shallower than the Yugguru, with a bank of high rounded boulders lying on soft, grey silt. The torrent rushed by, cutting a wide flat swathe through the thick forest. We dropped down to the water's edge, turned to the right and headed upstream.

Our group had spread out and the rain was driving hard. The Indonesians and Bill were some way ahead and Mark and Martha were far behind with Silas. Anna, Annette and myself were alone with two Nduga men. The water level was rising so we clambered up on to the slippery boulders along the bank as the river foamed between them. The men came to an abrupt halt and looked at each other anxiously. Deep murky water lay on all sides. We had run out of rocks.

'The river is flooding!' one of the men shouted to us through the heavy rain. The water below us was eddying gently but twenty feet to the left the main current was crashing along ferociously.

'Do we go back?' I asked. 'We should wait. Wait for Silas and the others.'

Anna crouched down on the rock and hugged her knees, shivering in the cold. She was covered in mud from skidding down the hillside. Annette was standing unsteadily in her sodden T-shirt, slipping on the lichen-covered stone and holding tightly on to one of the men's arms. The other man was lowering himself tentatively into the muddy waters. He reached solid ground at waist height and motioned for me to follow.

'Here, take my hand,' he called.

I slid off the boulder into the water and landed on something hard and curved. I felt its shape with my foot. It was a tree trunk. On either side there was nothing, just bottomless water. He held my hand and walked backwards very slowly as we felt our way along. The sunken platform ended suddenly and he almost toppled backwards.

'Can you stand alone?' he asked, righting himself. I nodded and he left me balancing as he lowered himself off the edge of the log. I followed him and the water rose up to my chest. This time my feet met the soft river bed and I waded towards the bank. Anna and Annette appeared like swamp creatures behind me, bedraggled and exhausted as their clothes drained around them.

We followed the river for maybe another half hour, climbing in and out of the water, crawling over slippery boulders, even swimming some sections until we came to a crowd of about thirty people waiting on a flat stretch of the bank ahead. Bill and the Indonesians had already arrived and there were yet more new Papuan faces. A long, narrow tree trunk had been levered up and dropped between the bank and a boulder mid-stream. It was wedged firm and a man balanced along it, just inches from the water. Two more men followed and they pulled more logs across behind them and used them to bridge the gap to a second boulder. Arms waved and voices shouted across the din of the water and rain. Darker clouds were rolling down from higher in the valley. I was very cold and found Bill sheltering in a tiny grotto under the rocky bank. He was huddled in a dank corner, surrounded by moss. Water was dripping steadily from the ceiling.

'Is there room for two?'

'Not really,' he said quietly.

'What about down here, by your feet.'

'You can try.'

I crouched down next to him, but still one shoulder was sticking into the rain. He looked pale and shaky, his eyes wide in an empty stare.

'What's up Bill? You look ill.'

'Bit cold, that's all.'

'Me too.'

I shivered to myself for a while.

'I talked to some of the Amungme men,' he said at last.

'Trying to persuade them to release us?'

'No. Asking them where they're taking us.'

'And?'

'They're taking us to caves, Dan. They want to keep us there until they have a free Papua.'

The land around was riddled with caves, some large and complex. The Mapnduma people had told me of them. How long would we remain sane imprisoned in an underground hole? How long would they hold out for a free country? All I could picture was a warm fire around which to dry myself. I was too cold to worry.

The river had risen further but the bridge was finished and men were stationed along it to help us cross. We wavered along the submerged poles, fighting against the current as the water flowed around our ankles, too exhausted to be afraid.

Yudas, Murip, Silas and Kwalik had arrived with about twenty more troops, who carried our bags and boxes. They crossed, too, and the last man pulled up the poles and pushed them into the stream where they hurtled away like torpedoes.

'There are no paths or bridges on this side of the valley,' said Yudas. 'The army cannot follow us.' He was proud of his cunning. We followed the river through the forest, lulled by the monotony of our slow trudge. By late afternoon the rain was dying and a mist had descended. I was ahead with Tessy, Lita, Annette and two OPM men. Silas called through from behind. 'It's late,' he said. 'We will build a house here.' We collapsed among the dripping foliage, heady with relief.

We were in a grove of pandana trees that stood around us like triffids in the haze. Each crown was supported by several straight,

splayed legs. These buttresses were roots sent down from the narrow, spiny trunk and several hung rigidly above us, growing slowly
towards the ground. Tessy pulled out a packet wrapped in a plastic
bag. He took out a clove cigarette, straightened the wrinkles,
checked carefully for tears and lit it. After a few drags he passed it
on to Annette who was watching him hopefully. She smiled and
rested her head on his shoulder.

'Only one drag each,' he said in Indonesian. 'We keep going
around.' The men watched and laughed at our game. One took
down a cigarette from behind his ear, added the leafy stump to the
rotation and joined our camaraderie.

'*Buah merah* trees?' I asked, pointing to the palms.

He took his drag, held the smoke, nodded his head, exhaled in
a gush and smacked his stomach. 'We cook *buah merah* and eat all
night,' he said.

I smacked my stomach, too, and we shook hands.

While some men cooked *buah merah*, others built crude lean-to
shelters among the palms. Our group was exhausted and only Mark,
Navy and I would eat the strange, savoury fruit. Yudas, Murip,
Silas and Kwalik sat apart, plotting, scheming and drawing patterns
on the ground. But the day was over and, for now, I could let my
worries go. As I sat by the warm fires watching the twilight fade
it seemed there was nothing in the world but the rumble of the
river, the scent of burning eucalyptus and dark clouds moving in
a cold night sky.

The sound of the rain woke me in the night. The floor of the
lean-to was so wet I couldn't lie down. Markus was next to me
and together we sat with our heads on our knees, cursing the rain.
I dozed into a fitful sleep and was glad when dawn came bringing
Petrus with hot potatoes.

Silas ordered us to sort through our luggage and throw away
anything that was not essential. He said that now we were on the
run, his men couldn't carry useless things. Navy and I went through
the papers, sealing the expedition results in waterproof bags. Anna
sorted through the medical boxes and made an emergency kit for
her bum-bag. A pile of bric-à-brac grew: marker pens, bird books,

solar panels and magazines. The men gathered around eagerly but we let Petrus make first choice. He picked a biscuit tin, a magazine and an old torch.

It was a clear, bright morning and the high hills of the valley loomed up around us. The atmosphere was relaxed and no one seemed in a hurry to move. I went down to the stream and washed out some of my clothes. Bill joined me.

'So where do you think we're going?' he asked dunking his socks and shorts in the freezing water. 'I heard you talking to Markus last night.'

'He wouldn't tell me anything, although I think he knows. They seem easier today, so maybe we'll stay. We're a long way from Mapnduma now. This whole army thing could be paranoia. Remember when they told us they had burnt down the missionary house. That was rubbish, too.'

Bill stood up and looked around. He seemed more at ease. 'It's not a bad spot here. Bit open though.'

Suddenly he plummeted to the ground. 'Shit, did you hear that?' he whispered, crouching next to me.

'What?' I croaked. I quickly collected my things together. My heart was thumping in my ears.

'That noise. A helicopter.'

I shook my head.

'That's it!' It was loud and clear this time and I saw it clearly, low in the valley, perhaps half a mile downstream. It was dark green, tilted forward and coming straight towards us.

'It's going to see the house. It can't miss it,' stammered Bill. I looked over to our camp. Silas was storming through the grass towards it.

'We need to be with the others,' I shouted. 'Come on, come on.'

Bent low, I sprinted across the grass with my wet washing and Bill followed. We got under the roof and crouched down with the crowd. I could hear other OPM men in a camp nearby. There were wet clothes from the day before hanging outside and someone was frantically pulling them down. Silas grabbed a red rucksack

A Papuan family stands beside the Indonesian army's graffiti on the walls of a building in Jayapura, Irian Jaya: 'Live to support one country and one people'.

above Dani men and women in front of a Indonesian-run shop in Wamena.

left Central Square in Jayapura with its advertisements for imported Chinese war films and the Victory statue of the Indonesian occupation. The roads into Jayapura are lined with concrete figures of Javanese policemen and soldiers to warn the Papuans of their strict rule.

above right Enjoying a smoke
in the shade of banana palms.

right An older-style round
house with cassava plants
growing to the left and a pig
fence in the foreground.

Nduga warriors.

In ceremonial dress with 'West Papua' scrawled on arms.

Metal axeheads have made the stone axe obselete. This man has pig tusks through his nose.

Nduga and Dani OPM. One of the men is wearing a coloured *nokin*. The string is made from bark and dyed with plant extracts.

29 February – our first contact with the ICRC in the pig village. From left to right: (top) Bill, me, Navy, Martha, Mark; (middle) Dr Ferenc, Tessy, Anna, Bram; (bottom) Markus, Annette, Sylviane, Lita, Adinda and Petrus in his brand new clothes.

Huts in the pig village. Silas's 'double-ended' house is in the background. We stayed in the right-hand half.

inset Yudas and Murip.

Kelly Kwalik makes his speech on 8 May.

OPM waiting in ranks on 8 May.

lying on the grass. Two other men began praying. Petrus was calm, with his tin and *nokin* close at hand.

I could no longer see the sky but I could hear the helicopter. The tone kept rising and falling as the thumping rotas echoed off the valley walls. It was coming nearer and nearer. It would see us and land. Thank God we were all together. We would lie down, very still. Army troops would pour out. They would shoot anything that moved. They would surround the shelter. There would be blood. Maybe we would get shot, but we would get out. We were going to get out of this hole. Maybe this afternoon we would eat chips and drink gin and tonic with Ivar Helberg.

Anna was next to me scratching her shins impulsively.

Annette was hugging her body and rocking back and forth. 'This *has* to be it.' Her words were muffled by her trousers. 'It's going to be over.'

The huge sound was almost overhead.

'Oh, Daniel, Daniel,' Markus pleaded, half crying, holding on to my arm. 'What if they shoot me? What if they think I'm the OPM?'

And then the machine passed over and was gone, gaining height up and over the ridge. We waited motionless for its return, but there was nothing. Murip appeared from behind a bush and other men came out from hiding. I saw Kwalik looking into the air. He swung round and shouted an order to Yudas.

'Pack up, pack up. Quick, quick,' Silas shouted.

We pulled on our shoes and tied up the bags and were off along the swampy path. Had they seen us? Would they come back? Should we have tried to escape? These were pointless questions. Our best chance yet was gone. The terror had faded, but the disappointment was crushing. For a moment I had imagined release and now I could think of nothing else. Despair overwhelmed me. The army had not rescued us and now they were driving us further into the forest. Every miserable mud-filled step took us away from Mapnduma and any chance of freedom.

We trekked all morning, following the river north, climbing across boulders, cutting through forest, wading through silty water.

Silas goaded us on, constantly telling us to speed up. Then Annette fell and hit her shin and he shouted at us, telling us to slow down and take more care of ourselves. At lunchtime we stopped on a tributary of the Kilmid river and were told to rest. I laid my washing from the morning on the hot stones. Kwalik arrived and summoned Mark and Navy while the rest of us waited anxiously.

They returned and we crowded around them. 'What did he say?' we asked.

'Well,' Mark began. 'Number one, he said that we could trust him whatever. He said that he, that Catholic man and Silas were the only ones we should trust. The others might cheat us or kill us.'

'Can we believe him?' asked Bill.

'Yes. He seems honest,' said Mark.

Martha asked something in Dutch and she and Mark began talking together. She smiled and nodded.

'What else did he say?' I asked.

'He says he wants to release us. He said that this is his land so if he chooses to die here that's his choice. But it's not our land. We should be free to die on our homeland so our souls can rest. That was the general gist. Anyway the main thing is, in theory it's over. Apparently all the leaders agree. Yudas especially. They say its stupid, just running. It achieves nothing.' We looked at each other smiling. The OPM were talking common sense. 'But the army have to withdraw first. He won't release us to them as he says they'll torture and kill us. He wants to give us to the church or our government representatives. He is going to send a letter to Mapnduma demanding this. Tomorrow they will take us somewhere safe while they sort it all out. We'll stay here tonight.'

We waited by the river for several hours while the men built houses nearby. It began to rain and we huddled together under a tarpaulin which Tessy and I held up on sticks. None of us mentioned Kwalik's comments but the possibility of release pervaded our mood. When our house was ready it was still pouring so we walked there together, all huddled under the blue plastic sheet. We looked like a huge pantomime horse as we shuffled across the stream and through the forest, making animal noises below. Even Silas smiled.

I was determined to have a dry night so I layered the roof with plastic bags, dug a ditch around my bed space and laid a tent out on the ground. As I did, the tent poles fell out of the bag.

'What are these?' Silas asked me, examining them. 'I said to throw away useless bits of junk.'

I tried to explain their purpose, but he had no concept of a tent.

'What do you mean: special sticks? These are broken sticks.' He waved the poles in the air and they wobbled sadly. They were short rods sprung together with elastic. I tried again but it was no good. My Indonesian did not have the right tone or he did not have the patience.

'Look around you, stupid,' he shouted. 'If you want to make a house there are plenty of sticks in the forest. Why carry them in a bag? Do you not have sticks in the city?'

He went through all the tent bags removing the 'sticks' and throwing them on the fire where their plastic coatings smouldered.

The next morning Yudas and Kwalik organized the day with military precision. They split the thirty OPM men into two teams, Amungme and Nduga, and briefed them as they stood to attention. One group was to take the slow walkers and the other would take the fast. We protested, saying the women could not walk alone, so Kwalik's group took the baggage while we stayed together with Silas, Yudas and Murip. (Daud we hadn't seen for days.)

We began climbing out of the Kilmid valley, heading west again. There were no paths through the thick forest and we ascended in a slow queue, waiting as each section was hacked out with machetes ahead of us. I was walking with Annette who insisted on making her own way but liked to have someone behind her just in case. Bill was with Anna, who was a much less confident walker. By mid-day we had reached the high plateau of the ridge top and began to descend, presumably into the next valley although I could not see ahead through the low mossy canopy. The hillside was blocked with fallen trees which created a network of broken branches and rotting tree trunks up to thirty feet above the ground. I heard Anna cry out some way ahead. I looked down and she was trying to jump between two slimy tree trunks.

'Of course you can do it,' Bill snapped. 'Just do it! Just jump.'

'Hold my hand. No, like that.'

'Oh, for God's sake, Anna, just pull yourself together,' he said. 'We're all tired.'

She was near to tears and this frustrated Bill even more. He walked off in a huff. He had been Anna's resentful husband all day.

'Go on, Dan, save her from Bill,' said Annette. 'I'll put up with him instead. God, he's a pain.'

I tried to be neutral and with some moral support Anna got across the logs, but the route was so difficult she couldn't manage without constant help. The fallen trees gave way to a series of steep mud slopes, each about twenty feet high. It was possible to climb down them using roots as handholds and footholds but Anna could only slide down on her bum, out of control. I would hold her at the top or try to catch her at the bottom but finally she fell and tumbled down into a crumpled, sobbing heap in the grime below. I sat her up and Murip came to see. He placed his hand gently on the back of her head and stroked her hair.

'I can't do it. I'm too dizzy, dehydrated,' she said swaying from side to side. All the water bottles were long since empty and there were no streams this high. She took some moss from a tree and tried to suck out the drips.

'Don't, it's poison!' Murip called. He pulled her hand away. The men at the front of the line called up the slope. 'Turn around,' he said. 'We're going back.'

'What?' I asked in disbelief.

'We can't get down this way. There's a landslide below.'

'Why didn't someone find out before bringing us all down here?' I started shouting at the men who were climbing up. I was livid. 'This girl's half dead and you say go back?'

The men shrugged in embarrassment; there was no choice but to start climbing back up to the ridge. Murip and I helped Anna all the way while the rest of the group went ahead.

'I think I've got a fever,' she whispered.

I felt her head. It was boiling. I guessed she had malaria.

'No, you're fine. Just dehydrated. You'll be okay. Keep going.' We had to get off the ridge and down to the forest before we could build a house.

We continued for several more hours, eventually finding a way down into the new valley. The men called it Ilare. 'This is forest for the spirits and the forest animals,' one of the OPM men explained. 'Men should not come here. The rivers come from all directions and it is easy to get lost.' As we got lower, I caught glimpses of the new land below. It looked even more wild and remote than Kilmid. There was no obvious north–south axis and the sun was setting in what I had thought was the east. I had finally lost all sense of direction.

Murip and Yudas helped Anna, who was almost too sick to walk by now. They stopped often to feel her head and I was thankful that they had realized how serious her condition was. Maybe it would take an illness to make them understand we could not go on like this.

It began to rain and the undergrowth darkened. We came out on to a fresh landslip; a wide river of grey rock, loose shale and buried tree stumps that ran straight down through the forest and disappeared far below. We zigzagged cautiously down it for over an hour in the downpour, praying that we would not send an avalanche of rocks on those below. It ended above a short, deep gully and stream and I climbed down into it to drink and fill water bottles.

'They've found a piece of flat land and are making a house,' Bill shouted down from above. I climbed up and out and followed footprints until I found the group huddled beneath the dripping canopy. They were trembling and speechless with cold. Anna was hotter than earlier, shivering uncontrollably. Martha gave her the red anorak and everyone looked anxious.

'Where's this house, Bill?' I asked, jumping up and down to keep warm.

'No machetes, no axe, no house,' he replied.

'And the bags? The tarpaulins and spare clothes?'

He shrugged. 'Only those.' Three soaking bags lay in the mud.

As darkness fell there was only Silas, one machete and a handful of men. Not even our trusted Petrus had made it. They put up a small frame and covered it with sticks, but there were only a few palm leaves for the roof. A huge pile of firewood was stacked in the centre of the 'house' and logs were laid on each side to make benches above the waterlogged floor. The damp stack began to smoulder and pump the house full of thick smoke and soon yellow flames licked to the top of it. I stood warming myself as my cold, wet clothes began to dry. A small tin of corned beef was found, heated and passed around. It was our first food in thirty-six hours.

By eight o'clock the fire was burning out, the wind was whistling through our exposed hillside shelter and I was beginning to shiver again. There was a patter on the roof and I dropped my head into my hands pleading that I might stay dry. Soon I felt a steady drip on my back. I moved a few inches and a different drip began to soak my trousers. My head ached with tiredness but there was nowhere to lie. I could sit, but the log bench was sticking cruelly into my backside. My stomach rumbled in hunger and I began to count, second by second, the ten hours until morning.

Late in the night a boy arrived through the darkness. At first I didn't recognize him but then I realized he was a spoilt brat from Mapnduma who had always bullied the other children. He had changed his boyish penis gourd for a T-shirt, shorts, fur hat and man-size bow. He had been in Mapnduma just two days before.

The army had landed, taken over all the buildings and moved into Aptam and six other villages nearby. Some villagers had tried to run into the forest and had been shot in the legs. All the pigs had been rounded up and slaughtered, but nobody had been allowed to eat the meat. The army had found our second camp, the church on the hill. Yesterday they had thrown in grenades and blown the roof off. Naftali had run with the radio further into the forest, but the army had found and beaten one of his family who had told them the place. Now Naftali and the radio had been taken away in a helicopter. And there were trackers, the boy said. Some were Nduga and knew this area well. When they heard that, the OPM were scared for their lives.

As the night drew on I curled up in a tiny space by the edge of the fire, but Silas woke me up and said my head would boil. I sat back on the bench, next to him and he put his arm around me and we shivered together into the early hours. He told me that the Nduga often stayed awake all night when they slept in the forest because of the cold. I dozed for a while with my head on his musty shoulder and felt safe. He fell asleep too, his head on mine but he awoke in the small hours crying out from a nightmare.

I curled my body over a stump of wood and inserted my head into a space beneath Annette's feet. There were roots in my back and neck and a constant drip. Soon I was shivering uncontrollably in my wet shirt, lying motionless and too far from the fire. On a make-shift washing line above me I saw a T-shirt hanging idly. I draped it over my shoulders and it eased my trembling.

It was first light. I was dozing but conscious of the noises around me. Silas was angry, questioning and accusing those around him. His T-shirt had been stolen. I realized quickly where it was, but at the same moment he saw it on my back. He grabbed it and screamed in my ear: 'Do you want me to garotte you?' I sat up with a start. He had wrapped the T-shirt around his fists and was pulling it tightly between his hands.

'I'm really very, very sorry,' I mumbled miserably.

'You will be.' He began to examine the cloth carefully, holding it up to the light. 'If I find a mark or hole, I will use it to hang you from a tree!'

In his anger he ordered me to carry one of the few rucksacks we still had. The pace that morning was depressingly slow as we stumbled and slid down the sheer hillside, clambering through the thorny, entangled undergrowth. Anna's fever had come back and she tottered in delirium on the end of my hand. A fungal rot had eaten the skin from Martha's toes and she hobbled along in agony. Her lower abdomen was also in pain and she was concerned that it was something to do with the baby. Suddenly I heard her cry out behind me. 'It's biting me. Mark, help me.' I turned around alarmed. She was pulling down her trousers and groping for a creature. Mark found it and pulled it off. It was just a leech. She pulled her trousers back up, apologised to me, sank her head into Mark's chest and held him tightly.

We came to a steep river of jagged, black boulders and sheer waterfalls descending relentlessly, one after another, into the valley. As we climbed down each rock face the freezing water, abrasive rock and exhaustion numbed our unspoken fear. I felt myself stumble but caught myself in time. Below me was a hundred-foot drop. Would it kill me, I wondered, and if it didn't which bones would it break?

For Martha the worry was worse. Just one small knock and she could miscarry, haemorrhage and die. 'They can't push us on much further,' I whispered to her. 'Nobody can live like this for long.' The thought of how or when we would ever make the return journey was beyond our imagination.

TWELVE

THE SICK HOUSE

Murip and Yudas caught up with us later in the morning. All the leaders were tired, hungry and spiteful. We were forbidden to talk and Murip made us carry more bags, threatening us from behind the barrel of the gun. We climbed down deeper and deeper into the sacred forests of the Ilare, so tired and frightened that we had no energy to protest. We left the steep, rocky river and followed a route through the forest which showed signs of having once been a path. Mid-day brought us to a wide open riverbed of flat, sun-baked stones. A clear stream flowed on one side and on the other was the triangular frame of a half-built shelter. About twenty men were sitting around and some of our missing bags were propped up against a boulder. But Anna's rucksack, in which I had placed my bag, was not there. Over the last three weeks I had kept a diary and suddenly it seemed the most important thing in the world to me. Were even my most private thoughts not sacrosanct any more?

Petrus was inside the house, working alone, pulling up the sharp stones from the ground to make the floor flat and comfortable for us. He didn't hear me until I crouched down right next to him and called, 'Petrus,' in his ear.

'I am making you a house,' he replied, holding on to my arm and smiling devotedly. I told him the story of our trip here. He shook his head and bit his finger. 'Poor Anna, poor Martha, poor you,' he said.

When I went back outside I found Mark with a note from Kwalik. He looked strained, rubbing his brow as he read. I looked over his shoulder and he handed me the scrap of paper without turning. 'It's not all bad news,' he said.

31st January 1996

Dear hostages,

I have gone home but have left instructions that Yudas should release you at his earliest convenience, and once the army has withdrawn. In the meantime you must rest and eat well.
  Greetings,
    Kelly Kwalik.

The prospect of rest and food registered as weak smiles of relief on all our drawn faces, but the thought of walking back to Mapnduma and persuading the army to withdraw muted any immediate enthusiasm at our prospective release.

Silas said we would stay a few nights until everyone was well. As the afternoon wore on men returned from the forest laden with *nokins* of *buah merah* and forest tubers. That night fires raged up the wide bank sending dancing embers into the night sky. Rocks were heated and pits filled. I sat with the men, most of them Amungme, and talked with them in Indonesian.

One was wearing a Lorentz 95 expedition T-shirt which had obviously been taken from the house in Mapnduma. His name was Jamie and he looked about my age. He wasn't a real OPM soldier, he told me, but a student at the school in Wamena. He had been walking home a couple of weeks ago to his village, Alama, when he met a group of OPM friends and villagers fleeing into the forest. They said the army had invaded Alama and it wasn't safe to go back there, so he had joined them. One of them had given him the T-shirt. I questioned him about Manuel, the Frenchman, who had been working in Alama. Jamie knew him well. He had been his translator and guide and was building him a hut in which to live when he returned. He said the OPM had been angry with Manuel the first time he came to Alama, but now they didn't mind him.

'So, do you speak much Nduga?' asked Jamie.

'*Wa wa*,' I replied.

'You must learn some of our language now you are with us. Say *Amole*, Jamie. It means hello Jamie in Amungme language.'

'*Amole*,' I said, emphasizing the word. '*Amole*, Jamie. It's easy.' I shook his hand to complete the greeting.

'Good, good,' he said. He smiled shyly and looked to his friends. They clapped enthusiastically and watched with wide grins. 'So when I come into the village from the gardens you say *amole*, then I say *amole* back, and then you say *beysa t'amole*.' He waited for me to try the dialogue.

'Okay, I've got that, but when do you do this?' I mimicked the special Amungme handshake I had seen. The knuckle of one man was inserted in between the knuckles of another. The interlocking hands were raised and released with a flick and a sharp, loud click.

'With *beysa t'amole*,' another man called out. He was older and had a tall, straight penis gourd tied up against his stomach with thick coloured bands. He showed me in slow motion. 'Try it, try it,' he said, clicking his gourd.

Others had gathered around, waiting for me to try.

'And say *menadas* at the end,' another man called. He had white feathers above his ears and they shone brightly in the firelight. The others laughed hysterically. I didn't know what it meant but I was sure it was rude.

I completed the routine with a clear click at the end of the knuckle-shake. The older man slapped his thigh, bounced up and twisted around in a full turn.

'Here try this instead,' I said laughing. 'This is how some young English people shake hands.' This time I did the Amole greeting and Amungme knuckle-shake but added on some extra moves. I clasped his hand sideways, thumped his clenched fist, gave him five, waited for him to slap my hand in return, then linked thumbs and brought our hands up like flapping bird wings. There was silence from the crowd, then applause broke into whooping.

They talked among themselves and I lay back against a flat rock and gazed up into the clear sky. Against the faint gossamer of galaxies the stars shone out brighter and clearer than I had ever seen them before. I searched for the familiar pattern of the Plough or Orion's Belt but realized that from this place on earth even my view of the universe had changed. So little linked me to home, so much had been taken away, so uncertain was the future and yet, despite all these things, I felt supremely content. It was as if adversity had freed me of my bonds and allowed me to live for just that moment.

Someone prodded about in the fire with a stick and brought out a forest tuber. He scraped off the charcoal and shared it around, passing the largest piece to me.

'Eat,' he said. 'It's like *ubi*, but from the forest.'

'Thank you. Is it nice?' I asked throwing my piece from hand to hand until it cooled.

'Strong, but very good.'

It was irregular and knobbly, with sharp prickles. I bit off a corner, chewing tentatively. Inside was white flesh with a potato-like texture and taste. I swallowed and took a much larger bite, nodding my head enthusiastically, thinking of how I would feast on them to make up for our days without food. Then the aftertaste came, welling in my mouth like quinine. I ate more and more, frantically trying to smother it, but my mouth throbbed so badly with the bitter and repulsive sensation that I had to stop.

I was thankful that there was still plenty of *buah merah* to come. Several pits were being opened while others continued to steam. By the light of the many fires the softened fruit was broken up and the long thin seeds pulled from the fibrous rind. They were mashed with water on a large palm leaf which dissolved the oily coating to form a bright red slop. Inside the house some groups of men had already begun to eat. They squatted on the dusty floor, scooping, sucking and spitting with silent satisfaction. I moved to join a circle and the men shuffled to the side to make a place for me. They pushed the leaf closer towards me and I joined the steady rhythm; scooping with a folded leaf, sucking the blood red fluid through my mouth and spewing the spent seeds into my hand.

Silas was behind me, crouching alone in the eaves, his angry black eyes watching the dim scene.

'Eat *buah merah*. Delicious,' I said turning to him, my mouth smeared with the red dye.

He shook his head. 'It is not right for me to eat with these people,' he said, shifting awkwardly in his place. 'I once killed a man from their clan.'

The oily consistency was rich and filling, with a smooth and creamy texture. The taste was savoury with a slight bitterness, like dark chocolate or coffee. I moved from circle to circle, trying all the fruits. Even when I was full I ate compulsively, unsure when the next meal would be.

That evening Annette began complaining of stomach pains and fever. She lay groaning on the floor and ran intermittently into the forest. Several of our sleeping bags had gone missing so Anna, Bill and I shared one while Annette slept alone. We were woken in the early hours by Anna, delirious and sweating, muttering in her sleep. Her temperature was close to 106 and her knee had begun to swell. We brought her water and gave her more chloroquine and waited until morning, but as the hours passed Bill, too, developed stomach cramps and diarrhoea. By morning it was clear that illness had ripped through our camp. Lita and Bram had the same bug as Bill. Adinda had kidney pain and was feverish, Markus was liverish again and Navy had a huge agonizing boil on his elbow that had doubled in size overnight. Most worrying was Martha. She had woken in the night with a fever and abdominal pains. Mark was stroking her brow while she lay sleeping.

'How is it?' I asked gently.

'Her temperature is 105,' Mark said. 'She thinks maybe it will kill the baby.' He was crouching close to her and she began to toss her head from side to side in a feverish dream. He pulled the sleeping bag up to her chin and touched her cheek to try to calm her.

'Is that possible?' I asked aghast.

'Anything is possible in these conditions.'

'We still have two chloroquine courses for malaria.'

'You cannot take chloroquine in pregnancy. They can abort the child. Martha should never have travelled to a malarial area.'

'But if this is cerebral malaria,' I lowered my voice, 'she could die in hours, and the baby with her.'

'But if the baby aborts from the drugs she could die of hae-morrhage.'

I sat down and chewed on my knuckles as I 'thought. 'Does Yudas understand that we can't take this sort of treatment, that our bodies just can't cope?' I asked. 'We're out of malarial prophylactics and antibiotic creams. Have you seen Navy's boil? And God knows what's wrong with Adinda and Markus.'

Bill walked over.

'So are you ill, too?' Mark asked.

'Bit of a dodgy stomach and headache, that's all.'

'Even if Yudas agrees this is madness,' I continued, 'what can we do? It's at least six days back to Mapnduma. If we could all walk.'

'Maybe we could get a longitude and latitude reading from the global positioning unit,' Bill said. 'Silas should have it in his bag with all those other valuables. Then we could send a messenger with a note and get a white MAF helicopter to come in.'

'It's a possibility,' said Mark, staring at the floor.

'Yudas and Silas have to understand that people could die.' I said. 'It is not in the hands of the Lord any more. It's in their hands. They can make a decision and save a life.' Bill and I looked bleak.

'You stay here and keep an eye on Martha,' Mark said. He got up and gathered Yudas and Silas together outside.

We could see them sitting outside the house. '. . . In the lowlands they have white beards,' Silas said, pulling on his own. 'We highland people are not the same as them. We have different bodies. Kelly Kwalik wanted to take you to the lowlands but I knew we would get sick.'

Yudas was looking glum, arranging pebbles in a pile. Mark was nodding encouragement. 'It's like that for us. We're not used to these forests. Look inside. See how sick we all are,' he turned to

Yudas. 'Do you want the life of a woman and child on your conscience and on the conscience of Papua?'

'Remember who caused this, who made us run into the forest,' said Yudas pointing at Mark. 'We were talking peacefully with the Bishop when the army came.'

'But you can make a difference now,' Mark said.

There was a silence again.

'We should be praying now,' added Silas. 'The Lord is the only one who can help us now.'

'No,' said Mark emphatically. 'Kwalik had said we are free, yes?'

'When the army has withdrawn,' Yudas corrected.

'The Lord wants you to help us,' pleaded Mark. 'But *you* have to take responsibility.'

'Responsibility?' shouted Yudas. 'What about the responsibility we have for our country? What about the responsibility to our people? The army will follow any helicopter that comes here. No. We must trust in the Lord.'

Mark got up shaking his head. His lips were pursed in anger and frustration and he thumped his leg as came back inside. 'I'm sorry, Mark,' I murmured as he passed.

For four more days we stayed in the sick house. We had never been so low. Now we were confronting the real possibility that someone might die. Before there had always been doctors and hospitals. And what would we do if an army helicopter flew overhead? The OPM would want to move us even further into the forest and then people were bound to die, sleeping cold and exposed in the rain. We would have to refuse, I decided. Even if they threatened to kill us.

Martha took a small dose of chloroquine and the fever seemed to drop but it came back again the same night. Mark developed what seemed like malaria soon after. Anna's fevers came and went in cycles like Martha's, and her knee inflamed until her whole leg was near paralysed. Markus's and Adinda's illnesses were a mystery, and there was little anyone could do except care for them as much as possible.

At times Tessy and I were the only well people left who could fetch water, wash clothes, take temperatures and check medicines. We tempted the sick with cold *buah merah*, helped them to the loo and cleaned their wounds. I took to sorting and cleaning to calm and relax me. I made an inventory of remaining medicines but the current illnesses had finished almost everything off. I cleaned Bill's rucksack which had become coated with a sticky resin. In the depths I found some chewing gum.

'What's this for?' I asked, waving it at him. He was lying inside the house, feeling nauseous and miserable.

'Making friends with an Nduga man in an emergency,' he replied. 'Leave them.'

In a side pocket I found a note dated about fortnight before. It was a short letter to his girlfriend in England; a last goodbye. Bill was staring up at the tapestry of leaves on the roof. What were his thoughts? What despair must he have felt to write and keep such a note? I had no lover waiting for me at home and I was thankful.

Like rats on a sinking ship the OPM abandoned us. First Murip disappeared, then Yudas left with most of the troops. Eventually even Petrus deserted us. Silas remained, hungry and crotchety, sitting by the river with his own worries.

'Pack up, pack up, we're moving,' he called out sporadically, storming around the hut. We would ignore him until he gave in but we knew he was right. We needed to move; we needed to eat. Slowly we were wasting away. The tubers were inedible and the *buah merah* had little substance. We had searched through our remaining bags and found only flour and jam. Then, on our third day, Petrus returned in a blaze of exhausted glory. He was carrying a *nokin* brimming with sweet potatoes and he remembered he had a bottle of oil hidden somewhere. We rolled out dough, cut up *ubi* and fried and fried, watching the potato sizzle in hot oil and eating chapatis smeared with jam.

With real food to eat, we all grew stronger. Martha went for over two days without an attack of fever. Antibiotics brought Navy's

boil down and controlled Annette's fever and dysentery. Chloroquine had cleared Mark's and Anna's malaria. Her knee infection
seemed to come to a head and she squeezed a quarter of a pint of
pus, blood and rotten flesh from a small incision. With rest, even
Adinda, Markus, Lita, Bram and Bill improved. Silas was keen to
release us as soon as possible. He described a village only a day's
walk away where we could find potatoes and pig and wait for
Yudas to bring news from Mapnduma about the army.

We left our sick house in search of food and freedom early on
Sunday 4 February after four nights in the depths of the Ilare valley.
We were all still weak and Anna's knee joint was infected again.
Within ten minutes of setting out she and I were way behind the
others moving at a crawling pace. Murip had reappeared out of the
forest and he dropped back with Petrus to help. We tried to give
her a piggy back, but none of us could make more than ten metres
at a time. Petrus suggested putting her on a stick held widthways
between two men, but the trees were too close together. A stretcher
was impossible as the path was too steep. As the morning wore on,
Anna said she could feel the joint beginning to loosen and we made
better progress, climbing back out of the Ilare valley onto the
western ridge of Kilmid. We saw couscous traps set along branches
and a small derelict hunter's shelter covered in a thick layer of furry,
green moss. It was clear that other people had travelled the route
before and it felt as if we were walking back towards civilization
again. I thought of a little village with women and children, pigs
and potatoes, and a MAF helicopter flying in to take us home to
Wamena.

As the afternoon rains began we sheltered in a tiny hut near
some old gardens. Then in the drizzle and half light of dusk men
appeared to take us to a house they had built for the night. We
climbed back up the hillside, through the icy pools of a tiny stream,
ducking beneath palms and creepers in the gloomy forest. Soon
our guides had left us far behind and we had only their distant
shouts and yodelling to follow. It had become so dark I could only
feel my way. At last, through the trees was the shimmer of a fire
and the silhouette of a house, hidden deep within the forest. A

large pile of wood was being consumed by a noisy inferno and deep within the flames were two pots, filled with furiously boiling water and savoury bananas. As I squeezed under the sleeping bag with Anna that night I was feeling warm, fed and hopeful.

THIRTEEN

THE COLD HOUSE

In the light of the next morning, our house didn't look as snug as it had the night before. It was perched on a minor ridge top surrounded by dense thicket. There was no view, no light, no open space. And it was cold. I argued with Mark about how long we would stay, still convinced that we would continue our journey to the village as Silas had described.

'Look around you,' he said. 'You think this place was built for just one night?' He was so level-headed and sensible that he often made me feel all of the fourteen years I was his junior. The men began to work on extending the floor and more palm leaves were brought for the roof. Miserably, it dawned on me that it was an excellent hiding place: enclosed, remote, with a stream which disguised the tracks of those who came and went.

When Yudas appeared later in the day he apologised about the house but said we would only be there while he went to Mapnduma to organize our release. It was not right to keep prisoners, he said. Now all he wanted was for the army to go home and our representatives to come in and collect us. We said he was very wise and began writing a letter for Bishop Munninghoff.

5th February 1996

Dear Bishop,

Finally we are in a position to write you a short message. This note is written from yet another shelter. We are still alive but both physically and mentally at the end of our reserves. Especially the last week was very hard.

181

Due to military activity close by, the OPM felt itself forced to change our location frequently. Extreme walks, unhealthy living circumstances and a lack of food have seriously weakened our physical condition. Three of us have suffered from severe malaria attacks. Martha's condition especially gives us many reasons for concern. She is now over eighteen weeks pregnant.

We stress that the army's attempts to set us free have endangered our lives more than the treatment of the OPM. Release by the army is just not feasible. As we have discovered the OPM is capable of hiding us for as long as they want.

It has now become very clear that the OPM has the intention to set us all free as soon as they can. The only condition is that the zone around Mapnduma is demilitarized (so that we can travel safely). We sincerely hope that this can be achieved at very short notice with your help and that in the meantime we are not forced to move again. After a month of imprisonment we desperately long for freedom.

Many thanks for your help.

We all signed it, put it in a bag and gave it to Yudas and waited expectantly for him to leave. As it was almost mid-day and it looked like rain he said he would set out the next day. When that came, he had developed an infection on his foot. He showed it to us pitifully and Lita put plasters and medicine on it. He would have to wait until it was better. More days passed and we sat around impatiently with sweet potatoes and pig meat, but with little to occupy our frustrated minds. It seemed that our latest chance for release was slipping further away. What if he changed his mind or we were forced to run again? More news arrived by messenger about the trouble the army was causing the local people and Yudas became restless and paced the hut. Why would no one help his people? Why were they left to suffer like this? He wanted to write his own letter, he said, and asked Navy and Annette to help.

To the Ambassadors of the Dutch, German and British Governments.

We the Papuan people have a rich land with beautiful nature. We hope you will keep in touch with us and we will share the natural resources if you help us in some way:

1) Acknowledge a Free Papua

2) Provide guns.

We need the guns because we have to fight the Indonesians. They always bomb us from both land and air, even though they know we don't have weapons. We suffer because the Indonesians fight us with modern weapons even though they know we don't have anything. They fight us without giving any thought to human rights.

Why do all of you not pay any attention to us? The OPM do not want to return the hostages without any feedback. We want:

1) Acknowledgement of a Free Papua

2) Guns.

You, the families of all the hostages have to think carefully and make a decision about this. We require your reply as soon as possible and then we will decide about the hostages. If we do not receive a reply you can forget about the hostages: they will die on Papuan land.

We have already shown you our kindness by sending back several hostages. For the others we require your answer. We do not want the army to take action. We do not want any bloodshed because our actions are based on:

– God's Law

– Traditional Law

– International Law

Why in 1963 did the Dutch promise to give us independence? Who is working here to colonize our land? I hope the Dutch, British and Germans will take responsibility for the hostages.

So, we want acknowledgement of our freedom and guns. We promise if there is a reply then there will be a decision about the hostages.

We wait in hope for the reply to our demands. If we do
not receive one, the hostages will die on Papuan land.
Thank you
    Daniel Yudas Kagoya.

Yudas was pleased with his letter but he asked us if we thought it
was too rude. He still wanted to release us, he said, but he was
angry: he had asked the Bishop, we had asked our representatives
and yet no one had had the courtesy to give the OPM a reply.
How long did it take them to decide whether they could have a
free country or not?

Finally, by the end of the week, he declared his foot fully recovered. As he strolled off down the hill towards Mapnduma, with his
gun on his shoulder, a baked *ubi* and the letters in his pocket, we
were optimistic. Compared with Silas he was rational and resolute
and he was certainly more trustworthy than Murip. If anyone could
organize our release it was Yudas.

The biggest hindrance now was ABRI. How likely were they
to withdraw when they had only just moved their troops in? Then,
one evening, about three days after Yudas's departure, the Radio
Australia Indonesia news service announced that the army was creat-
ing a demilitarized zone from Mapnduma twenty miles west to
Alama to encourage a peaceful resolution of the crisis. Silas and
Murip were sitting by the fire as the announcer's voice crackled
across the forest.

'Did you hear the news?' Mark asked them with suppressed
excitement. 'On the radio?' Often they did not understand the
rapid Indonesian of the broadcast. They looked up and shook their
heads. 'The army are withdrawing from the area,' Mark continued.
'This is a victory. The OPM have pushed out the army.'

He waited for their reaction.

'Oh *that* news,' said Murip indifferently, staring blankly into the
fire. Silas was nodding slowly on his left. 'We knew *that* when we
saw the white cockatoo fly past this morning. White cockatoos
always bring good news.'

The next day the air was filled with green helicopters moving back and forth across the mountains as troops were ferried out of the forest.

'It's all the work of the local women,' said Murip, rubbing his hands together, 'making magic.'

'Pregnant ones are the most powerful,' Silas explained to Navy, taking him into his confidence. 'Their witchcraft brought the rains. It washed out the army and it will wash away the President of Indonesia.' There had indeed been torrential rain in our area over the last week. We had heard reports on the radio that Indonesia had the heaviest rains for three decades. In Jakarta there had been floods that had left hundreds of people dead. 'But if, when I return to my village,' Silas continued, his tone louder and more threatening as he pointed his finger around the room at each of us, 'if I find the army have killed one of my sons, then I will take you,' his finger locked on me, 'in compensation. And if they have killed one of my daughters, I will take you,' and he picked out Lita.

The obvious military withdrawal convinced us that Yudas had reached Mapnduma and would return within a matter of days to take us to a rendezvous point and a helicopter he had arranged with the Bishop. We were wrong. Three miserable weeks passed as we waited for Yudas in that forest camp. I have never grown to hate a place so much.

From all our other camps I had derived at least some comfort: either the mountains and valleys were dramatic; or the Papuan villagers inspiring; or the sunny rivers beautiful. Here, the forest was impenetrable and the trunks and foliage stretched into a tedium of brown and green as far as the eye could see, still and seemingly lifeless, except for the mosquitoes and biting flies that were drawn inexorably towards us. There were no birds, butterflies or mammals to watch in sun-dappled glades or grassy clearings. The trees were tall and tightly packed, blocking out the sun and the land around us and the undergrowth was like chest-high gorse. The stream was just a far-off dribble through a series of thorny pools, in a dank, insect-ridden dell and our only company was Silas, Murip and a measly collection of sulking, sneering men.

The thought of food preoccupied me twenty-three hours a day. Petrus would return from the gardens at about the same time every afternoon, panting and heaving with his *nokin* of *ubi*. We would cook all the food together in a big pot and then I would eat my three potatoes and two spoonfuls of leaves in a ravenous frenzy. For ten blissful minutes I sat, happy and satisfied, my mind lulled and contented by the feeling. Then the hunger returned, gnawing at my stomach through the night, keeping me from sleep.

Sometimes, near midnight, Murip would stand over us and watch us silently. While Anna and Annette slept, he would touch their noses with a long stick until they tossed and turned and fought in their dreams. Once when Annette went to pee late in the night she returned shaking. She had met Murip and he had groped her. 'I told him: God would not want that, and he stopped,' she whispered to me furiously. 'That man is just a low-life toe-rag.'

We slept on widely spaced wooden slats which formed a platform above the forest floor. We had only one mat between four and only one sleeping bag between two, opened out over the top of us. The cold air would blow beneath me and cramp the muscles in my back and the ache would wake me in the early hours. I would pull my legs tight to my chest to stretch but only sitting up cross-legged was comfortable and this was how I waited out the nights.

Perhaps it would have been more bearable if we had been resigned to a long captivity, but freedom always seemed so tantalisingly close. Each morning I was convinced that Yudas would return with arrangements for our release. I would imagine the euphoria of the helicopter ride out, the delicious food, the excitement of being an ex-hostage. At dusk I would taunt myself with thoughts of weeks or months waiting in that camp with little to eat and nothing to do. Sometimes I dreamt that I was buried alive, crushed and asphyxiated. The more I squirmed and the faster I dug the more gravel and soil enclosed me.

The boredom drove me to levels of distraction I had not imagined possible. I would cut my nails again or trim my beard with Martha's scissors, climb down to the stream to drink water so I could go for yet another pee, change sitting position, count the leaves on a vine, arrange the charcoal in the fire, pull fibres from the floor, pluck lashes from my eyes. But the more I urged the day to end the slower the seconds seemed to pass.

Annette's diarrhoea and fever returned and for several days she could not eat or talk. I wondered if I might make myself ill. In sickness there would no boredom or hunger. While my senses were healthy they needed stimuli just as my stomach needed food. I had tried to sit all day in silent contemplation but I hated the dull, predictable output of my mind. A monk would have spent all day deep in meditation, but I when I tried the mosquitoes attacked me.

I wondered: was restlessness a natural human condition? or was I afflicted in some abnormal way? As a child my mother said I fidgeted; at school my teachers said I did not concentrate. In recent years I had been in a constant hurry, either to make an appointment or to finish a project. It was as if I needed activity and feared what might happen if it stopped. Was this part of an innate tendency to explore and search out new experiences? Was my current frustration a mirror of the drive that had brought me to Irian Jaya?

The others seemed more at ease. Anna whiled away the day making hair-braids and learning Nduga words like a child, far away in her own world. Annette, when well, would burrow down inside her sleeping bag and play out fantasies of millionaire lovers, black-tie balls and Mediterranean cruises. Bill played endless games of Patience, using the scores as a means of predicting our future.

There were plenty of activities that could have occupied my recalcitrant mind. I could have written a novel in my head, learnt Dutch, memorized my 13 to 99 times tables or become an expert at balancing sticks. I had neither the patience nor will. I could have trained every day to become super-fit, but calories were at a premium. Even standing up made me dizzy enough to faint. I was able, though, to relive memorable journeys I had made and I was surprised by my memory for detail: the price of a curried egg in the window of a white-pillared cake shop on the shores of Lake Malawi; the cellulite-removing cream advertisement on the side of the yellow tram that passed the 'Sleep In' hostel in Amsterdam. I devised several business and employment opportunities. I planned enough extraordinary birthday parties to keep me going for another fifteen years. I routed my career in twenty different directions. Sadly, each line of thought could fill only a small fraction of the day, before, with torturous inevitability, I reverted to fantasizing about food.

When Bill remembered that Petrus had packed two magazines carefully in his tin there was great excitement. Any reading material at all was welcome since we had thrown all our books and papers away but these were Australian editions of *Women's Weekly* from the late 1980s and they were packed with references to food: features on Grandma's Biscuit Barrel, Bar-B-Q Treats, Classic Chicken Dishes; recipes for cookie ice cream, banana fritters, chilli con carne, vegetable kebabs; adverts for Fudge Sauce, Angel Delight, Cheese and Chive Dip, Banana Cake. I would stare with glazed eyes and sniff and lick the paper, conjuring up the smell, the texture, the pleasure. And then I would wake from the hallucination, shaking myself into real world, pushing the magazines away from me. By then it was too late, the images would pervade every part of my empty mind. Six mindless hours to wait until the boiled potatoes were ready.

When food was served the tension was tangible. Any move was interpreted as a possible assault on the pot. Paranoia dictated that my portion of potatoes always looked smaller than anyone else's. Even if they were riddled with brown fibrous knots there was no time to complain. It was a race to see who could finish and be back for extras first. Those without a spoon had no excuse: it was possible to shovel just as quickly by hand.

The hunger, like the boredom, seemed to have a particularly bad effect on me. It made me hostile and selfish at a time when we needed to support and care for each other more than ever. Navy often eyed me disapprovingly. He was always generous and restrained. Sometimes I watched him give food away and I wondered what it must feel like to do something that selfless. One evening, when Anna dropped a potato through the floor, I decided to see. With great effort I offered her my last potato. I was dismayed when she accepted but I felt as if I had taken the first step towards regaining control of my life and overcoming my animal instincts.

My manic attitude to eating was fuelled by more than just greed. If we had to run or hide, our fat reserves would dictate how long we would live before starving to death. While Anna and Annette seemed quite content to lose some excess pounds, my already lean body was becoming alarmingly skinny and I was frightened.

I felt as if I were being stripped of everything. The missing rucksacks had still not been found. Everyone had lost a few things but I had lost everything. A month before his prospect would have terrified me but now I was getting used to living a basic life in the forest. It didn't matter that I owned only one set of clothes – I just washed half of them at a time. I had no toothbrush, so I shared with the others or used a stick. I had no compass, so I watched the sun and tried to pay attention to the lie of the land and the position of the mountains. With poverty came an extraordinary feeling of liberty. There was nothing to pack, nothing to be stolen, nothing to worry about. I was as poor as a Papuan.

Many of the valuables that Silas had taken from us in the river house for safe-keeping had been shared out for the greater wealth. With Navy's permission, Silas had distributed our Walkmans and cameras while we lay ill in the sick house. I had watched the men prod the strange machines, twist them and shake them, pull the lids up, snap the levers off, prize out the rotas and crack the frames to pieces under rocks. From the wreckage they had removed the possessions they prized: a shiny mirror for a necklace, a smart black strap for a penis gourd, a battery for a nose piece.

One bag of valuables was still intact. Silas carried it wherever he went and was obsessed by the objects inside. Almost every day he would shield off a corner of the house, shoo away the other OPM men and empty the bag for inspection.

First he lined up the binoculars, tape recorders and global positioning units in height order, gently wiping away any dust or grime. Then various microphones and bits of wire were spread out in front. Finally he sorted the cash, stacking the notes in piles according to colour and denomination. Originally, there had been eight million rupiah ($4000): more money than Silas could possibly imagine – enough to buy one hundred pigs, five hundred machetes or fifty wives. He insisted the money was ours although he seemed to control how it was spent. While we were waiting for Yudas's foot to get better, Silas had used some of it to buy three pigs from a local woman. Then, instead of saving them and eating one pig a week, Silas had insisted we slaughter, cook and eat them all that day, in case the army came and we were forced to run. We had made ourselves sick on pork and now, of course, we were starving. Binge and fast seemed to be the principle by which the OPM lived: walk twelve hours a day for days then sit idly in the forest for weeks; ambush your enemies with machetes one moment then invite them in for a smoke the next. Nduga life was built on passionate extremes.

Silas was hungry and bored like the rest of us. His brain filled with ill-conceived ideas and one afternoon he took his confidants, Navy and Mark, into the woods for a secret meeting. In huddled whispers he explained how the three of them would run away to Wamena that night, with a letter for the President of Indonesia. The church would send helicopters to find the rest of us and Papua would be freed. His plans soon dissolved but, as the days passed, he became increasingly frustrated. He asked what month it was and we told him it was the middle of February.

'Two moons have passed, two whole moons, and we are still here,' he lamented as he strode around the camp. Then he turned on us, trying to justify himself. 'Don't blame me for being hungry. This is God's way. It was the army who caused us to run into the forest just when things were good. Anyway, hardship is good for you. See how you have all grown from this. Daniel, here,' he put his hand on my shoulder, 'he was just a boy. Now he is a man. And with hair like that he should be a Papuan man and wear a *nokin* on his head!'

As his anxiety grew, Silas threatened to go home. He had wives and children to think of as well as us, he said. Suddenly we were frightened of what would happen if Silas left. None of the other leaders spent so much time worrying about our well-being or were likely to ensure that the Indonesians were not mistreated. Silas had grown fond of us, especially of Mark and Navy.

'But Silas, you have been with us since the beginning,' Navy pleaded, kneeling down next to him, 'feeding us, housing us and looking after us. You know us and are like a father to us. We trust you and know you will not harm us. Please do not leave us now.'

When we woke two days later a strange calm had descended over the camp. Silas, his *nokin* and the precious bag of valuables were gone. We had been abandoned – only Murip and a few men remained.

Yudas had left his radio and we checked it every day for news. The Radio Australia Indonesian Service was still covering the hostage story although it was over three weeks since the army had come in and all contact with the OPM had been lost. ABRI said there was a small chance that at least some of us were still alive. Apparently the church, our embassies and even the ICRC (International Committee for the Red Cross) were trying to make contact with the rebels again.

Then, one evening, we heard the voices of our parents on the radio.

'These are our sons and daughters. They are completely innocent. We believe them to be alive,' came the strong clear voice of Annette's father. Anna's mother and Bill's girlfriend followed before I heard my mother's words: 'Daniel only wanted to help the Papuan people.' In that dark, silent forest through the muffled hiss of a battered radio held in the arms of Murip, our guerrilla leader, it was chilling and surreal to hear our families speak out. On the other side of the mountains was another world and that evening it felt farther away than ever. Nobody cried.

'It will be my father's fiftieth birthday tomorrow,' whispered Annette that night as we lay in the darkness beneath a sleeping bag. 'I really, truly thought I would be home for that one. My next date is Simon's wedding, in three and half weeks. I'm sure we'll be out for that.'

I turned to stare at her in the dark. 'And presumably you've got a whole list of dates stretching into the future?'

'Yep.' I could barely see her nod.

'So tell me about Simon. You mentioned him last night . . .' And she began, as she often did, to fill me in on another chapter of her social life.

I awoke as usual in the coldest part of the night, with pain searing down my back. I knew I had about thirty minutes to snooze with my knees pulled up tight until even that became unbearable. I tried to catch my dream before it was lost, but I was too late. I lay thinking of things to think: the food I ate on a picnic last summer in Granchester Meadows with friends; the food I would eat in May to celebrate my birthday with my family. The thoughts stung me only with hopeless desire and I tried to shut them out, to focus my mind on the now.

There was a breeze. That was unusual: the air was still in tropical forests, except before a storm. I turned over but moving was excruciating, and the ache was the same in every position. I had lost my half of the sleeping bag in the manoeuvre and felt too paralysed to retrieve it. On this side the slats were too far apart and they dug into my skinny hips.

I tried to take my thoughts elsewhere. Family, food, parties, food. It tormented me. God, why did I always think of food? Why did I always wallow in the past or dream of the future? Why did I spend so much time longing and yearning? Could I not just be satisfied to be alive?

I heaved myself up, moved to the fire and warmed my hands on the red heat that ebbed and flowed across the coals. I poked a few with a stick and they broke into glowing shards.

Anto was sleeping close by. He was our trusty wood chopper and the one man in the camp I liked. No, I liked the young boy, too, the one with the black plastic pipe around his neck. And Petrus, of course, poor Petrus, even though he had fallen out of a tree when he was young and hit his head. Anto was gentle and considerate. 'I don't understand why you are prisoners,' he would sometimes say. 'I don't understand why they take innocent prisoners to get a free country. Seems all wrong to me.' Now he stayed with us all the time, sniffing next to the fire, joking quietly to himself and walking bow-legged in his black T-shirt and red shorts.

He woke, shivering. '*Dingin*. Cold,' he muttered. He pulled down more wood from the stack above, layered it on the fire and began to make his first smoke of the day. Long flames of burning gas hissed out from between the fibres of the timber as he dried his fragile fragments of tobacco by the edge of the fire. He took a large rolling leaf from his arm band, creased it and folded the tobacco inside. I never asked but after the first two drags he would always offer the cigarette to me. I took one drag, offered it back and with a kindly jerk of his head he insisted I take more. It was our little ceremony.

The nicotine was strong and took away my hunger. For a moment I allowed myself to indulge in dreams of all the comforts I did not have, to wallow in self pity and blame my problems on the world. I tried to conjure up my family, imagining the feel of their touch and the timbre of their laughter. One by one they appeared, their faces shimmering, their eyes sparkling. I felt their love for me and I knew I would see them again one day.

For a moment I felt at one with the present: seeing, feeling everything. There was no boredom, no hunger, no longing to be elsewhere. The billowing hot air from the fire was scented with witch hazel. The bright flames beat against the silent night. Dreaming bodies slept around me. There was something about this morning that I knew I would not forget. One day, I thought, I will remember this fire on a hill in the night and it will give me inspiration. In every day there are beautiful things: one must find them and live with them.

I watched the dawn, savouring every minute. Clusters of the trees in the thicket emerged from their blurred night shapes. The inky darkness drained away from behind the stars visible through tiny holes in the canopy of leaves. The first mosquito whined slowly through the cold air, its tone shifting as it swooped and climbed. The fire quietened and I became conscious of the gentle swish of the stream in the gully below. For once there were birds, mainly parrots and lorikeets, calling from high in a tree nearby, flapping from branch to branch in a rustle of bright feathers. From certain angles through the forest I could make out narrow sections of the eastern ridge picked out by an early morning glow. As the sun broke the horizon, the others awoke. One by one they plonked themselves down next to me and I felt slightly superior, as if to say, this is my day because I have been with the dawn.

'Hi, Dan, how are you? Did you sleep well?' Anna sang out, hanging her knickers above the fire. She had tried drying them at the bottom of her sleeping bag but they were still damp. Annette sat silently, sending curt replies and cold stares at anybody who infringed on her personal space. 'For God's sake, Anna, take down your knickers. Do you think Murip needs any more encouragement?' Bill stood staring out through the forest then sat worrying quietly about what the day would not bring, holding his knees in a comforting embrace. Murip woke and began pointing, fussing and bullying, hammering my head with his constant taunting:

'Why are there no potatoes? Where is one I baked last night? Petrus! Where is Petrus? Daniel, what are you boiling? Why do you want to drink hot water? Give me that stick! See there is too little water. Petrus! Is this water from the roof? Fetch water from the stream. Why are clothes hanging here? They will burn. Anna, you sit here. Why is your knee still ill, you should wrap it in paper. Why won't you teach me English. Petrus, there are no potatoes. Quickly, kill the fire! Can't you see it's already day?'

During those long difficult weeks an unbreakable bond formed between Anna, Bill, Annette and myself. By the end we knew that we would stand by each other, maybe lay down our lives for each other. But this loyalty was never spoken of and was different from friendship. Although we struggled with the same feelings of hunger, boredom, longing, hopelessness and fear we rarely opened our hearts. Much of our time was spent retracted into our own lonely, frustrated worlds. Our feelings made us too fragile and were too deep-buried to be shared. 'Even if my best friend was here,' Annette told me one day, 'I wouldn't share my feelings. Once I started to let go I wouldn't be able to stop.'

Around us there were other unions and pacts. Navy, Adinda, Tessy and Lita shared everything, never speaking in more than a whisper lest the OPM hear. Bram and Markus were distantly connected to them but spent much time apart. Bram also suffered from a bad back and would sit alone in prayer much of the night. Markus was often with the other Papuan men, talking and sharing cigarettes. At first Mark and Martha thought they should hide their love for each other in case it made them more vulnerable but the more visibly pregnant Martha became, the more they became a case apart. The OPM understood that Mark would be a father and must take care of his wife.

Mark and Navy were the prominent figures in our extended family and they led by example. Mark was sensible and even tempered, while Navy encouraged generosity and selflessness for the good of the team. They were also the only two who could speak both Indonesian and English fluently and they had both earned respect from Silas.

Often it was humour that kept us all together. We joked endlessly about boredom, food, our captors and our general plight. We developed code names for the OPM leaders so we could talk about them in secret. Silas was '*babe*' which was Jakarta slang for father; Murip was Robin Hood for his taste in green clothing and habit of stealing from the rich; Kwalik was Marlboro; Yudas was green beret; Daud was old nutter; Petrus was our helper, and Anto, black T-shirt. The OPM itself was sometimes known as Dad's Army for its comical similarities to an aspiring military force.

Bill and I developed an excellent conversational relationship. He was eloquent and very highly informed. We discussed and debated any subject of which we both knew a little: the role of Ugandan conservation projects in community development, the last years of apartheid in South Africa, the technicalities of sailing a tall ship across the Atlantic, the economy of Romania. He filled in the large gaps in my knowledge of current affairs. I talked from my broad scientific background about electric eels and quantum physics.

He told me about his family's herd in the Borders, explaining the characteristics of each breed, the techniques of artificial insemination, the production of the feed from molasses and oats. I explained darkroom colour printing, homemade rockets, bicycle repairs and long-distance footpaths. He talked about his brother Tom who worked at an auction market, about his Dad who had built up his business from nothing and about his mother on the Borders tourism development board. I talked about my mother, image consultant and therapist, my father's love of go-carting, surfing, croquet and Hamleys, and my brother's computer business. He told me of his isolated teenage years, living miles from any town, too musical and intelligent for the other lads, and how he had seduced his first girlfriend in a shed at the bottom of the garden. I talked about my early years in Herefordshire making tunnels though the woods, rafts on the lake, about my schooldays and social life in London.

We drew tremendous enjoyment and entertainment from our conversations. They took my mind from my stomach and satisfied my desire for knowledge; they drew Bill from his pensive, anxious moods.

Annette hated our talk. Every voice was an irritation and in that small forest shelter every sound was audible. She only joined our discussions if she had a strong opinion and then would attack us ferociously. In fact her whole tone had hardened. In day-to-day communication she said as little as possible with cutting honesty. She no longer had time for small talk. When I drew her attention to the change she was surprised. So much of her energy was used to keep herself strong and disciplined that there was little left for tolerance or social niceties. I noticed the same change in myself, to a lesser degree. Annette and I both shared a determination to keep positive and as the weeks passed we turned to each other more and more often for support.

Anna's never-ending reserves of geniality and patience, even during her bouts of sickness, were extraordinary. She was always kind and generous and seemed irritated by no one, not even Murip or members of the OPM. Even the constant boredom did not obviously frustrate her. She preferred to let others worry and talk about our situation, trusting fate to take its course. Only occasionally did the stresses of the situation build up. Then she would break down in tears and only Annette was able to comfort her.

Anna and I shared many spiritual and philosophical beliefs which we sometimes discussed and once even Navy joined in and told us about a friend he had seen levitate in meditation. Most of the time, however, Anna and I found it difficult to talk. I was too aggressive, she too passive, and we would grind to an awkward halt.

The influx of news from Radio Australia continued. The army was still in Mapnduma and Alama but had withdrawn from the areas in between. The ICRC were now stationed in Wamena and were working full time to make contact with the OPM. One morning we saw a white helicopter flying high overhead and then several days later a note was brought to us by messenger. It asked the local community and the OPM to make contact with the ICRC helicopter to help resolve the hostage crisis. We knew the OPM held the ICRC in high esteem so they seemed to be the perfect intermediary.

Less helpful were a series of radio interviews with a man named Moses Werror who claimed to be of the leader of the OPM in exile in Papua New Guinea. He stated that we would not be released until the UN had convened a special assembly of the Dutch, British and Indonesian governments to discuss the issues surrounding the theft of West Papua from the Papuan people. Thankfully, Murip and the other OPM men had never heard of him and paid little attention to the broadcast, and we remained hopeful that Yudas would return any day with news of our freedom. With ABRI out and the ICRC in everything appeared to be set for our release.

Then one afternoon, after almost three weeks in the cold house, Jamie, the pleasant Amungme man who I had met at the sick house, came panting up the hill, smiling and talking excitedly about good news. He sat cross-legged on the floor, caught his breath and asked how we all were. He said he had been thinking of us and was sorry for us, that we looked skinny, but he had brought us sugar cane and news.

We seemed to have been waiting for this moment for ever. We sat patiently. Jamie had walked far that day, from Geselema a village at the north end of the Ilare valley. The ICRC had come there, he said, in a white helicopter. The doctor had spoken with Yudas and given them a Red Cross flag to put in the centre of the village, and a walkie-talkie so they could talk to the ICRC in the helicopter and be sure it wasn't the army tricking them. They had brought rice, noodles and cigarettes and there would be a ceremony on Sunday. He didn't know what would happen but it was very important that we were all there. The Red Cross were going to help the OPM and the hostages.

We were elated. Maybe this was the release ceremony that the leaders had talked about at the river house. Yudas had obviously gone to Geselema when he heard about the ICRC, thinking it would be easier to arrange our release through them than the Bishop. I bit into my stick of sugar cane, sucked out the sweet juice and licked at the dribbles that tried to escape down my chin. It was clear that things were moving again.

'I have letters for you as well,' said Jonny. He coughed and looked a little sheepish, 'from Kelly.' He withdrew a folded wad of paper from his *nokin* and began to flatten it out on the floor. He handed two handwritten sheets to Mark. ' These he wants you to type.'

Alarm bells were ringing in my head. What did Kwalik have to do with anything? He had gone home and told Yudas to release us. And why type? What did typing have to do with us going home?

Dear friends,

Happily I can tell you that we have secured the support of the ICRC for our cause. We have asked that the UN convene a special assembly of the Dutch, British and Indonesian governments to discuss the issues surrounding

the theft of West Papua from the Papuan people. I have
thought of this idea myself. When this has been completed
you will go free.

You must eat well and keep healthy.

Kelly Kwalik

Regional Commander, OPM, Division Fak Fak III.

For a split second I could not believe it was true. Everything we
had been through was in vain. After seven weeks it was beginning
all over again. My eyes slipped out of focus, I shuffled slowly on
my buttocks to the edge of the hut and slumped back against a
post. My arms fell limply out of the hut, swaying in the cool evening
air as desperation engulfed me. Every ounce of hope was draining
away. Each day I imagined as an eternity in hell. How could I keep
going?

I thought I might be dreaming. My skin was numb and I was
breathless. I got up and walked like a ghost to one of the sleeping
bags. Fumbling with the zip, I pulled myself inside and curled up
in a tight ball against the tapered end.

'Dan?' It was Annette, calling me kindly. Her voice had lost all
the harshness of the previous weeks. 'Dan, don't go there.' I stayed
still for several seconds, suffocated by self pity. I wanted to cry but
could not. Annette touched me. 'It's not worth it,' she said. Suddenly I felt resolute. There was always hope. There was hope in
everything.

I crawled up and out with bleary eyes. Annette smiled and patted
my arm. 'It doesn't mean anything,' she said lightly. 'Give them a
day and they'll want to release us again.'

Jamie spent the night and the next day Murip suggested we write
letters to our families.

Thursday 22nd February 1996

To all my family and friends on the outside,

I am hungry but well enough. I think of that incredible Isles
of Scilly fudge cake everyday. Yesterday was a difficult day.

Three weeks ago all the leaders, including Kelly Kwalik, promised we would be released *asap* with no demands. Now after waiting in a dark, wet camp with no food or books they tell us their new absurd demands for a UN meeting etc. We are sure that this change of mind has been caused by a Radio Australia interview with Moses Werror last week, combined with the attentions of the Red Cross. Unless their new demand can be faked, they need to understand the following: 1) No government will negotiate with hostage takers, this can only happen after our release. 2) The imprisonment and maltreatment of innocent people contravenes the exact human rights that they are so fiercely fighting for. 3) This action is solely their responsibility and not the fault of the army or the will of God. 4) Public opinion for their cause decreases day by day.

I miss you and love you every day, Daniel.

Navy selectively translated parts of the letters at Murip's insistence. He was not impressed that we all moaned about being hungry. He said that everyone was hungry right now, and for Papuans hunger was normal.

It was Thursday and the ceremony was not until Sunday. Murip sent the letters off to Geselema with Jonny but was then unsure what he should do with us. He had dreamt badly the night before and that was a bad omen for travel. 'What if it is all a trick?' he asked us. The next morning men arrived to help carry the bags to Geselema but still Murip would not budge. Then suddenly we heard the distinctive whoosh of a hornbill beating its huge wings nearby. The black and white bird with a long conical beak alighted in a tree nearby. Murip needed no more persuading: we packed our bags and were off.

After weeks with little food or exercise we walked the path like drunkards, wheeling off logs and falling down holes. We moved slowly, holding tightly on to each other until, in the afternoon, we arrived at a tiny village down near the banks of the Kilmid river. Plenty of OPM troops had come from Geselema to help us with the onward journey. I questioned them about the Sunday ceremony and some seemed to think we would be freed.

The walk had been very difficult for Martha, who arrived with pains, holding her stomach. Mark was angry and said there was no way she could endure any more. The baby had dropped very low and they thought it would miscarry. Murip said she could be carried but Martha refused. The tracks in the area were as steep and dangerous as any we had seen and Mark explained that a fall would certainly kill the baby and maybe Martha. He suggested a ICRC helicopter pick her up before the party on Sunday. Murip whispered with his cronies. The new men began to rant and shout. The ICRC would trick them, they said. Petrus tried to defend Martha but he was punched in the face. We wished that Silas was there to stand up for us.

We could not go back, as the cold house had been destroyed. We could not stay more than one night in the tiny village as it was too open. We knew it was important to be at the ceremony in case we were due to be released. Despite all our vows that we should never split, early the next morning we did. It was already Saturday and Martha wanted us to go ahead to make the meeting. She and Mark would rest and join us later.

The ten of us dropped quickly to the Kilmid river. We were higher up so it was smaller and easier to cross. We splashed from bank to bank as it twisted and turned through forest and palm groves. The sky was overcast and our mood was heavy and oppressive now that we had abandoned Mark and Martha. Mist was hanging around the hill tops and the river narrowed into a steep rock gully. Our slow steady march through this prehistoric wilderness had an epic feel. I felt that at some moment a pterodactyl might swoop squawking from the craggy mountain tops and snatch one of us away.

Instead, there was a whirr of blades in the trees above us. We ducked instinctively, then hid ourselves in the undergrowth. A machine was close above, moving east, with a large red cross on its belly. We stared in awe as it climbed higher and higher to clear the valley ridge. It was our first sighting of the legendary Red Cross.

The OPM guides took us up and over into Ilare crossing the ridge at a low pass. We were much further north and it looked nothing like it had nearer the lowlands. After several hours we came down to the river which was wide but fordable. There were some huts and flat space on the bank to land a helicopter. But it was not Geselema and the OPM goaded us on. 'Is it near?' we asked our guides. Always it was the next hill, or the next hut.

By late afternoon we reached a high plateau on the hillside and staggered into a filthy village, awash with mud and pig shit. The rotting trunks of the felled forest lay this way and that, forming broadwalks across a tiny toxic stream running yellow with urine and detritus. Three huts stood among all this and at the far side was one which was long and double ended.

Large knuckles covered by saggy skin clasped the first door frame. An old woman peered out from the dim interior with beady eyes and jerked her head towards the other end. I tiptoed cautiously along the side of the house.

'Hey! Who's that?' came a loud familiar voice from inside. 'What time do you call this, eh?'

Silas appeared from the other doorway of the house, his lips quivering in a smile.

FOURTEEN

THE PIG VILLAGE

'Silas! What do you think *you're* doing here?' I said, pointing my finger at him. I was delighted.

'Young Daniel still has a snake's tongue, good, good,' he said grabbing my shoulder and embracing me with one arm. 'And Mr Navy.' He gave him several good slaps on the back and laughed loudly. 'This man could be my brother if his hair wasn't so straight and his skin so yellow. And you, yes, and you,' he said looking fleetingly at Anna, Adinda and Annette as they came by. 'And Mr Ben.'

'*Bill*, not Ben,' hissed Bill with a look to kill.

Silas stood proudly as he watched his flock file into the tiny hut. From the eaves he brought down a wok filled with pieces of cooked meat. Navy rubbed his hands in glee and shuffled forward to dunk his nose in the aroma. '*Wam, wam, wam, wam*,' he repeated excitedly to himself. *Wam* was the Nduga for pig.

'Sit back, sit back,' said Silas. 'I cooked this pig for you yesterday. Where have you been? This is my very last pig. The army shot all the others before they left.' He began picking pieces out, carving them in the air with his serrated knife and handing them out randomly.

Never believe in the pig until you're chewing the lard. With so many false promises I had got used to muttering this to myself whenever I felt my expectations rise. Now we were here in a real village, in a house, with pig meat to build up our bodies again. I sank back against the wall. The ache of my tired limbs was almost a pleasure. For a moment I forgot that we had left Martha and

Mark behind. Then, like an apparition, they were at the door; Martha stomping and puffing, Mark's face in a wide and comical grin. 'I smell *wam*,' he said twitching his nose. 'I smell the scent of a roasted *wam*.'

We bombarded them with questions. Martha said she was all right but she was obviously exhausted and still worried. Silas cut off a triple-size portion for her, about the size of a half-pound steak. She just looked at it in amazement and asked, 'Hey. Is this all for me?'

Each chunk of pig was a thin band of dark meat beneath an inch-thick layer of white lard backed with a charred coating of skin. The cold, jelly-like fat wobbled in my mouth, melted and dribbled down my chin and the skin was tough with a waxy flavour but Markus was happy to take what I couldn't eat. The meat was delicious, a little undercooked, perhaps, but we didn't worry. Even Anna was nibbling like a rabbit at the corner of her piece. We egged her on, reminding her that she needed protein to repair her knee and build up her strength.

There were potatoes as well: tasty small ones, not the over-sized fibrous freaks that Petrus had been digging from the old gardens and forest around the cold house.

'Tomorrow we will raise the flag,' announced Silas. 'The ICRC will come.' We all stopped eating and looked at him.

'Will we go too?' I asked hopefully.

'Maybe,' he said, hesitating a little. It was clear he didn't know and I wondered just how much involvement Silas had in the decision-making of the OPM.

'Where is Kwalik?' asked Mark.

'In Geselema with the flag. The Amungme brought it from the lowlands.'

For a moment I panicked. I had thought this was Geselema, but I checked myself before I began to ponder our fate too deeply. Speculation just wasn't worth the energy.

We spent the afternoon sorting out our new home. It was undoubtedly the smallest yet. There was a central fireplace, as in Aptam, but the back section was taken up by pig pens: too small to sleep in but perfect for hanging rucksacks and bags. Petrus busied himself building steps down the steep bank which led to a particularly unappetising long-drop loo. Silas pointed us to a washing area he had made by damming the dribble of a stream that ran through the village to create a putrid brown pool.

It was not a perfect location but the very fact that we were back in a village cheered us all. It was open, with a view to the north, and meant the chance to get news and food more regularly. There was likely to be more going on around us. Already I felt much less isolated and I went to bed that night tingling with life again. As I lay thinking of what the next day's ceremony might bring, it was excitement not cold that stopped me from sleeping.

I crept out of the hut early the next morning to see if there was a view of the mountains. Bram was up, holding on tightly to the side of the hut, swaying gently backwards and forwards in waves of giddy nausea. The pigs had already spied the pool of vomit and were shuffling and licking greedily around his feet. 'Good morning,' he whispered, forcing a smile, before he heaved again.

Within an hour of dawn we heard a helicopter land behind the ridge further up the valley. It took off quickly afterwards and it was obvious we were not expected to go to meet it. By eight o'clock Lita, Annette and Tessy also had diarrhoea and vomiting and Petrus had begun building a second loo. Navy, Mark, Markus and Bill were using it by mid-day and after the helicopter came and went again in the early afternoon Martha, Anna and I were feeling pretty queasy as well. The hut was filled with groaning bodies cursing Silas, his festering pig meat and his squalid village.

When Silas, Murip and various onlookers arrived later in the day we were pleased they could see the pitiful state we were all in. Silas blamed Petrus for fetching us bad water; Murip blamed us for eating too much. They both looked fairly guilty, though, and emptied goodies from their *nokins* which provided some distraction: six tubes of toothpaste, eight packs of sanitary towels, four bars of soap, two bras, three tins of pilchards and two packets of noodles. Murip offered us a cigarette each from his pack and we wondered what other things had not quite made it through to us.

They had brought a large brown envelope stuffed with mail, this time for everyone. Annette's father's words went through my head again: 'These are our sons and daughters. We believe them to be alive.' After so many weeks of bottling up my emotions I knew I was about to give in.

Reading the compassionate words of my parents, realizing that they were suffering and worrying with me, I no longer felt alone. Feeling so close to them gave me the strength to let go at last. As the pent-up tensions of the weeks poured away I felt that mixture of grief and expectation that accompanies a rite of passage. I had lost an innocence and a part of me had changed forever.

The OPM were humbled to see us cry. Silas produced a camera from his bag and asked Navy to take a photo. 'Your parents must know how much we all want to be free,' he said. For a whole hour they just let us be, without nagging or shouting. I even saw Silas hold Navy's arm and tell him softly that it was only natural to miss one's family and that patience would see him through.

For some strange reason only Bram received nothing. I knew he was longing to hear about his baby girl but I wondered if he had the energy to be miserable as he sat pale and gaunt with his head between his knees retching stomach acid into a plastic bag.

By evening Annette's condition had worsened, too, although the others were getting better. She had bad diarrhoea and she thought it might be the dysentery she had got rid of in the cold house. I sat with her on the veranda late into the night, helping her every few minutes down the steep path to the loo and waiting for her in the darkness.

'Here, take this,' I said, giving her a wad of tissue paper saved from weeks before. 'Better than leaves, eh?' She smiled thankfully. 'I've got a candle saved, too, if you want to read your letters again.'

'No, I don't want to read them again.'

'You want to save them?'

'I suppose. They make me worry. My dad will be fine, rushing around being practical about everything. I worry about my mum.'

'I couldn't let myself start worrying about everyone else. If I did I'd crack up under the strain.'

'I spoke to Navy the other night in the village,' she said, changing the subject. 'It was the first time I saw him down. Really down.' I had noticed that he had seemed a little depressed as well but I still found it difficult to talk to him.

'What was wrong? Apart from the obvious. Does he know something?'

'I don't know. Probably just a mood. I think he takes on a lot of responsibility for Adinda, Lita and Tessy. He worries for everyone, does everything for everyone.'

I laughed a little. 'Do you think I should be like that, in my role as a team leader?'

'I'd kill you first.' She looked serious.

'Is Navy scared, do you think?'

'Scared of what? Sickness? Accidents?'

'Well, there's that.' I felt a little foolish. 'But wouldn't you be scared if the OPM had beaten you on the first day?'

Two days later everyone had recovered from the poisoning except Bram who was still on a water diet, although even that he found difficult to keep down. Adinda was also ill again with kidney pain and fever. It kept her awake through the night and she was so weak that Navy would carry her down the steps and hold her when she needed to pee.

When Kwalik honoured us with a rare visit he poured scorn on Adinda's pains, suggesting that it was a venereal disease she had caught from Navy. They were strict Christians but under the circumstances there was nothing Navy could do but gape. Kwalik said there was no need to worry about sickness because he had agreed that we could see the ICRC doctor. After talking a little more about how kind and good he was, he began to preach about his new demand for a UN meeting. Bill and I dared to suggest that there would be more sympathy for the OPM from the UN and our governments once we were released. He got angry and started shouting, 'Kwalik is not a fool, I am Kwalik, Kwalik is not a fool,' over and over like a demented despot. We were thankful when he had gone.

We were so depressed by his visit that none of us dared to hope that the doctor would come but two days later on Thursday 29 February, we heard the sound of the helicopter, this time right above us. The OPM men quickly pulled in our drying clothes and stood in front of the door but I watched the thundering machine circle above the village and land nearby. Twenty minutes later we heard a group of people squelching slowly along the path towards the house.

Yudas had rushed ahead and was at the door waving his arms at us. 'Quickly, quickly, clear up, sit up straight, the doctor is coming.'

Many people talked excitedly outside. We heard a voice speaking in French, and I caught a glimpse of some blue jeans standing amongst the bare Papuan legs. All our fears of being lost for ever just melted away. We had finally been found.

'My name is Dr Ferenc Meyer. I am a delegate of the International Committee for the ICRC in Geneva.' He spoke English with a strong French accent which was calm but formal. He was maybe forty-five, rugged, with a moustache and a large ICRC badge on his shirt. He squatted outside, looking in at our dim hostage hovel.

'First I must ask your permission for us to photograph and film this meeting for possible use by the media. As you can understand, there has been worldwide interest in your plight.'

We shrugged and nodded, overcome by the significance of the event. This man had brought the world to see our tiny, pathetic home.

'I am here to make a medical examination. Outside you will meet René Suter and Sylviane Bonadei, also delegates of the ICRC.' He turned to Yudas and spoke in broken Indonesian. 'You want me to do the examinations in the other hut?' Yudas nodded. He was enjoying himself.

As we walked out of the hut René, a tall, slim young man, was filming us and I waved at the camera. Sylviane, wearing a padded

bodywarmer, her hair in a ponytail, met us with a big smile. Annette
gave her a big hug while Anna bobbed up and down nervously as
if curtseying to royalty. Bill looked uneasy and slightly confused. I
felt the same. I followed Sylviane to another hut, shuffling along
in my filthy T-shirt and broken shoes and staring at their clothes:
more freshly laundered blue jeans, a smart Swatch watch, a purple
Gortex anorak and new Timberland boots. There was just a faint
memory that I, too, had been like that once – affluent and free.

'So while Dr Ferenc is examining, the rest of us can just talk,'
she said taking out a crisp red packet of Marlboro cigarettes.

'May I?' I asked nervously.

'Of course, of course. They're for you.' She began emptying her
pockets and handing things around. 'Take a packet. I have packets
for everyone. And some sweets for those who do not smoke.' I
took them like a street urchin and hid them quickly in my pocket.
'You know we almost didn't get in today because the weather was
so bad. After so much talking with Kwalik to get him to allow this
visit, we couldn't believe our bad luck. But here we are! The
helicopter will be back in three hours so there is plenty of time.'

'So here you are,' we repeated, nodding. There was an awkward
silence and I looked around and realized Kwalik was nowhere to
be seen.

'So how are things?' she asked.

'Okay, I suppose,' I said nodding again, 'except for this hostage
thing.'

'Yes, we heard about that,' said Sylviane with a smile.

'We've been ill and there's Martha's baby,' Annette began.
'There's too much walking and not enough food. But we're okay.
We've been on the run or in hiding for ages.'

'Have the leaders talked about our release?' Bill asked.

'Right now we're just building things up bit by bit. We've been
bringing in supplies for the people here, rice, meat and things and
Ferenc has been doing some medical work.'

'You have to try and talk some sense into them,' I blurted out,
'what with this free Papua thing and now the UN thing they heard
on Radio Australia. I mean, the Red Cross is everything to them

and so much could be achieved for the area, for the people, but they've got to be realistic.' I felt exasperated already.

Sylviane was nodding slowly. 'Yes, sure, sure. There is a lot of confusion right now and I get the feeling they don't know what they want. Is it political freedom or is that the pretext for development and human rights? But we will do *everything* we can for you. Our reason for being here is the hostages.'

While Dr Ferenc examined us one by one in his hut, Sylviane and René chatted with the rest of us outside in English and Indonesian. At first I felt nervous and introverted, as if I had been locked in an attic for too long. Then we began to laugh, joke and relax.

'We didn't know what to expect,' said René. 'Ferenc brought bottles of anti-depressants but you don't seem to need them.' We shook our heads and felt proud. We wrote notes home and took Polaroid pictures of each other for our parents. The OPM seemed quite happy with the situation. I asked about Ivar, our Defence Attaché in Wamena, concerned that he might give up on us.

'No, Ivar is dedicated,' Sylviane reassured us. 'He was with us loading up the helicopter in Wamena at five o'clock this morning. He wanted to come, too.'

'But how is he surviving without his gin and tonics?' Bill asked facetiously. 'Wamena is a dry town.'

'You think his personal stock is finished?' said Sylviane laughing. 'His room is the social focus of the hotel.'

Finally, Ferenc came out and sat on the porch of the hut. We gathered around him. 'I will telephone each and every one of your families tonight and send them the messages from you that I have safely in my book.' He patted his breast pocket. 'We hope we can meet you every week or so from now on and bring some things to make your life a little easier. We have here four rucksacks packed by your embassies and a box of food. And don't worry too much about Moses Werror. We plan to go to Papua New Guinea to speak with him soon. Kwalik says he cannot release you until Werror gives the word. So we can be hopeful. We won't abandon you now.' He smiled. 'So now I try the other business.'

'What's the other business?' I whispered to Navy.

'He wants to take Adinda for tests in hospital,' he said shaking his head gravely. 'She is not well but he doesn't know what it is. Or maybe he doesn't want to say.'

I saw Ferenc at the bottom of the village with Kwalik and some other men talking in agitated fashion. After a few minutes Ferenc came back up shaking his head.

'I said to them: you wanted a doctor. Here I am. I said: in my professional opinion that girl needs a hospital. They said I should bring in the tools and do the operation here and I tell them that's impossible.' He threw his hands in the air. 'So what can I do?'

Over the ridge from the east was a high whine and a black dot. Sylviane pulled out a walkie-talkie and talked to the pilot. 'The weather is building over the mountains,' she said. 'We need to go.' The helicopter circled above the village and landed a little way down the hill. The three of them packed up with some urgency and we shook hands hastily.

'Keep strong, eh? You're doing an incredible job,' said Sylviane. 'We'll see you again really soon.' She hugged us all and went down the path after the others.

'Well, that's that,' I said, sighing. 'Back to the real world again.' There was a sinking feeling inside and I tried to ignore the helicopter taking off behind me. The OPM had rushed down to watch it go, leaving the village empty. Only Petrus stayed and helped us back to our hut with the rucksacks from Ivar. We allowed our excitement about the contents to mount, to take our minds off the helicopter, and we crammed into the hut as Tessy stood guard by the door. Hands prodded the pockets. Some said we should wait, others that we should stop wasting time. Hands felt inside and suddenly all control was lost and everyone was diving in.

'Books, one, two, three ... ten books. And a chess set. Two packs of cards and newspapers!' shouted Bill. He sat on the floor reading the cover of one of the books with the biggest smile I had seen for months.

'Rice, noodles, chilli sauce,' Navy called out and Tessy began to improvise rice and noodle songs between puffs of his fag.

'Chocolate, six bars. Boiled sweets, three jars. Crackers, two packs. *Cheese*, Kraft cheese slices, *ten* packs.'

'Did some one say six bars of chocolate?' Anna's face lit up and she leant over the bags. 'Is it fruit and nut?'

'And chocolate Haagel Slaag flakes!' cried Martha. 'Our embassy packed these rucksacks too!'

Petrus was smiling and shaking his head as the goods were pulled out, cooing in wonder and patting us all on the arms and legs.

'Writing paper, pens, torches, notebooks, disposable pants, tooth-brushes, soap, T-shirts, more sanitary towels. Loo rolls! Ten whole loo rolls!' A huge cheer went up through the hut.

'Shhh,' whispered Tessy with sudden urgency. 'Murip *datang*!' We frantically shovelled everything into the nearest pig sty, covered it with hay and sat around innocently on the floor. We didn't want Murip or any of the OPM men seeing the goods and helping themselves.

Thankfully in the tiny hut we did not have to endure Murip, Silas and a whole host of OPM living with us constantly. Murip still made a predictable appearance around meal times, Silas did some shouting every other day and there were a growing stream of passing spectators but in comparison to other places the hut was cosy and private. Only Anto and Petrus stayed with us at night and over the next few evenings we sorted out the goods, sharing them around and allocating quotas of sweets and chocolate to each person. Petrus and Angin were included as well in repayment for all their hard work and loyalty to us. But it was clear that what Petrus wanted, more than anything, were clothes so that he could be like us and the 'real' OPM men. We donated one of the new white T-shirts and Bram gave him a spare pair of his shorts. Petrus was overjoyed and paraded about the hut and village with a huge smile. He washed them every day, watching and copying our scrubbing actions then checking them every five minutes to see if they had dried.

It was like Christmas for everyone in our hut: Mark and Martha sat engrossed in trashy novels, sucking boiled sweets contentedly; Anna learnt Nduga words from Petrus and wrote them into her new notebook; Tessy rolled endless cigarettes from squares of air-mail paper and Bill cut out all the crosswords and spent hours chewing his pencil. There was a new treat every day: cheese slices on crackers; packet soup with noodles and corned beef; milky drinks with sugar, and coffee. The ground below the hut was littered with the happy wrappers of confectionery and other factory food.

Our chocolate allocations tormented Anna and me. Should we save all ten squares for the next depressing walk, when we were half dead at the top of some mountain? Should we be controlled and eat just one square per day, with the thought of the remaining ones haunting our every waking moment? Or should we eat the whole thing in one go in an orgy of indulgence?

Soon the party foods were finished. Bram was better but Adinda was still ill and Anna had developed malaria again. One afternoon old friends appeared at the door. Philipus and Naftali had trekked from army-occupied Mapnduma. Many families, he said, were still living in the forest with little food or shelter, too afraid to return. Many were sick and very hungry. We linked hands and Philipus prayed for the plight of everyone trapped between the army and the OPM.

The ICRC visit had reminded us vividly of the possibility of freedom. Having ample food and a warm environment gave us plenty of time to think beyond hunger and cold and out to the real world. I began reading a gripping thriller based in Europe but when I closed the book our situation flooded back, making me reel. We had a few copies of *Newsweek* and the *Weekly Telegraph*. I became aware of life out there beyond us, rushing past while we were stuck in suspended animation.

'We have to do something. We have to,' Bill pleaded. 'We can't just sit here useless. Let's write to Moses Werror, do something, anything.' The rest of us just looked at him apathetically. As nothing we did seemed to have any effect, it seemed pointless to try.

Bill seemed to suffer most in the mornings. He stared at the ceiling, wide-eyed and motionless, with thoughts of home passing through his mind. He became so morose that we dared not go near for fear of catching his disease. And as his mood pervaded the tiny hut I began to resent him and struggled to feel sympathy.

'If it had been me who went to the radio, like Yudas suggested, I would be free right now,' he sometimes said. At other times he wondered if they would let him go if he broke his leg. Was that the only way out?

'Bill, I can't let myself dwell on my life at home,' I tried to explain. 'This is my life. I have to respect it as my fate not because it was ever *meant* to happen, but simply because it has. If you resent it, it makes everything worse.' But for me it was relatively easy. I had no girlfriend at home to think of and had made no definite career plans. I even liked the Papuans and their land.

As Bill withdrew he became dependent on those around him. Others were left to cook and do chores. This behaviour infuriated Annette who lashed out in private.

'Annette,' I would whisper, 'don't say that. He'll hear.'

'Oh, he'll never hear. He never notices anything or anyone,' she would reply crossly, although sometimes I was sure she wanted him to hear and take note. By sharing such slanderous thoughts we formed a secret alliance, made more secure by the gulf between Bill, who was so down to earth, and Anna, who was distrait. But as Bill revealed his own more vulnerable side his patience with Anna seemed to grow. I watched them play chess and cards happily together and sometimes he asked her quietly about meditation. He seemed to be searching for a faith that could help him through his crisis and was willing to consider ideas and beliefs that previously I would have expected him to scorn.

While we remained a loyal but lonely four my relationships with the Indonesians began to improve slightly. There was more food available now, mainly cassava and sweet potato, and I was able to control my greed. I would decline seconds and serve others before myself. Navy's example had finally shown me that the group would survive only if every one of us made a conscious effort to place others before themselves. Food still preoccupied many of my thoughts but I tried hard to pretend I had kicked the habit. Within days Lita, Adinda and Tessy were much warmer towards me and

I felt that Navy was at last treating me with some respect. Adinda and I grew fond of each other and would practice our Indonesian and English together and often Lita, Tessy and I would tease each other playfully.

Learning to fit twelve people into twelve feet by eight also brought us closer together. The tolerance and patience required seemed a small price to pay to feel so closely linked. Anna, Annette, Bill and I slept in one corner. There was not enough length to stretch out, so we bent our legs; there was not enough width to lie flat, so we lay on our sides. We were like a row of interlocking spoons turning together unconsciously in the night.

Although there were no pigs they had left their fleas and when the fire was dead and the hut was in darkness the creatures would begin to creep over our skin, biting intermittently. The tiny clusters of red marks itched terribly. Anna would lie next to me for hours at a time, scratching her legs uncontrollably, using both hands and all her fingers.

'You've got to leave them,' I would plead as I was jolted around by her movement. 'They'll get infected,'

'I can't, I can't,' she would cry. 'It's too much. They itch too much.'

Finally she would scratch herself to sleep, and I would drift off, but then the woman behind the partition in the other half of the house would begin to cough and groan. Apart from her and a couple of others, the village was empty except for OPM. The families had run and hidden deep in the forest when the army came. She was too ill to run and lay there alone, throwing up phlegm and blood through the long night. The scratching, coughing and groaning tormented me, filling my head with vivid dreams and then, in the half light of dawn, her pigs would wake me as they screamed like humans, clambering and fighting to break free of their pens.

With the very limited space it was easier to keep other visitors out as well. Many Amungme troops, who had yet to meet us, were in the area. Each day a few new people would wander up to our end of the village and try to sit with us. They were generally very friendly and their presence and curiosity were understandable. Not only were we extraordinary aliens, a certain amount of kudos went with being known and liked by the hostages. It was a delicate balance for us. On the one hand we wanted to nurture our popular status; on the other hand we did not want to appear too happy in case they assumed we were enjoying ourselves. More immediately problematic was that our privacy and space were compromised by large, gawking men.

'Why do you want to come in?' Bill would snap as a new group tried to squeeze into the hut with us. He would sit blocking the doorway and the men would crouch outside waiting for him to move.

'Look, see how small this house is,' I tried to explain to them. 'People in here are ill; too ill for visitors. Maybe if you go in you will catch the illness, too.' With some gentle persuasion they would usually leave disgruntled.

One afternoon Bill slipped on the path in the village while we were collecting drinking water. The frustration and humiliation poured out of him and he screamed furiously at the men standing nearby, 'I want to go home, I want go home.'

'Are you okay?' I asked.

'Yes. But we need to show them that sitting around like this is not a holiday for us.'

We spent ten days in our little house and became quite attached to it despite the poor facilities. It had accommodated us during a crucial period of stability and recovery. Silas and Murip visited less and less often, Yudas hardly at all and there were few of the original Nduga faces left. There were plenty of Amungme troops, though, and they did not think the house was good enough for us. Although the ICRC were visiting Geselema every other day, there was little for them to do so they began building us a shelter by a small river nearby. It was a good location but we viewed the move with some trepidation. Moves often meant leaking roofs and stolen baggage, and we had a lot of new things to worry about now.

Twenty Amungme troops arrived late in the afternoon just as it was about to rain. We persuaded them to delay until the next morning but then it was Murip who delayed us. He sent us back and sulked because he had not been informed. When, finally, he agreed Mark, Navy, Bill and I split up to monitor the progress of the bags on the short journey. I saw one group of men sneak behind a bush to share out our collection of precious magazines. I had seen them stare at the photographs of scantily clad white women before. Like a headmaster I crept up on them and snatched the pile back with a 'I'll take those, thank you *very* much,' and left them to scowl. Within an hour we had collected all the other rogue porters and their bags from around the village and had directed them down to the new house.

The house was large, beautifully made and close to a babbling river. There was a washing pool and waterfall with a spectacular view up the valley. But quickly we realized we had conspired in an unfortunate and covert political coup. This was a definite Amungme snub on the Nduga and a move designed to win influence in the control of the hostages. Yudas, Silas, Murip and the other Nduga troops stayed away and Petrus and Anto said they felt uncomfortable with the Amungme. They were the traditional enemy of the Nduga.

The Amungme men insisted on living on top of us but complained that there was no food in the village for them. Even if they knew where the gardens were the potatoes would not belong to them. They talked about their home in the lowlands and the abundance of fish and sago there. Our unspoken solution was simple: they should go home and take their fanatical leader with them. Hadn't Yudas, Silas and Murip always promised to release us? But there was little hope of the troops leaving while the ICRC was still bringing in gifts. Perhaps, if they waited long enough, they would bring a free country as well.

Although Kwalik did not visit, other Amungme leaders did and we talked to them, trying to make them understand our perspective on the situation. Sometimes I felt there really was a chance. One man explained to me that a paper war was the best way, just as Silas had said at the beginning. We talked about an OPM office with a telephone and fax machine in communication with organizations around the world, forcing the Indonesians to give the Papuans better human, land and development rights. Suddenly we heard news that Kwalik had changed his demands. Now all he wanted was a promise that the ICRC would set up offices in Timika and Wamena to watch over the area once we were released. At last, sense was prevailing and our spirits were high. There was even talk that we would see the doctor again within a few days. But we had only been in the new house two nights when there were renewed concerns about ABRI.

FIFTEEN

ELMIN'S GARDENS

The morning had been uneventful: Mark and Martha had sat about reading in the sun; Bill and I had discussed what the ICRC might bring; Navy had cooked the remaining rice for lunch and Annette and Anna had written some letters home. Suddenly a large group of Amungme men came walking up the river. They looked agitated and aggressive. 'Pack up, quickly. The army is coming,' they called out.

I hated those words. Surely this was paranoia. Or was it a more sinister ruse to take us away from our Nduga leaders? It was late in the day and clearly about to rain. Adinda had a temperature and kidney pain as she had had every day for the last two weeks. Images of freezing nights on hillsides went through my mind.

'How can the army be coming when the ICRC is here?' asked Mark. 'The army have promised to stay away now.'

'I tell you we know. The army is nearby,' said one of the men. 'Pack up, pack up. We must run.'

'God, we can't just keep running,' cried Bill in English. He put his head on the wall of the house and thumped the wood in desperation. 'When is this going to end?'

'Mark, we can't do this,' I said, loud enough for everyone to hear. 'We should get the Nduga leaders to agree first, otherwise we're undermining them. God knows where these men will take us if we go with them.'

The men were whispering nervously. Mark looked at them and then at me. He carried on packing. 'How do you think Adinda and Martha will be after a night in this?' I asked, pointing to the sky. 'Remember what happened last time we ran from the army?'

Mark was still silent. I looked around at the group for support. Everyone avoided my stare.

I turned to the Amungme men. 'We're not going until Silas gives the order,' I announced, impressed by my own audacity. The men were unsure what to do. We had started packing so we finished then sat on top of our rucksacks as the skies grew heavier around us. The first drops of rain fell on the dry, grey stones of the riverbank.

'Silas has given the order,' said one man eventually.

'Where is he then?' I asked, gaining confidence.

They whispered again then one came forward, swung one of the rucksacks on to his back and walked out of the house. I went after him. 'Where do you think you are taking that?' I said firmly, putting my hand on his shoulder. 'Put it back.' He stopped and put it down slowly. I turned round calmly and walked back to where I had been sitting. My whole body was trembling.

There was more whispering among the Amungme and I looked away. Everyone else was totally silent, staring down into their laps. I tried to concentrate on keeping calm but my mind was running through all the possible scenarios. This was a gamble, but I knew I still had some way to go before they would hit me. We had to make a stand.

One of the men picked up an axe and hurled it with tremendous force at the frame of the house. The main support buckled and the roof shifted above us. Another of the men began to pull the tarpaulins off the roof.

'Walk!' shouted the eldest man, glaring at us. Our strike was over. The men continued to demolish the house but I had too much pride to leave so I stood among them trying to be calm and cheerful. Usually I played the joker and charmer and now I was scared that they would hate me. The others set off while Bill and I waited to check the bags. Then we were led off through the torrential rain and into the dark forest.

A floor and an inclined roof had been built out from the steeply sloping hillside. It was like a great grandstand looking over the

eastern side of the valley through the murky forest. Fires were
roaring at either end of the long house and a crowd of children
were fighting around a pan of *buah merah*. The toddlers were shovel-
ling the slurry into their mouths with their fists and forearms while
the older ones stood above, delicately balancing heaped spoonfuls
to their mouths. Large red globules were dropping on to the bodies
and hair of their siblings below. Two mothers were scolding and
controlling the children around them, seemingly oblivious of the
suckling babies in their arms. As we approached they dragged the
pan and children into a far corner and for a moment the youngsters
stared fearfully at the white, bedraggled monsters appearing from
the mist.

One of the women got up, put her breast back through a tear
in her ragged dress, deposited the baby with a little girl, wiped her
hands on her thighs and came over. She shook us all by the hand,
looked us in the eye and welcomed us in articulate Indonesian.

'Welcome, welcome, Elmin is not here. I am his wife, Gita.'
We smiled wearily and nodded. She seemed to know all about us,
about Adinda and her pains, Martha and her baby, but we had
no idea who she or Elmin were. She gave curt instructions in
Amungme to the men with the bags, greeted Petrus in Nduga and
began talking to us in bursts of Indonesian so rapid I had no hope
of understanding. Then she sat the women by the fire and began
rolling cigarettes from a pouch of factory tobacco and a packet of
papers, handing them out as she completed each one. I sat, damp
and chilled, looking around our new home from behind the comfort
of my cloud of smoke. It was about thirty foot by ten with one
length and the two ends open to the elements. There were twelve
hostages, fifteen children, two wives, twenty Amungme and Elmin,
whoever he was. It was going to be another cramped night.

We were amazed when Silas appeared later that evening. Gita
knew him and, indeed, was furious with him. She began pointing
and shouting at him in Indonesian. 'Elmin, look at these poor
things, half dead from cold!' At first, he snapped back at her, 'I did
not give orders for them to come here,' but soon he shrank away
and sulked in the corner as she started shouting at him again.

We realized that Silas had a completely different identity and status with his family. He had built this house in the forest to hide them. When the army had come in the pigs had run loose and eaten all the potatoes so he was making a new garden in an adjacent area of cleared forest. He had two wives: Gita and another woman who cowered when he spoke and later disappeared with her share of the children. There had also been a third wife, we discovered, but she had been a witch and placed a curse on Silas's father. He had become ill and died so Silas had killed her.

We were about two miles outside the pig village and by nine o'clock the next morning people had come with more news. It seemed that the army rumour was correct. A platoon of about thirty soldiers had crossed the demilitarized boundary from Alama, fifteen miles to the west. They had advanced as far as the next valley and hidden, but a group of villagers had stumbled across them. The terrified platoon had shot at them and run. Jamie was part of the group and had been heading back to Alama to find his family. They had got him in the leg and he was missing. The men wanted to move us further into the forest.

The OPM expected the ICRC to visit them in Geselema that morning and we prayed that the weather would clear so that they could come in, placate the OPM and stop the military. The situation seemed so fragile at the moment. Just a day or two was enough for the peace process to be set back months. The white helicopter was spotted late in the morning and a wave of relief went through the camp. By mid-day a messenger arrived from the meeting. There was a note from Kwalik summoning Markus to the village to help with some typing, there was a food package for us and also letters for us from our families.

'Stunning news from my mum,' called out Anna as she sat reading the messy scrawl of the fax machine. 'Dear Anna, etc, etc, The Foreign Office have told us that Kwalik has changed his demands to just 1) Information about OPM organizations around the world, 2) Promise from the army of no retribution when we are released and 3) Orders from Moses Werror in Papua New Guinea that we should be freed. It seems that the doctor, Ferenc Meyer has been to see Mr Werror and the signs look good.'

Our parents seemed to know more than us about the state of negotiations but they had no idea how delicate our situation really was. Just one slip by the army or a bad dream by one of the OPM and we were back to square one again. The morning's ICRC visit had reduced fears about the army but Kwalik's new demands and the chance of freedom had been forgotten in the panic. The men were excited about the food and cigarettes the ICRC had brought. They were becoming used to the frequent visits from Sylviane, René and Ferenc and were treating them like a flying shop. What incentive was there for us to be released?

Over the next few days there were so many rumours that our moods swung from high to low almost hourly. We had no radio and only occasional letters, so our speculations relied on the interpretation of the OPM's casual comments or guilty glances. Silas repeatedly claimed that we should be released, that enough was enough, but he lacked the ability to put his ideas into action. It was easier to avoid the issue and he became preoccupied with finding the rucksacks that had gone missing over six weeks before. He claimed the Amungme were guilty and insisted that the Nduga were not thieves, yet he sat there wearing Bill's watch and had already handed many of our valuables out. When we asked to buy another pig with our money he explained that it was finished, all $4000 of it.

He eventually set out in search of the rucksacks leaving us with a handful of men, Gita and the children, who brought us potatoes, frogs and, occasionally, a handful of forest grubs for Martha. Despite the food parcel we were relying heavily on potatoes. One day Martha, Bill and I took it upon ourselves to cook the evening meal and, for a change, we made a potato and leaf stew with some packet soup stirred in. It was delicious, relatively speaking, but the Indonesians would not eat it.

'Tessy,' whined Lita in her Malukan accent, 'can't *eat* it, Tessy.' She sat on the floor poking it with her spoon.

'Hey,' said Martha, 'you haven't even tasted it.'

'We can't eat this,' sulked Tessy, who was serving. He let some of the stew plop unappetisingly back into the pot.

'Indonesians can't eat sloppy food,' explained Navy, who at least had the courtesy to try a little. Now he pushed his bowl away. 'It's just not in our culture.'

We were a little offended, but it was their choice if they wanted to go hungry. The stakes moved up a notch when Navy went over to the noodle box and took out half the remaining packs.

'Hey,' said Martha again, more firmly this time, standing with her hands on her hips. 'You think we have enough food to be fussy? Where do you think you are, Jakarta?' She sat down and tutted loudly, shaking her head.

'Navy!' I said pointedly. I had wanted to stay out of any further confrontations with Navy, but unfair distribution of food resources was a serious offence. I went over to the box, took the remaining packets and dumped them unceremoniously in a pile on the European side of the house.

Bill shrugged, 'Well, I'm never going to try and help with the cooking again.'

'Nothing's changed there, then,' retorted Annette. Lita and Tessy began to bicker as well and it seemed as if the whole camp was breaking out in civil war.

Anna was trying desperately to keep out of it and had sunk back into the shadows pretending to read her book. Navy cooked his noodles and glared at me every few minutes. But when the noodles were ready they looked so good that we all ate them. I put the packs I'd taken back in the box and nothing more was said about the incident.

Three days later Silas and Markus returned. Silas had not found the rucksacks or their contents and was angry. He strutted about the house blaming the Amungme for all our problems. Markus, however, had finished his typing in the village and had different views.

'The typing was nothing. The Amungme want to release us, probably within a week,' he explained to Tessy and me in a hushed voice as we sat outside sharing a rolled cigarette. 'It's the Nduga who are delaying. Kwalik is happy to go along with the decision of Moses Werror.' It seemed this was our best chance yet.

Silas continued to mutter about the rucksacks but occupied himself in his gardens: cutting trees, clearing the undergrowth and planting crops. We spent much of our time reading the books and newspapers that our embassy had sent in. Bill had read almost everything within a week and was left with his crosswords, Patience and occasional card and chess games with Annette. I had always hated these games and Anna wasn't very keen either. She played her recorder, made juggling balls and sewed. One of her creations was a sleeping bag stitched together from Red Cross blankets. It wasn't very warm but she was happy to use it and it meant Annette, Bill and I could have our own sleeping bags. While the three of us were prone to argue among ourselves, Anna was more tolerant. She gave away food if there was a dispute and would squeeze up at night to make more sleeping space for the sake of peace and goodwill. She was always a pleasure to be with: there was little that she needed and little that bothered her.

The only thing about her that really irritated me was the amount of junk that she emptied from her bag every morning and spread around the house in heaps. There were cotton reels, scrunched-up knickers, furry socks, loose expedition notes, chocolate foil wrappers, summer frocks, letters, old hair braids, bandages and pots of unopened body lotion. As I went around, slipping and tripping over the heaps and piles, I would make space by tidying the things neatly into corners. There was something about the cleaning and sorting that I found therapeutic, but I think she found her mess rather homely.

One afternoon I spied Anna through the floor slats creeping underneath the house for a pee.

'Anna!' I shouted out, raising the alarm. 'You're not peeing down there are you?'

Everyone looked and I was joined by a chorus of 'Oh, Anna!'

'But it's raining,' she pleaded.

'So what?' said Bill. 'Use the forest like the rest of us.'

I was particularly cross because I had spent all afternoon clearing up the sweet wrappers and noodle packets that had accumulated below. They were an eyesore but I had been careful not to clear up everything. We had been meticulous about litter while living in Mapnduma, but in hiding we had lost all our environmental tendencies. Now our litter formed a paper trail. Should we disappear off the face of the earth again, there would at least be some indication of where we had last been.

Late one afternoon about a week after arriving at the new house, I wandered up and out into the large open expanse of Elmin's gardens. The sun was breaking beneath a band of low clouds as I balanced along the fallen tree trunks that connected the two acres of sugar cane, sweet potatoes, cassava and banana palms. As I walked further in among the head–high crops and buzzing insects I heard music wafting through the air. I got closer and recognized it as 'A Whiter Shade of Pale'. There was a tiny lean-to hut ahead in which two men were smoking and listening to a decrepit radio set. We had not had a radio for weeks and I asked if I could borrow it.

Bram, our expert tuner, found Radio Australia Indonesia immediately. The batteries were very low and the reception poor but the news was intelligible. Irian Jaya was still making headlines, but it was not good news.

An OPM leader, Thomas Wanggai, had died in a Jakarta prison after being sentenced to twenty years for raising the West Papuan flag in public. Riots had been sparked off in Timika following an incident at Freeport. Thousands of disgruntled Papuans had taken to the streets and ABRI were trying to regain control.

We all took a deep breath as we considered what effect this might have on our release. The next day we received typing instructions from Kwalik. One was a new letter, re-demanding a free Papua. The second was a circular to be sent to OPM factions around Irian Jaya calling on them to declare war on Indonesia, take more hostages and carry out acts of sabotage. Our plans were collapsing around us. The Papuans seemed to be on the brink of revolution and we were pawns in the middle of it.

The following morning we heard the ICRC helicopter and put

our faith in their ability to bring peace and calm. Bram was summoned by Kwalik and told to bring his belongings. By the end of the day Bram was free.

'Look, if they've released Bram we can't be far behind,' I said, looking on the bright side. No one thought much of my sentiments.

In Papuan culture all relatives must be present at a funeral or the spirit of the deceased will haunt them forever. Bram, or Abraham Wanggai, to give him his full name, was a distant relative of Thomas Wanggai. The release was Kwalik's way of honouring the Wanggai family.

The fate of the rest of us now seemed highly uncertain. The feeble radio died, but not before we heard reports of riots in Jayapura, much larger than those in Timika. That night Yudas and Murip arrived by torchlight. They talked secretly with Silas outside the house. When they came inside Yudas sat on the ground between the two fires, offered his packet of cigarettes around and asked how we all were. He always seemed to be overcome with guilt when he visited us and saw us as prisoners. Tonight we looked desperate.

'They flew the body of Wanggai to Jayapura today so he could be buried on his home soil,' Yudas said. He bowed his head and looked at the feet gathered around him. 'Jayapura is in war, like Timika. Everywhere Papuans are fighting against the Indonesians. It is a problem for you to stay here, you understand?' he said looking up gravely. 'The gardens are empty and there are no potatoes for the troops or for you.'

'And we can't trust Bram's tongue,' Silas interrupted abruptly. 'He could lead the army straight to this place tomorrow. We'll have to move.'

'Kwalik and his men want to join the uprising in Timika,' Yudas continued. 'He wants the hostages with him.'

'Ah, a frog's arse to Kwalik,' heckled Murip. He was standing slightly away from Yudas and Silas, leaning against the fireplace, rolling a leaf cigarette between two fingers of his right hand. 'Who started this? On whose land?' No one answered. 'The Nduga did. So the Nduga will finish it.'

Silas and Yudas began whispering again. 'Could you make it to

Timika?' Silas asked half-heartedly. I couldn't believe Silas was even considering it. Five days on the move had been bad enough. The journey through the lowlands to Timika would take us more than two months. With no food, medicine or shelter, treacherous paths and river crossings, surely we would not all make it alive.

We shook our heads. Silas turned to Yudas as if to say, I told you so. I thanked God that Silas had at least learnt something about our walking ability. Silas turned to us again.

'What about if we split you up; a fast group and a slow one?'

We shook our heads again, much more vigorously this time.

'Anyway, we do not agree with Kwalik,' explained Yudas, 'We want to end this thing. Tomorrow we will move with the Nduga men. Early.' He looked to the other two and they nodded.

At first light we were packed up, sitting on our bags in the chill air and waiting to go. A group of Nduga men arrived through the forest and we set off with Murip and Yudas. The mood was tense: everyone was suspicious and no one would talk to us. After a couple of hours we arrived at the remains of the previous house, now a heap of ashes by the river. I followed one of the men up to the village but it was deserted. Had the Amungme already left for the lowlands? I quickly returned to the river, counted the bags and waited for the others. An Amungme man I recognized appeared but ignored me. Then Yudas arrived with the others. He looked up and down the river then led us down a series of paths that by-passed the village and came out the other side. We were left in a hut for an hour and then suddenly he and Murip returned and told us to move quickly.

We were off again, marching through the forest. This time I was relieved to be walking, the farther away the better.

We trudged in slow convoy for several hours away from Elmin's gardens and the pig village until we arrived at a tiny hut in an open area by a large river. There was standing room only as we sheltered from the rain but by late afternoon a larger shelter had been constructed on the river bank. It had no floor and that night a stream formed under our sleeping bags and mats. By candlelight Navy and I dug a trench with our hands, channelling the water away.

When we woke the next morning, Yudas, Murip and the Nduga men were nowhere to be seen and within hours the Amungme had found us. They were friendly and pleasant as they tried to tempt us back to the village. We would be able to see the ICRC doctor, they said. But on cross-examination they admitted that they wanted to take us to the lowlands and Timika.

No sooner had they gone than we saw Kwalik approaching. 'Ignore him to show we only follow the Nduga,' whispered Mark as Kwalik walked in, wearing his giant fur hat. The atmosphere was icy as we avoided his gaze.

'You have enough food?' he asked quietly. Only Anna nodded. The rest of us were motionless and looked at the ground intently. He stood silently for several minutes trying to break our resistance with his implacable stare. It gave us strength to know that even though we were his prisoners we could hurt him with our contempt. Finally, Annette got up to leave. He shifted awkwardly and then walked out. We had humiliated Kwalik and I wondered just how wise that was.

We sat all afternoon in that cramped shelter imprisoned by the rains. No time had felt as critical as this. We wrote letters to the Red Cross explaining the danger we were in, praying that they could do something to prevent us being taken away. Petrus agreed to deliver them for us the next day. 'Give them directly to the pilot,' we said. 'Do not show them to anyone else.'

As the rain turned to drizzle I went down to the river and headed upstream. Once I was out of sight I broke into a run; clambering over boulders, climbing up waterfalls, jumping from rock to rock with images in my mind of the Amungme chasing me, coming to take us on the long, slow march to the lowlands.

After twenty minutes the river met a fifty-foot cliff that forced me to cut into the forest. I climbed the steep, wooded slope coming out at the top of a waterfall and sat exhausted and panting on its lip, peering down to the rocks below and across the valley to the opposite ridge. If I had to I could carry on up this river until nightfall, then cut through forest, follow the rivers, climb over ridges until I reached the army in Mapnduma. Always there was the option of escape. For twenty minutes I sat in quiet meditation in my own free world.

That night there was a huge electric storm. The rains beat torrentially on the tiny lean-to, the thunder shook the ground and the lightning lit the forest in blinding flashes. Thirty yards away, invisible in the pitch darkness, the river was in massive spate. As the rain eased I went down towards it, stepping across the streams that now crossed the path. There was a deafening noise all around me. I turned off the weak beam of the torch and peed in the darkness as the rain pelted on my shoulders.

Suddenly there was a brilliant lightning flash. For a thousandth of a second my surroundings were imprinted on my mind, painted in a milky light: a fifty-tonne tree trunk was tumbling by; man-size boulders grated as they rolled along the riverbed. The twinkling pools of the morning had erupted into a wall of churning mud and debris eight feet high and only yards from where I stood.

Within a second the thunder had exploded above me and I was alone again in the thick darkness. I fumbled for my torch. Fear engulfed me and I stumbled back towards the safety of the house.

In the morning the little river was barely recognizable. Boulders, tree trunks and debris bordered the banks for twenty feet on either side. The vegetation was flattened and twisted and the mud had been sculpted into ribs by the currents and eddies from the night before. In the early light we spotted twenty or so Amungme men picking their way through the wreckage towards us.

We looked around. Murip was nowhere to be seen, Petrus was in the village and the other Nduga men were finding potatoes. Only two young boys sat huddled by the fire.

'Go find Murip,' we whispered. 'Quickly!'

The Amungme men were soon in the house surrounding us. 'Pack up, pack up,' they said. 'We are going to the village to see the doctor.'

We refused.

'These are orders from Silas. Pack up now.'

Again we refused. The men began to pull at the bags.

'Hey!' shouted Murip. He was running down the slope from the tiny hut in the gardens. The Amungme men looked afraid as the Nduga leader approached. 'What are you doing? What is going on here?' He ordered them out of the house and argued and shouted with them on the bank until they turned to go.

That afternoon Yudas, Silas and Daud appeared. For the first time in ten weeks the Nduga leaders were together. Daud, lanky and toothy, was hopping from one leg to the other as we had seen him on the first day. 'We fought them, we smacked them, we fought them,' he repeated, smiling in glee.

'They wanted to take you,' said Yudas sitting quietly. 'We said: you have the flag, we will take the hostages. They wanted both but we said no; the Nduga started this, the Nduga will finish it.'

'I hit Kwalik with my fist,' Daud said proudly. He swung his right fist through the air in slow motion. 'We showed the Amungme men and now they have gone home for good.'

'I have brought official paper,' said Yudas, opening up his *nokin*. 'So now we can write our own letters and end this thing.' The paper had the OPM stamp at the top. He handed a sheet to Navy and told him to take notes.

'We, the OPM, still have received no answer to our demands,' he began. 'We demand recognition of a free Papua, we demand guns . . .'.

The cycle had begun again.

SIXTEEN

DAUD'S HOUSE

Daud returned three days later and decided to take us to his village, Geselema – where we had been told we would meet the ICRC before. We were confident that this would bring us closer to them again and move us further from the Amungme threat, so set off in relatively high spirits. We followed small rivers and steep paths deep into the forest. After six hours, to our dismay, we arrived at an exact replica of the cold house where we had been so hungry, bored and frustrated before. The structure was quite large with a raised floor, a good palm roof and open sides but we were surrounded by forest and the nearest water was a tiny stream that ran through a dank, mosquito-filled hollow far away. Daud had gone ahead and was now sitting inside smiling innocently. I scowled at him angrily. 'You said we were going to your village. You promised there would be a river.' We had been tricked again.

That evening, as Daud cleaned and polished his musty Dutch rifle and laid out his four precious cartridges on an old rag, he told us that he was the *Ap Noe Wimbo*, the Head of War, for Geselema and that we were now in his jurisdiction. He said it was time to organize a party. He eyes lit up with the thought of it. 'There will be a pig feast and speeches and you will be released.'

But the next day, Daud, Silas, Yudas and Murip had disappeared without a trace, leaving us in the hands of Petrus, Anto and some random troops. Several days passed before a young runner arrived with a message. He said that representatives from each country were required to attend a special meeting of the ICRC in the village that morning but only fast walkers should come or else they would not make it there in time.

It had been almost a month since our meeting with the ICRC. Mark, Navy and I set off immediately assuming that we would be going to Geselema. But the boy took us on the path back to the lean-to by the river and on to the pig village. As we neared the village, several men came down to meet us. The only two I recognized were Amungme.

'Mark,' I whispered, 'I thought they had gone.'

'So did I,' he said. He called to them, 'Has the ICRC arrived yet?' They shrugged awkwardly.

'Surely they must know if a bloody great helicopter has come down in the village,' I said. 'Is Kwalik in the village?' I called sharply. One of the men nodded. What was Kwalik doing here still? We thought he had left several days ago. 'Mark. That boy with the message. Who sent him?' I was becoming very anxious.

'Murip, I assume. I don't know for certain, do I?' He was defensive now and breathing heavily as he climbed the hillside.

'Why would they want a representative of each country? And why fast walkers?'

'What? How do I know?'

'What if Kwalik wants to take the fastest walker of each of the three nationalities and move them to the lowlands? How do we know this is not a trap? They've tried it before, luring us with promises of the Red Cross.'

We walked in silence as we neared the village. I considered running or trying to return to the house but now there were already eight men with us. I looked nervously around the forest. Kwalik and his men could appear at any moment and force us away at gunpoint. I couldn't bear to think of being taken away from Anna, Annette and Bill. I wasn't sure if I would be able to cope as a hostage in this forest without them. Now it was just the three of us; three fit men whom they could hide easily, move quickly and treat badly. They would win sympathy for releasing the others but keep the political edge. I couldn't believe we had been so foolish.

'Shit,' said Mark, 'They're taking us in the back way.'

I wasn't sure what this implied but it seemed a suspicious way to be entering the village. We came out of the forest at Silas's hut, where we had opened those first rucksacks from Ivar and the ICRC. The house was bare, the village was empty.

'Should we do something?' Navy asked quietly, turning to look at us both for just a second. I hadn't seen him look so scared since the very first days. His face had softened and lost its proud restraint. He looked young, almost angelic.

'What can we do?' I said. We had walked straight into it.

I have never been so happy to see white faces in all my life. Dr Ferenc Meyer and René Suter were sitting inside a beaten-up, lopsided hut in a small clearing just below the main village sur-rounded by squatting men. Ferenc stood up and walked slowly out towards us, trying to pretend that Murip was not following him closely with his rifle. Sion, who had beaten Navy in Mapnduma, was standing with his arms folded, looking particularly hard and mean. Yudas and about ten other men were there too but Kwalik was nowhere to be seen.

'Hello, hello,' called out Ferenc. 'I'm glad you could make it.'

'Speak Indonesian only!' Murip ordered, brandishing his gun aggressively.

'It is very difficult for me,' said Ferenc dipping his head and opening his palms to the sky in a shrug. His Indonesian was smothered in a thick French accent.

'Okay, so we try in Indonesian,' he said to us, looking slightly exasperated. 'So you are well? Good. How is the health of the other hostages?'

We explained the various ailments: Adinda's kidney problem, Markus's liver, Martha's baby. We were glad Murip could under-stand all this.

'So, I think I must see them again,' Ferenc suggested to Murip. 'All the hostages, but especially the sick.' Murip and Yudas talked for a minute and then agreed to summon them for the next morning.

We took shelter in the derelict hut. An entire wall was missing and I trod carefully to avoid the great gaps in the aged bark floor.

'René, you promised you would bring me a new backpack,' Murip said. He took off his backpack and pointed sadly at the tears and holes. 'See, it is no good, and I am a leader of the OPM.'

'No, I never promised,' René said firmly. 'I cannot bring special things for special people.'

'And what about my watch strap?' Murip asked, pointing to Anna's watch which was held on to his wrist by string.

René sighed. 'Would you like a cigarette?' He took out a packet of Marlboro from his bag and pulled off the cellophane. 'You've got to see the funny side of this farce,' he said to me under his breath. I smiled as he offered the cigarette packet around to the tangle of grabbing hands. 'Careful, careful,' he called. The pack was empty in seconds. 'Now Murip,' he said. 'Sit here and let's talk about the hostages.'

After a few hours the atmosphere relaxed. Murip left and we began to speak English with Ferenc. 'So after six weeks do you think they trust you yet?' I asked. I had been depressed watching Murip herding Ferenc around at gunpoint. I thought the OPM already trusted the ICRC, especially for their support after the killings in Hoea the year before. 'Kwalik always wanted you to help. He even had a copy of your brochure, you know.'

'Yes, we received a letter from him in January asking us to come in. But, to be honest, it is very difficult with Kwalik and it is much better now he is gone. He has suffered so much and is so bitter and full of resentment that whenever we reminded him that you are innocent, he said his family were innocent, too, and they were all killed by ABRI. I think maybe Kwalik would have released you if it was not for all these new problems in Timika and Jayapura after Thomas Wanggai's death in prison. He had already promised. And you know the reason Wanggai died? He was my patient and refused to be seen by any other doctor, but I was in Irian dealing with this mess. The irony, eh? I did the autopsy too. It was his heart condition but Kwalik still insisted the Indonesians murdered him.'

'What about Moses Werror?' I asked. 'The radio said the ICRC were flying to Papua New Guinea.'

'Yes, we went there. Kwalik said Werror was boss and should make the decision about the hostages. Werror agreed straightaway that the hostages should be released unconditionally. He wrote a letter to Kwalik and I made him read it into a tape recorder, so the OPM could hear his voice. Also, I had photos taken of us in his office with the Papuan flag, so they would believe me. Then I came back and Kwalik said: Werror is a city man with easy living. So I said: What is the command structure, who makes the decisions? They all shrugged. Nobody wants to take responsibility.'

'We keep saying, the Nduga started it so they should finish it,' Mark said.

'That's exactly it,' said Ferenc emphatically. 'Kwalik has left, now it's up to the Nduga to sort it out. It was the Nduga who we met first. Kwalik came along later.'

'So how *did* you make contact?' I asked. 'We saw the white helicopters when we were in that cold forest house for all those weeks in February.'

'In early February we began combing the area using two helicopters hired from Airfast, the air-freight company,' explained Ferenc. 'One worked from the east, the other from the west.'

'And this was with military clearance?' asked Mark. 'The radio said there had been a problem.'

'Yes, a little misunderstanding at the beginning. Now we have the highest clearance in the land, from Major-General Prabowo. He is the President's son-in-law, you know. A very powerful man and commander of the Kopassus Special Forces. He is very supportive of this mission but not everybody in the military is. Some just want to come in and go smack.' Ferenc's fist went into his hand. 'So it is sensitive, but Prabowo is a good man and stands up to the other generals. I think maybe he understands that the military solution is not always the best. And, of course, there is a lot of international pressure to pursue a peaceful solution.'

Ferenc paused, trying to remember his train of thought. 'But you were asking: how did we find you? First we dropped notes in all the villages explaining what the ICRC was trying to do. Then we hovered above every village waving our flag. We hoped the people would know us and signal us down. For almost two weeks we tried to land somewhere with no luck. The people were just too scared to come out, because of the army. You see, in Indonesia the army have the right to commandeer any civil or commercial aircraft, so it is impossible for the people to know who is inside. Eventually, people in one village waved us down. There were a whole line of men with bows and arrows lined up in the trees, aiming right for us. They ordered us to leave the helicopter and lie on the ground. They wanted the helicopter to go so it circled around nearby while we were in contact with the walkie-talkie. I thought at that point, maybe I am another hostage now.'

'Is that something you still worry about?' I asked. 'That you will be taken too?'

'Well, there are always, how you say, occupational hazards.' Ferenc laughed. 'I have seen many dangerous situations with many more guns than this. The villages here are in a state of such fear and confusion. They had heard stories that the ICRC would be coming in on foot and then we come in a helicopter. They hear the Red Cross are good, then they hear they are the military in disguise. Anyway, at that point we were very lucky. The headman was very ill with bronchitis, almost dying the people thought. I gave him a shot of antibiotics and he was better by the next day. It was like a miracle for them. If he had died, maybe I would not be here now!' he laughed and patted Navy on the back. 'But I was a hero then and could do no wrong. We brought in food, treated the other sick people and then they agreed to take us to the OPM.

'Three of the men came in the helicopter to guide us. We took off and they were shouting, go this way, go that way, this hill, no, that mountain. It was impossible; the helicopter was swerving all over the place. There was an old man in the back holding on for dear life terrified that the floor would fall away. But he knew the land best and we listened to him. He took us to the village further up the valley, Geselema. The people there did not want to trust us either, but eventually the men said they would call Yudas. We met Yudas and he sent a note for Kwalik.'

We heard a far-off whine. The clouds were building up over the valley. Sion went out of the hut and spoke to the pilot on the OPM walkie-talkie. He raised his thumb to Yudas, confident it was not the army.

'This is another one of our problems,' Ferenc said, packing up hastily. 'Airfast are scared after all the troubles in Timika and Jayapura. We have to hope that MAF allow us to use the mission helicopters if Airfast withdraw.'

The helicopter manoeuvred down on to the tiny landing space next to the dilapidated hut. The turbulence ripped the palm leaves from the roof and sent them twisting into the air. Ferenc packed up his bag then he looked at us intently. 'Listen. This is an unpredictable world. If it comes to the worst, just lie down on the ground and don't move. Statistics say that is the safest way.'

We followed Ferenc and René up to the chopper. A large ICRC emblem had been stuck on to its curved nose. The body was sleek and white and inside the seats were plush and the display panels crammed with technology.

'Here,' cried Ferenc above the roar of the swirling blades. 'I have a package for Navy from BScC.' I could only see his lips moving now as the engine tone rose and the rotas began to accelerate. He grabbed a box from the back seat, handed it to Navy and then climbed inside. Murip led us away, stooping and running, and we watched from a distance as they strapped themselves in and put on their radio helmets. The pilot flicked various switches, opened the throttle further and nodded to us. The machine tiptoed and then began to lift. It tilted back, banked to the side and was off across the valley. I tracked it as it passed in and out of the heavy cloud until it shrank to a dot above the opposite ridge. We were alone again and I felt incredibly homesick.

Opening the package from Navy's friends and colleagues in Jakarta the three of us were like children rummaging naughtily through the box of noodles, soap bars, cigarettes and sweets.

'We really should keep all this until the others come down,' I said sensibly.

'Oh *gooo* on,' tempted Mark. 'They'll *never* know! Just one more mint chew!' He grabbed the pack and crammed another sweet into his mouth.

'Maybe we can buy and eat a whole *wam* before the others arrive,' Navy joked, measuring the imaginary pig with his hands. 'Then we can declare the day a real success.'

It was refreshing to see a less serious side to them both. As the senior representatives of our group they bore a large burden of responsibility. Now, away from the rest of the team, they could relax and be themselves again.

That afternoon Mark read a book in the hut and I chatted with Navy on the porch until late. There was none of the usual tension between us and we talked together of how we would both like to return to Lorentz to carry out more biological work sometime in the future. He told me that he had already written to his friends at BScC about his plans to work in the Asmat area to the south where there were fewer OPM problems. We shared an enthusiasm and a friendship that I had not known since our times planning together in Jakarta.

When Mark joined us he asked about how the team had got on while working in Mapnduma. It lead to an open and frank exchange of views that helped me to understand some of Navy's often ill-concealed disdain of me. He believed that women should be given protection and that Bill and I should look after Anna and Annette properly. I said that I thought his treatment of Adinda and Lita was overbearing. We realized that these were cultural as much as personal differences. He felt that I should be more dominant and take more responsibility for my group's behaviour but I explained that the four of us strove to be as independent and self-supporting as possible. Everyone could lead and be an inspiration in their own way.

The next morning the others stumbled exhausted into the village after the long journey from Daud's house. Adinda was very weak – walking always brought back her fever – but Martha seemed to be bearing up well. Within half an hour we heard the ICRC helicopter land. It was several hours before Ferenc came up to see us. He was upbeat and confident and handed us a letter from Moses Werror.

'This explains exactly why the OPM should release you. Yudas and Murip seem to understand.'

'Then you are a man of miracles,' Mark said, looking at the letter.

'Even better, I spoke to Henry Fournier in Jakarta last night. He is the head of the ICRC in Indonesia and has received the final approval from Geneva for a long-term commitment to the area. There will be clinics, medicine, regular doctors' visits and SB Radio.'

We were very impressed. It was a brilliant plan, and more than we ever dreamed the area would get in return for the OPM's desperate actions.

'We're going for Easter Day, 7 April, as the release date,' said Ferenc. 'We've even got the Vatican to write a begging letter.' He pulled a photocopy from his file and passed it around. 'That only gives us ten days but I'm confident Murip and Yudas will go with it.'

'Have they agreed?' asked Annette.

'They are very positive. Obviously they want a few days to decide. Even if they want to ask Kwalik, they should be able to get a message to him by then. I should warn you that, in the meantime, we will be bringing in fewer supplies for you and the OPM. We hope it will focus their minds on the real issues.'

With all the activity Ferenc had time only to examine Martha and Adinda before the helicopter returned. 'We'll come again tomorrow,' he promised and that night we stayed in the village feeling hopeful for the future, amazed by how quickly our fortunes seemed to have changed.

The next morning we trudged back to the forest sullenly. A helicopter had returned but it had delivered only a brief note explaining that the ICRC had been called away on other business. Murip, mistrustful as ever, decided they had betrayed the OPM to the army. He ordered us back to Daud's house in the depths of the forest. Our optimism about Easter had turned quickly to disenchantment.

'I don't think it's going to happen,' said Bill adamantly the next afternoon as we played Scrabble. 'And I am not going to let myself be swept along with hopeful thoughts just to be knocked down at the end. It's easier to give up now; then at least I know where I stand.' Anna had little enthusiasm either. She had taken to working out complex mathematical problems that whiled away many hours of the day. The latest was calculating the intensity of sunlight that hit the earth as a function of latitude and month. 'I'm not really thinking about it,' she said when I asked her what she thought about Ferenc's plans. 'Maybe it'll happen, maybe it won't.' She picked up her pen and began chewing the end. 'How many degrees did you say the tropics were from the equator?'

I could not ignore the possibility of release and my nights filled with frustrated dreams. The discovery of a new path led me to a small shopping precinct in the forest below. The No 23 bus to Wamena was waiting to go but I could not board because I did not have the right fare. Another time I found Ferenc sitting in a white helicopter which had landed silently on a new football pitch nearby. I got in and strapped up but the pilot could not take off with me because I was too heavy.

Everything was set now, and it made so much sense for the OPM to accept the ICRC's offers and release us. But it was becoming clear to me that the world in which we were captive did not pay heed to sense or reason. There were omens, superstitions, emotions, dreams that no one but the spirits understood.

And what real incentive was there to release us? The OPM did not trust the ICRC. 'What if you trick us and send in the army,' they said. 'Give us a free Papua first.' Nor was there any excitement or fun in releasing us; no big raid like when they had taken us. There was only the admission that they had failed to get their free country.

I imagined us in thirty years' time, still sitting in some forest hideaway. Martha's baby would be almost twenty-nine, but each time we asked why we could not be set free the men with us would say, 'Oh we don't know, we're just here to guard you. There was a man who knew once, but he died long ago.' No one seemed to want to break the stasis. We knew how much the OPM disliked making decisions or taking responsibility.

The more I chased my freedom, the more distant it seemed to become. 'Release will come when you least expect it,' my mother had written in a letter to me and this I now truly believed. I knew that each day brought us closer, but how could I put my hope in an ending that was as likely to be one year away as one day? And if I gave up hoping how would I survive? How would I keep from spiralling into despair?

I would have to give in and resign myself to living here for ever. It was the only way to cope. I had always wanted to live in a forest, perhaps one just like this. If only I could forget that I was a prisoner, perhaps I could find pleasure in life again. While the Papuans sat making bracelets, arm bands, rain mats and bows and arrows, Petrus and I began to make steps and a handrail down the long, steep muddy path to the stream. There I constructed a bamboo aqueduct to channel water from above, so we could wash under a good head of water and I dammed the area below to make a shallow pool where clothes could be rinsed. Up in the house Navy helped me build shelves for shoes, potatoes and vegetables and a stepladder to climb in and out at the back of the house. There was a tiny clearing nearby which caught the sun for two hours each morning. I crammed in several washing lines and benches so that we could dry our clothes and sit and feel the rays. I made my own portable bench so I could catch the smaller sun patches as they moved between the trees.

Once the house and yard had been equipped with the essentials I moved on to more inessential items like garden furniture. Petrus and I built a very good table, with benches around the sides and a smooth top made of thin bamboo strips woven tightly to the frame. We felt quite civilized around that table in the forest: eating together, talking politely about the weather or the quality of the latest potatoes. When I sat there writing letters that described the world about me I often felt as if I was sitting at my desk at home, writing from my memories instead. Sometimes I wrote through the afternoon and into the dusk. As it got dark Petrus would come and hold flaming wood as a torch and stare, mesmerized by the movement of my hand. Writing was a therapy and I poured my heart into it. I was devastated when I heard that Murip had been burning our letters, believing them to be full of deceit. Thankfully the incoming letters arrived fairly regularly by messenger boy after ICRC visits. It was strange to think that we knew so little of the negotiations in the forest around us, but were up to date with affairs back home.

I set myself a swing as my next task. Its neat rectangular seat was hung on lengths of rattan from a high crossbar supported on large A-frames. It belonged in an elegant English country garden and was unrecognizable by the Papuan boys who were with us. Their version was a much better ride than mine: a one-hundred-foot piece of vine that hung down from the canopy on which they swung like Tarzan. My model gave a more measured pleasure. Creaking gently in the seat, dragging my feet, resting my head, I whiled away the long, gloomy dusks which came so early to our overcast hill location. The darkness seeped slowly through the forest like a gently rising tide and when it was true night I would set myself swinging high into the air, tempting the frame to uproot as it lumbered dangerously beneath me, thumping like the footsteps of a lame giant roaming through the dark forest.

Petrus built even more than I and set about producing an elaborate complex of aerial walkways with foot-bars and handrails. They stretched down to the loo, along the side of the house, to the clearing with the washing lines and round again to the front. There were branch lines stretching off to the table and the swing. The other men thought his constructions were folly but we loved them. Now we could walk around the entire plot without needing to put on our shoes and this was a great boon during the inevitable night-time loo trips. Alone in the pitch black, feeling along those walkways with my toes, I challenged my fear of the dark and discovered that I felt safer in those forests than I have felt anywhere.

Petrus moved on to smaller household items and began what looked like a wicker basket, about the size of a football.

'That will be his helmet,' Mark joked, 'for when the army send the bombs!' But it seemed to be for the two eggs a woman had brought us the day before.

Women now came regularly with cassava, *ubi*, leaves and *kopi* and sometimes plantain, watercress and sugar cane. Quantity of food was no longer a problem but, without the ICRC, protein was very rare. Martha always had extra portions but we worried for her and the baby. We complained to Murip on one of his fleeting visits but he was unsympathetic. 'Sweet potatoes are a complete and nutritious foodstuff for pregnant women,' he declared. 'If you want fancy food, you should pay for it.' As he and Silas had spent all our money we put together a collection of T-shirts, sarongs, plastic bags and boxes as payment and sent out the word that we would barter for meat.

The first offering was from an old woman who brought fifteen tiny frogs, smoked and dried. She offered them shyly in her wrinkled hands but refused to accept any payment. This was a truly generous gift as we knew how scarce meat was for the Nduga. We added the frogs to our watercress broth and christened it pond stew.

Over the weeks we ate giant rat, which tasted of sewers, and bat, which was mostly cartilage. The most repellent variety of meat came wrapped in leaves and vine. Initially I thought the parcel contained chillies or ginger roots but then I saw it begin to squirm. Inside were more than twenty beetle grubs taken from the pulp of a tree. Each was the size of a man's thumb, and they wriggled like huge maggots, hairy and translucent. But after five minutes baking in the coals of the fire they made a tasty snack: creamy, wood-flavoured syrup coated with thin, crunchy skin.

One day the women brought a few large leaves of fresh tobacco. We dried them and mixed them with our carefully hoarded Marlboro tobacco. Annette, Bill and I shared our rations but there was only enough for a few drags per day. To smoke more, I joined the men around the fire at night. Here they sang extraordinary Nduga songs. A young man or boy would sing a high, sweet melody and the rest of the group, maybe ten, twenty or more, would join in at the end of each refrain with a loud, nasal groan that sounded like a noise squeezed from the bowels of the earth. Sometimes they would click their penis gourds a-rhythmically, beating faster and louder as the song progressed, building into a crescendo of frenzied tapping. One evening I tried tapping rhythmically to the song but the men did not like it. There seemed to be no dance in their culture. The only kind I had seen was when they moved their arms and hands through the flames like charmed snakes, conjuring lustful powers. They were flirting, they told me, with imaginary women. Most of their songs were about love, they said. 'A woman always looks for a man with a good voice,' explained one of the younger OPM men to me. 'And a man looks for a woman who will take good care of his pigs.' He sighed. 'But there is never a chance to find a wife for a man who is constantly on the move with the OPM.'

The Papuans would sing late into the night, happier to sit by the fire than sleep in the cold. Even after curling up and going to sleep, they woke often to pile more wood on the fire and pray. Petrus prayed loudly at least three time every night. His rambling Indonesian monologues asked the Lord to protect the hostages and he always tried to list all our names but missed some and repeated others. We became used to his praying but when he developed a cough and groan *and* decided to sleep on top of Bill, patience began to crack.

'Petrus,' Bill scolded one night. 'I – need – to – sleep.' We all woke immediately but Petrus was partially deaf and could not lip-read at night.

'Ahh,' he groaned and then coughed again.

Bill gave him a good kick.

'Ahhhhh,' Petrus groaned, much louder this time and Bill began shaking him awake.

'Please, please,' Petrus whimpered. 'Petrus is half dead with disease. Maybe he will die.' He coughed again to gain sympathy, by which time we were laughing under our sleeping bags.

Bill held a torch to his lips so Petrus could see. 'Ahhh' he groaned, trying to mimic Petrus. 'No good,' he shook his head. 'Don't do it. Understand? Egh, egh,' coughed Bill softly. 'Okay, no problem. But Ahhhhhh, egh, egh, egh is not good.' He took great pleasure this time in imitating Petrus' rasping cough and loud moan. 'That's why I kick you. See?'

Petrus had missed Bram terribly since his release and always included him in his prayers. Bram had promised to write to Petrus and when letters arrived from the ICRC he would look hopefully at us to see if there was anything for him. 'I must make a letter to Bram so he does not forget me,' he would say, and Navy would get him some paper, a clipboard and a pen and Petrus would sit and practise his writing.

Looking after us had given Petrus a role in life and with his new clothes he had grown enormously in self-esteem. He had become attached to us. 'You will stay here one, two, three more months,' he told us enthusiastically, counting the time on his fingers. He couldn't bear to think that he might one day lose us. 'You are my family now,' he said to Navy. 'And when you go home I will go home with you.'

Easter Sunday approached with no news and no sign of release. I counted the days in the back of my notebook and realized that I had spent almost thirteen weeks in captivity: a quarter of a year. It seemed strange to think that once we had counted our time in hours, then in days and now we were counting it in weeks. Would we one day be counting it in months or years? As the time passed I felt that my whole state was changing. I no longer needed so much entertainment. I was content with the basic living conditions. I moved about more slowly. I spent more time in contemplation. I was learning to appreciate the almost monastic existence. Time was passing much more effortlessly and I began to understand how the human body could adapt to long imprisonment.

Sometimes there were depressive periods but they never held me for long. I had grown strong with the determination to live with joy and passion no matter what the circumstances. I was thankful for what I had and I knew that others were not as lucky as I. Adinda was still unwell and was now passing blood in her urine. Martha was having malarial attacks again. Markus was in constant pain from his liver. I was grateful that I did not mind the walking, that I liked sweet potatoes and that I enjoyed the Papuans' company. I had one argument with Navy about food which became quite vicious but on the whole Navy and Mark were an inspiration to me. They were cheerful, positive and always worked hard to cook and help out. I tried to follow their example as best I could.

The men around us still showed us little sympathy. Even though Martha was a kind of Virgin Mary and we were emissaries of their new country, the OPM bundled us around like baggage and stared at us as if we were zoo animals. Everyone was friendly, eager to please and in agreement that we were not guilty of any crime, but they did not seem to have any comprehension of what a long and gruelling ordeal this was for us. Maybe it was because we were so different and from such unimaginable backgrounds that they found it hard to imagine that we, too, had homes, families and lives that we missed. More likely they saw our capture as part of some grand masterplan pre-determined by the sprits and far beyond the responsibility of mere men. And in many ways I agreed. Being a hostage was no longer a regretful accident in my life, it *was* my life. Did I really have the arrogance to assume that I could understand the larger significance of the events?

On Easter Saturday about fifteen new OPM arrived, mostly from the Dani tribe in the Baliem valley to the north. We questioned them anxiously but they had no news of the ICRC negotiations or our supposed release. After breakfast on Easter Sunday we asked the men to join us for a special Easter service. Anna, Bill, Annette and I sang two verses of 'I Vow to Thee My Country', because that was the only hymn we could remember. Navy read a passage of the Easter story from the Bible then gave a short sermon explaining its significance. Petrus proudly read the Nduga version from his Nduga Bible. Adinda and Lita sang another song and I ended with a prayer in Indonesian focusing on why Easter was a time for new beginnings and for families to be reunited.

The service was a sad attempt to take control of our lives and try to influence those around us. But many of the men were just passing through and left quickly afterwards. The people with us changed so often that we had little hope of persuading them to release us. Even Anto, who had been with us since the very beginning, announced that he was leaving. He had made bracelets for each as goodbye gifts and we thought it unlikely that we would ever see him again.

One of the Dani men who remained was an old man with a large curved penis gourd, a band of brown possum fur around his head, and black cassowary feathers behind his ears. He had a crooked gait, communicated in sign language, and watched us with quizzical, sparkling eyes that twitched and blinked as if blinded by the sun. I watched him pick up a metal axe and eye it suspiciously. He attempted to chop a tree with it but seemed confused. One of the young boys ran out and demonstrated how to aim it at an oblique angle. Later that evening I saw him fumbling with a cooking pot, examining and tapping it. 'It was all pits and stones in my day,' I imagined him saying and I wondered if he was still unfamiliar with these pieces of technology. I watched him as he sat in the camp alone, weaving bracelets and making rain mats and I asked one of the men about him. He was from over the mountains in the Baliem, they thought, but he spoke no Nduga or Indonesian. He had heard of the white hostages and had set out on a solitary quest to find us. I liked this old Dani man and I was sure he would bring us good fortune.

The morning of Easter Monday a new batch of letters arrived from home. Bill's face paled as he began reading and I was alarmed.

'What is it?' I asked gently.

'It's a letter,' he replied anxiously. 'In code.'

Both of us had wondered if we might start receiving this sort of thing. It meant a new military operation was inevitable. I leant over to see. It was just a normal-looking typed letter but the signature was 'your uncle, Old Bill'.

'I don't have an uncle Bill,' said Bill quietly.

'You're sure?'

'Of course I'm sure. It's those Scotland Yard detectives in Wamena . . .'

I read on. '"My Aunty Jane and I have moved into Sunhill, a lovely area. I hope you are being treated well, your Aunty Jane tells me that lots of nice people take care of you. How many? Are they armed?" – Code? It's not very subtle is it, Bill? – "Aunty also says they move you about the forest a lot. It must be very hard for you and the girls. How often do you move? How far do you walk? The scenery must be nice. Why not tell Aunty Jane about it? What can you see? How near are you to the village?"'

Annette and Anna were listening now. 'What is it?' asked Annette.

'A bad omen,' I said dryly. 'From the Old Bill, in Sunhill.'

The latest rumour had it that all the leaders had gone home for good except Murip. I worried that the ICRC would not get anywhere with his suspicious, aggressive attitude. Perhaps the Red Cross had finally given in.

That afternoon we heard the whine of an aeroplane high above us. The men were nervous and put out the fire. 'Operasi militer,' they whispered to each other. 'It's just the ICRC,' we told them, but it was clearly military surveillance of some kind. The next day it came again.

First I was filled with nervous excitement that things were happening and that we were not forgotten. Quickly that turned to fear. I could think of no way in which a military operation could succeed, even with all the technology and support in the world. Ideas went through my mind of CS gas, secret transmitters and satellite images but still I was sure we would be shot in the crossfire or forced to run deep into the forest.

As the week drew on, we all withdrew and for the first time I saw Mark and Navy, who had always been positive and strong, shutting themselves off in their own closed worlds. Each of us sat close to a deep pit of despair but in that week everyone was struggling and fighting to keep out of it. It was the unity of the group and the example we set each other that pulled us through.

There was more bad news. We heard a rumour that Irian Jaya

was being closed to all foreigners because of security risks. Then we were told that the doctor was coming to see us in the forest that weekend.

'Will he walk this far?' asked Annette.

'He will if its his last chance,' said Bill.

We wondered how safe it was for him. In these desperate times would the OPM kidnap him too? The weekend passed and there was no doctor but the following Monday a note from Murip arrived in his slender, rather elegant handwriting: 'Come to Purumpa village for examination by the doctor. Bring sleeping bags but leave heavy baggage. Greetings, Murip.' There was an ominous feeling that if we got to see the Red Cross it would be the last time for a very long time.

SEVENTEEN

PURUMPA

We left the next morning, a slow, stumbling group resting frequently for the sick and lame. Martha was large now, almost six months into her pregnancy. Adinda was still passing blood in her urine and suffered from constant fever. Markus was liverish again. We had never heard of Purumpa but the men said it was only one hour away. Three hours later we were still climbing and descending along switch-back paths when a messenger came running through the vegetation ahead. 'Go back, go back,' he said. 'Murip says you cannot see the doctor.'

It was typical of the OPM's capricious actions but it caused such exhausted fury that we erupted in united anger.

'What do you mean, turn back?' I shouted. 'We have sick people who cannot walk.'

'You can tell Murip we will *not* turn back,' said Mark, battling to sound restrained.

'You think you can come here and start telling us to turn back and not stop to think about how far we have come,' Annette yelled, approaching the messenger with an accusing finger, 'or what pain Adinda might be in, or how Martha is feeling.' The messenger stepped back, lost his balance, turned and ran back through the forest. The porters stood around awkwardly. We started walking again with determination and they followed.

The dark trail opened suddenly on to a sunlit gash of rubble and scree. Far above the ground had slipped and tumbled taking an avalanche of trees and debris down into the valley bottom. We crossed several such landslides and also a giant rent, zigzagging its way down the hillside. It seemed that an earthquake had ripped open the land and shaken down its forest. The trench was filled with rocks and was only ten foot deep but as I stepped into it I felt that it might once have reached down far into the centre of the earth.

The vicious terrain levelled out and the forest thinned as we climbed up towards a desolate, windswept plateau with just a few solitary trees and palms growing from the white clay. A deep valley was drifting in and out of view through the cloud below. The sun was ahead; a white disc behind the swirling mist which rolled quickly across the open hilltop. Two figures appeared silhouetted on the brow above us. They waited a while like strangers in the swing doorways of a saloon, then walked slowly down towards us.

Murip's gun was ready and his finger was on the trigger. His camouflage hat flopped over his brow and his lips were pursed in a wry half-smile. The man behind looked like his brother. He had the same hat and face but was leaner and had a long ragged scar on his arm. He stared at us malignantly. More men appeared on the hill. Some wore balaclavas and army webbing straps. Others had denim shorts and blacked-out faces. They looked more hard-line than any OPM I had yet seen.

Murip went up to Anna and shook her hand limply. 'Hello,' he said quietly.

'Hello,' she replied.

He moved on to Bill who was sitting next to her. 'Hello, Bill.' He held out his hand but Bill refused to look him in the eye or shake his hand.

'Why will you not shake my hand?' he asked angrily.

'I only shake the hands of my friends,' Bill muttered.

Murip swung around to face us all. 'I tell you,' he screamed, pointing the gun at us, 'those who shake my hand will live to see their families.'

He stood there glaring while the other men came down the hill behind him. Bill held out his hand reluctantly.

'Too late,' he sneered, turning away and continuing his round of greetings with the rest of us. Now none of us refused.

Martha was stumbling out of the forest below with a hand on her belly. She was crying and Mark had his arm around her and was stroking her hair, watching her as she walked.

'So will *you* shake my hand?' Murip asked as Mark approached, but somehow he misunderstood. I had never seen him shout before, but now he was livid, yelling and waving his arms. Murip began defending himself. 'It's not my fault the Red Cross try to cheat us. All I want is a free Papua. I am just waiting for the Red Cross to bring me their answer. Anyway, the Dutch government started all this! You are Dutch so you are to blame!'

'I am not the Dutch government,' Mark shouted back. 'I don't work for them! I don't agree with what they did!'

Murip stormed off. His brother scowled at us for a few seconds and then followed him. Stony silence fell.

'Come with me,' one of the men said after a few minutes. We trailed after him, entering a network of muddy rivulets between the low bushes. Several huts appeared and we were shown to one that stood alone, away from the centre of Purumpa. We clambered in exhausted and sank back into its dark recesses.

I ventured outside after the rains and sat on a wet log. A long line of men came running down the bare muddy hillside on the other side of the village. Their whooping and cheering echoed through the valley below.

'What are they doing?' I asked a man standing nearby.

'Celebrating,' he said, smiling proudly. 'The OPM ambushed two soldiers in Alama. They chopped them with machetes and stole their guns. And fifteen more were killed in Timika today. We will fight this war, even if we have to fight the whole of Indonesia.'

More OPM victory cries filled the mist like the calls of a great flock of birds circling over the hilltop. The putrid smell of burning pig fat wafted across the scrub. The sticky mud glued my feet to the ground. There was something sinister and surreal about the day that I could not make sense of. It seemed almost absurd.

The old Dani man appeared again, stalking slowly through the bushes. He waited behind one, spied me, winked, waited, then tiptoed over. He held my arm, pointed to his mouth, patted his stomach, twitched his head and said, '*Mino*! Eat!' He pulled me over to the hut and pointed to the pile of potatoes the women had brought. He hunched up pathetically, pleading with his palms together, repeating, '*Mino. Mino.*' I gave him three which he put quickly into his *nokin*, looking around him as he did. He took my hand, sang a little song and then disappeared into the bush.

'Well, it's clear enough outside,' said Navy climbing back into the hut after cleaning his teeth the next morning. It was our one-hundreth day of captivity. We sat there willing the helicopter to appear. If it didn't come that day we would be sent back to the forest for sure. There was an almost inaudible buzz and our only OPM guard ran off to the centre of the village. We got up and looked out of the door. We could see it now over the top of the ridge: the small white MAF helicopter. As it circled nearby we waved from the door. It swooped down over us and we could see a white hand wave back.

Three weeks lost in the forest and we were found again. Two OPM men came running back. 'Get in, get in,' they called point-lessly. 'Take in your clothes.' They stood blocking the doorway and I sat peering through a crack in the wall.

'They're here,' I whispered, 'Sylviane and someone else. There's Silas!' And tiptoeing along behind the procession was the old Dani man.

Sylviane sat bewildered and amused as she listened to our litany of worries and depressing thoughts.

'Will you have to pull out soon?'

'Oh no,' she said, comfortingly. 'Why would we want to do that when everything is going so well?'

'And the military. Is there pressure from them to pull out?'

'No, they are very cool about everything.'

'We heard people were packing up and leaving Irian. Riots everywhere.'

'No. Just some troubles back in March.'

'But the OPM have killed many people in Timika and Alama?'

'I think there is some exaggeration. The OPM killed two soldiers in Alama. As a result one of the soldiers in Timika went on the rampage in an aircraft hangar and shot fifteen of his colleagues and a New Zealand pilot dead. It's very tragic. What everyone needs is now is patience,' Sylviane continued. 'These are very difficult negotiation conditions and it might be another one or two months but I think the OPM are growing to trust us now. Progress is being made.'

I was incredibly impressed with how Sylviane managed the OPM single-handedly. When one man began cheering and describing how they had killed the army men in Alama, Sylviane was angry. 'They have families just like you,' she said. 'So is that any way to talk?' The man left very humbled.

It was a brilliant hot morning and we sat around chatting and chewing sweets as Patrick, a new doctor, examined us one by one. Mark and Navy joined Sylviane to talk to Silas. They had grown used to his idioms and slightly bizarre perception of things.

'Why do you not bring us a free Papua?' he asked. Together the three of them were able to explain again about what the Red Cross could and could not do and what could be achieved after our release. Silas said that he wanted to end things; it was wrong that we were kept in the forest with the bats and tree kangaroos. The next day, he said, we would move to Geselema which had a clinic where Martha and Mark could live together. The rest of us could sleep in the church. The Red Cross would see us every day.

Murip wandered in later, still sulking from the argument the day before, but we offered him cigarettes and tried to make some peace. He was angry that the OPM had not received a reply from any government about a free Papua. Why did our countries care so little about the hostages? How could they release us before they had a decision?

'They are not going to drop the demand for a free Papua until someone explains to them that for now it is impossible,' said Mark to Sylviane. 'They still think that our governments can just organize it and will do so if they hold out a little longer.'

'Your embassies have already prepared the replies,' she explained, 'but we are worried what the OPM's reaction will be. If the ICRC tell them to forget their demands they might think we are on the Indonesian government's side. We are hoping to divert their attention towards aims that are achievable.'

Dr Patrick and Sylviane left and we spent that afternoon in good humour, reading our letters, talking about the new village and unpacking the goodies we had been brought. There were three kilograms of chocolate, two tins of prunes, ten packets of asparagus soup, one Edam cheese, four salami and various sweets. In the space of a morning our world had changed around again.

I sat outside with Martha later in the afternoon.

'So what did Dr Patrick say about the baby?' I asked.

'He says it's good, just as it should be,' She patted her stomach. 'You know I can feel the baby kicking me sometimes.'

'Are you going to call it Lorentz. That's a good Dutch name.'

'I'm not saying anything.' She smiled and held her finger to her mouth.

I sat chewing on my stick of sugar cane dipping it into the orange sherbet in my hand. 'Are you very worried?' I asked.

'Patrick asked me to prepare myself for the possibility of having the baby here.' She was calm and relaxed. The change of mood had lifted everybody's spirits. 'Sure, I'd rather be in a hospital than a jungle, but the women here do it all the time. It'll be fine.'

The next morning we were packed up early and were keen to get off to the new village before anyone changed their mind. We organized the bags and men, rounding them up and ensuring they knew where to go. When Silas had given the go-ahead we set off up the slope towards the ridge at the top of the village. There was a large clearing with spectacular views. To the right was the Ilare river, almost a thousand feet below. To the left was a deep basin carrying its tributaries where Daud's house had been. But ahead, glinting like silver in the bottom of the valley, were tin roofs, several huts and a landing pad. It was a metropolis, bigger than anything we had seen since Mapnduma. A wave of excitement went through the group and we almost skipped our way down the clear wide paths through open gardens. Banana palms towered overhead in the morning sun and plots of scarlet plants grew among stands of sugar cane. The mamas working the gardens stopped and waved as their children ran up to us and joined our triumphant procession. This was Geselema, about which we had heard so much.

When we arrived in the sun-scorched village we lined up along the wall of the clinic in the shade of its corrugated eaves. There was a large gravel pad nearby on the edge of the plateau and I imagined the Red Cross helicopter landing and taking off. Within minutes, though, Murip's brother appeared and strode aggressively towards us.

'You can't stay here,' he said, shooing us on with his hand. We stood like dumb cattle, glued to the wall of our would-be home. If we had disliked this man before, we hated him now. What right did he have to be bossing us around when he hardly knew us? He jerked his head. 'Get moving. Quickly.'

'But Silas said . . .' we pleaded.

'It's only near. Don't worry,' one of other the men whispered, and so we began to move on, but as the path began to climb steeply and the village disappeared from view our resolve strengthened again.

'If it is so near,' said Mark. 'We'll wait here and Daniel can go ahead to check.' Everyone sat down in the shade of a large tree and looked to me. Our guides and carriers shrugged in exasperation and I headed off with two of the men, following the wide path through some woodland, across a stream and waterfall and into open gardens again.

I stopped in wonder to take in the view: soaring, rugged foothills climbing up beneath the mountain wall. They fed numerous rivers which fused in a melting pot of foam to form the Ilare river far below. Four huts stood among tall grass and wild flowers in the gardens ahead. I clambered over a pig fence on which two small boys were balancing, pushing each other and giggling. Several women were sitting on the grass, laughing and talking. They got up and stood primly as I approached, smoothing their grass skirts. My two guides spoke in Nduga to them and they pointed to a pair of huts on the hillside above. I went up the ramp of one, on to the neat porch and stepped inside.

It was dark and cool and the air was scented with pig. A row of penis gourds stood on the back wall. Tar coated the ceiling of palms and soft bark lined the floor. An elderly woman was sweeping with a straw brush.

'*Wa, wa, wa*,' she said, taking my hand.

The two guides and local women had followed me and were peering through the door as I looked around. 'The other one is for you as well,' said one of the men, poking his head further in.

'Two?' I asked surprised. I had never imagined such luxury.

I set off to tell the others the news, meeting the old Dani man on the path. He caught my arm and pointed to the huts I had just left. I passed him and broke into a run: splashing through puddles, leaping from log to root on the open path.

'Two huts, nice stream, brilliant view, ten minutes,' I called, panting as I arrived. I borrowed some soap from Annette and skipped back, passing the Dani man again coming in the opposite direction. Boiling hot and streaked with sweat, I reached the small waterfall and I stripped off. Before the air could cool me, I immersed myself under the torrent, drinking as it drenched me, opening my eyes to see it stream across my face, calling out with the shrill pleasure of cold water on hot skin.

That afternoon the village men and women baked *ubi* in pits and everyone, including the OPM men, gathered to eat on the grassy slope. A local man stood up to welcome us. He said we should feel free to visit the gardens, to go down to the river, to make the village our home. The OPM would stay away and the local people would look after us.

The two houses belonged to a man named Tabril and his two wives. I was sure he was the same man who had pinched mine and Anna's toes in the old church several months before. Now he had changed from his OPM uniform of shorts and T-shirts back into his penis gourd and claimed he was just an innocent villager. Sion had also changed out of his clothes and there was something almost ludicrous about him now as he strolled about looking mean

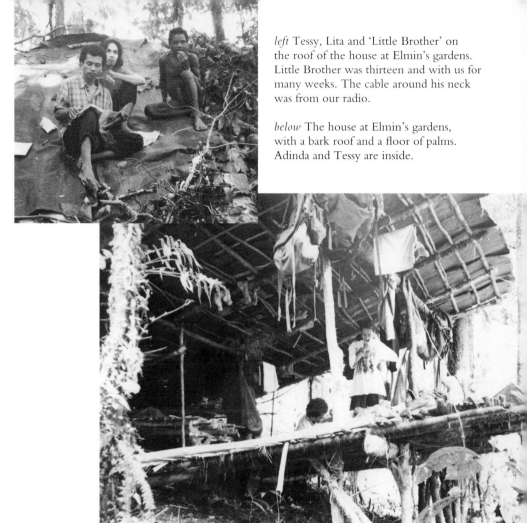

left Tessy, Lita and 'Little Brother' on the roof of the house at Elmin's gardens. Little Brother was thirteen and with us for many weeks. The cable around his neck was from our radio.

below The house at Elmin's gardens, with a bark roof and a floor of palms. Adinda and Tessy are inside.

Inside the house: Bill's feet, Anna, Adinda, Petrus with his Bible behind them and Markus, far right.

Murip wearing his Freeport McMoran jacket while watching his OPM troops parade.

A mixture of headwear on parade, including traditional possum skin and cassowary feathers, plastic bags and stolen Freeport helmets (see the boy on the right).

The most wanted men in Indonesia:
Silas, Kwalik, Kwalik's Catholic crony,
an Amungme elder, Daud and,
crouching, Murip and Yudas.

The OPM are about to raise the
West Papuan flag. This is a capital
offence in Indonesia.

Our host Tabril, with Navy on the left and Mark on the right.

Me, Sylviane, Markus, Mark, Bill, Bram and Silas all looking happy on our first meeting with the Red Cross on 29 February 1996.

Martha writing a letter home.

Anna and Petrus, our affectionate and loyal helper.

Tessy and Lita writing letters home. Our medical kit is in the white bag on the left.

In the front row: Markus, Tessy, Lita, Anna, Sylviane, René, Adinda and Navy. During this meeting, Ferenc tried to get Adinda out as she had developed a kidney infection but Kwalik refused.

Annette (left) and Anna, looking cheery after reading notes from home.

Mark (left) and Bill.

Murip (left) and Kwalik (right) giving out their pamphlets on 8 May. Behind them are John Broughton, Bill, Tessy, Annette, Sylviane, Henry Fournier, Martha, Ferenc.

far left Daud sits in traditional garb next to Dr Patrick.

left Although he could speak no Nduga or Indonesian, the old Dani man followed us around wherever we went and communicated through sign language.

below Nduga men and OPM on 8 May. The black facepaint is made from soot mixed with pig fat.

8 May: Ferenc, Anna, Annette, Mark, myself, Martha and Jan de Graaf lined up to watch the slaughter of the pigs. Several were left alive to show that we would be welcome should we one day return.

Eating pig stew, greens and rice at the 8 May feast. Markus crouches on the left. Henry, Ferenc and I kneel along the right-hand side.

Pigs are an important part of any ceremony or celebration as well as a way of measuring wealth. Eighteen were killed and cooked on 8 May.

As the 8 May feast was finished and the clouds came down, Kwalik still refused to release us.
There was an air of panic and despair as the helicopter returned.

with his Red Cross walkie-talkie hooked to his penis gourd strap.

Later that afternoon two women made us a fire and fried leaves in a wok using oil, salt and chillies. It was a generous gift given that oil and salt were hard to come by. As we sat eating the tasty greens with our fingers there was squawking and rustling in the coppice above. Men and boys rushed past the house heading towards the sound and within minutes the crowd had emerged, cheering and shouting, parading the hero on their shoulders. A young boy, smiling and delirious with victory, had a great red and black cockatoo skewered on the end of his arrow. They placed the boy hero down and he presented the squealing, flapping bird to Martha.

'The meat's no good on those birds,' one of the older women joked in Indonesian. 'Get nothing from that.' We gutted and cooked the bird anyway but she was right; the meat was only good for swallowing as indigestible lumps.

Tabril refused the meat, but not because it was so tasteless. 'I cannot make gardens, take wood or eat meat from that land,' he explained. 'It is the site on which I killed a man.'

I was beginning to understand the significance of the land to the Nduga. It was alive with ancestors and spirits. Each man was connected to it and his deeds were imprinted upon it. Apart from pigs and a little money, land was the only resource and it provided everything the Nduga needed. It was the essence of their life and culture. To lose it was a fate worse than death.

EIGHTEEN

GESELEMA

There was something homely and familiar about this small suburb of Geselema. The overgrown paths were filled with free-range children and gossiping mothers. Tabril was courteous and kind. The pigs and their shit were kept safely away on the other side of the fence.

Navy, Adinda, Markus, Mark and Martha slept in the bottom hut while Lita and Tessy chose to break away and join Annette, Anna, Bill and I in the top one. We took turns to visit each other's huts for candlelit dinners, returning home laughing and stumbling in the darkness. There was good-natured rivalry over food. Tessy or I would often lead raids to expose the contents of the *nokins* in the lower hut.

'How many did they have hidden down there?' I asked Tessy as he returned with an armful of confiscated cassava.

'Eight. There were bananas, too, which they say are for the sick people: Martha, Adinda and Markus.'

'More likely for Navy and Mark,' I joked. 'Husbands of the sick shouldn't get special priority.'

One night I found Tessy outside, watching the night sky. During the day we didn't talk much; we didn't have the patience or confidence to struggle with each other's language. That night we sat for several hours, rolling and sharing cigarettes, trying to pass the sleepless hours. I asked about Bandung and Jakarta, about the night clubs and music scene. We teased as we compared our different lives.

As we talked about the others I discovered that Tessy was often infuriated by Navy and his bossy ways. He and Lita had come to

stay in our house for a change of company. I asked about Adinda
and found out that she had met Navy at school. They had been
engaged for over five years.

'Did you know they plan to get married when they get home?'
Tessy asked.

'Really? That's excellent news. And they just decided recently?'

'*Ya*, but it's a secret.' He drew on the cigarette and then passed
the orange glow to me.

'So Tessy?'

'*Ya?*'

'Are there are lots of nice women in Jakarta for you . . . ?'

'Maybe.' He laughed coyly. Tessy was over thirty but I knew
he was single.

'So what about you and Lita?' They were always flirting, fighting
and cuddling under their sleeping bags.

'Shh,' he whispered. 'Maybe one day, eh?' The poles of the
porch creaked as he turned towards me. 'But what about Annette?'

'You like Annette?'

'No! But maybe you do!'

I slept eventually and woke at dawn. Lying in my sleeping bag
I could hear the croak of a toad in the bushes nearby and from the
huts above was the muffled voice of a mother as her baby began
to cry.

Outside smoke filtered through the roofs and diffused into the
still grey air. Mist filled the valleys and only the ridges and waterfalls
on the sheer mountain wall were visible through windows in the
fog. They hung high in the sky like fragments of heaven unattached
to earth. The black peaks of the mountains above were laced with
wispy cobwebs and the sky was a pale morning blue streaked with
high cirrus painted pink by the dawn.

We ate pumpkin, potato and cinnamon soup for breakfast and
then I asked Tabril to take me down to the bottom of the valley
so I could see the river. I packed my plastic bag with a book, some
tobacco and a square of saved chocolate. The sun had risen and
the mist was already beginning to clear as we walked along the
path through open meadows and steep forest.

After daydreaming for a while in the hot sun, Tabril left me and I set off downstream. I waded into crashing pools which churned like mill grinders and threw up rounded stones from the riverbed. I bathed under crystal waterfalls which towered up into the deep blue sky. I bounded from boulder to boulder until the river's course turned and the valley opened up with a view to the sea. On the bank above was a patch of old garden and I lay in the deep green grass, breathing in the freedom of the beautiful land.

Being so close to Geselema meant that Mark and Navy could join the ICRC negotiations more often. Five days after we had arrived they met Henry Fournier, the head of the ICRC delegation in Jakarta.

'He's a big guy,' Mark explained, 'and it gives him status. They can see from his size that he is the big boss. There were loads of noisy people packed into that dusty room in the clinic but no one said a word when he spoke, even though he can't speak any Indonesian.'

'So what did he have to say?' Bill asked.

'Well, it's all or nothing now. The new date is the 8 May: International Red Cross Day. Henry has promised a big feast. Our representatives will come in and meet the OPM and collect us and the whole thing will be filmed by CNN. There'll be the Red Cross health programme as before and promises of no military retributions. There's also a new offer that will give the OPM a real chance to make their case.' Mark handed us a copy of a letter from the President of the European Parliament, Klaus Hänsch, and addressed to the Free Papua Movement.

> Although we cannot under any circumstances condone the holding of innocent civilians against their will for whatever purposes, I can assure you that we are very aware of the difficult situation in Irian Jaya. Once the hostages are released unharmed I will put to my colleagues a proposal that we welcome a delegation representing your organization here in the European Parliament to give first hand information about the problems confronting your people.

'That's brilliant,' I said. 'When do they have to decide by?'
'1 May.'
'That's my birthday,' I said. 'Ten days' time.'
'And what about Kwalik?' Annette asked.
'I think they'll send a runner out to him, but the Nduga leaders were insistent that they can decide by themselves. Daud has appeared on the scene again and he's especially keen. He seems to have a lot of status in this village.'
'And you think the others will agree?'
'Silas said it would have happened earlier if it was not for the army. Murip is still suspicious and wants to see what Yudas says. Apparently Yudas got bored by the whole thing and went home weeks ago.'

In the ten days that followed the hopeful signs grew stronger and stronger. First Daud came by with ten of his men and sat with us telling us how pigs and cabbage would be helicoptered in from the surrounding villages. In Geselema the gardens were empty and all the pigs had been eaten or shot by ABRI. When Murip turned up he mused for a while in our hut. When I asked him how things were, he said only 'not yet positive', and accused Daud of being overexcited. But two days later Silas said that all four leaders were in agreement and that Yudas was already herding his pigs and family across the hills towards Geselema to join the party.

Markus was summoned for typing, but this time it was only to prepare invitations and shopping lists. Guest houses were built and people in our village began to plan and talk about the celebrations. Tabril and the local community were adamant that we would be released and said they would fight the OPM if they had to. We cornered every OPM man we could find and lectured them on all the things they had achieved for their area. Sion finally softened and agreed it was time to end it. There was a buzz in the air; an unspoken, unconscious consensus among the OPM and community that was stronger than the result of any logical reasoning. Even Petrus seemed to understand that we were finally going and that he could not come with us.

'You'll be arrested and thrown into jail if you come out with us,' we explained numerous times.

He made us promise to send him piglets from home. 'Then I can fatten them up for you and breed them,' he said, 'and there will be plenty of pig to eat when you come back to see us.'

I returned to the river almost every day. It was like a secret garden and I played there alone. I built dams wedging logs and boulders between the banks, spending days on each construction until they were washed away by floods. I found several sections of the river that were narrow, deep and fast in which I could swim like a runner on a treadmill.

My excursions became more daring and one day I followed a path that led me to a large, flat clearing above a gorge in which another even bigger river flowed. I climbed down and marvelled at the crimson bedrock and composite boulders made of yellow, pink and black pebbles bonded tightly by the heat of a subterranean furnace. There was fool's gold and the rock face was streaked green with copper.

The young man working silently among the trees did not notice me. When I caught his eye he was startled and for a moment I thought he might run. Then his face broke into a wide smile. He was teasing grubs from under the tree bark and showed me his handful proudly. We had no common language but he signalled that I should follow him into the forest. I found his family gathered around steaming pits of *ubi*. I continued my journey down the river and the young man followed with his three younger brothers and sisters. Already the news had spread and more children came running from out of an old garden. I felt like the Pied Piper of Hamlyn with my excited entourage.

Tall tree ferns lined the river. Each crown stood high upon a trunk, shading the forest with a parasol of six large leaves, each held at half-cock by a narrow leafy stem. Just one stone, if thrown with incredible strength and accuracy, could break the stem and cause the leaf to topple. In two teams the youngsters raced up and down the banks de-crowning every tree fern along a one-hundred-yard length.

I sat watching from a rock as they began chasing butterflies in the sun. I wondered if this was a utopia. Unburdened by worldly possessions the Nduga lived their life with an extraordinary passion and joy. They had so little and yet seemed so free.

The first of May came and Mark and Navy set off for the meeting in which the OPM would give their final decision to the ICRC. We wished them luck and waited anxiously for their return.

'Ninety-five per cent certain,' Mark called out as he appeared on the path several hours later. The only ambiguity seemed to be Kwalik. A note from him had arrived at the last minute. It had graphically described the killing of the two soldiers in Alama and it ended with the line: 'In principle I do not agree to the release unless there is some political gain.' But we were all confident that the letter from the European Parliament would satisfy him of that.

Sylviane had sent in two birthday cakes for me and there were some cards and presents: a packet of Bitter Mints, two packets of fudge, two books and some lovely words from my parents.

Navy had saved a packet of biscuits from the last box of ICRC goodies which we ate together at lunch, Martha presented me with a cup of hot milk made from her own special tin of powder and Bill gave me an entire Marlboro cigarette: perhaps one of the most generous gifts I have ever received.

I found a beautiful clearing in the woods and spent the rest of the day reading alone. It was one of my happiest birthdays, I decided, and I was struck by the mysterious and sometimes brutal way that life conspired to fulfil my expectations. I had seen the Nduga in a light the expedition could never have provided. We had suffered hardship which had exposed my darkest fears and I was still resilient and strong. I felt proud of who I was and what had been.

Later that day, just after dusk, Yudas came up from the village to see us. He had been absent for many weeks, building gardens, he said, for his family. We crammed into Navy's and Mark's hut and Yudas offered us cigarettes and politely asked after each of us. It was difficult to believe that we could ever have feared him or distrusted him. Annette had always maintained that he was the most decent of them all. We teased him about his new red cap. He laughed shyly, smoothing it on his head and straightening the fit.

'We'll have to think of a new name for him now that he has lost his green beret,' whispered Anna.

Yudas talked about the party and the hundreds of people who would be present. Many Dani and Nduga men from over the mountains were already arriving and more were on their way. He said that once we were free we should return and continue with the work we had begun. 'Mapping of our traditional land rights is important,' he explained to Mark. 'And when you return you will have the support of the OPM.'

He brought out a tape recorder, one of ours, of course, and played us a recording he had made of an Nduga song. We sat about the fire, as we had done many times before, with just the light of the flames and a solitary candle casting shadows across the contours of the faces. I could see the glint of the fire on Tabril's teeth as he crouched in the darkness at the back of the empty pig hutch. A young teenage boy, who I knew was slightly simple, was cross-legged in front of him. He stared with empty eyes, a trail of mucus running down a narrow path of inflamed skin to his mouth. Our Dani man sat opposite with the soles of his feet together, his knees spread wide, and his penis gourd almost touching his chin. He played his Jew's harp to the music, humming and moving his lips and body with each new twang of the vibrating reed. There was an older woman with us, sitting close to the fire turning *ubi* with agile, heat-resistant fingers before burying them to bake in the hot ash. She began to cry as she listened to the song. 'It is a very sad song for us,' said Yudas. 'It tells of the death of an old and wise village chief.'

An old man arrived. He had been hunting in the mountains for several days and he shared out some fresh possum meat.

'If a man returns with eight possums,' Yudas said, 'he will give two to his mother's kin and two to his father's. Two he will share with his village and two he will eat with his family. The man knows that all those people will give to him when they have meat. They will help if he is sick or in difficulty and they will defend him and fight with him if there is war. One day, when our land is free again, our society will be based around the village and family. Everyone will work together and share in the benefits just as we have always done. We will always keep our Papuan identity.'

As people arrived for the party over the following days our huts were busy with a stream of Dani and Nduga visitors wishing to meet the famous hostages. Outside there was the constant kerfuffle of women and children. Navy sat in the grass teaching the younger children songs and Martha gave them haircuts in preparation for the special day. The older children had an insatiable appetite for learning English. The Nduga and English language worked on an almost entirely different set of vowel sounds but the children quickly learnt a whole repertoire of awkwardly pronounced words, and would run around the village shouting 'Gud Mooning', 'How e You?' or 'win, tee, three,' at us.

Anna always had crowds of adoring women and children about her. As well as teaching them English she showed them how to make braids, how to draw, how to juggle and a whole host of other miracles. Their favourite treat was looking at the magazine photos.

We showed them pictures of skis: 'shoes as long as we are tall'; and satellites: 'man-made stars which people can talk to'. The mothers tilted their heads, hunched their bodies up and tutted in amazement. The children in their miniature grass skirts and tiny penis gourds copied carefully. When we showed them pictures from a book Martha had received on childbirth, the mothers bit their lips or fingers and squeezed our arms, but the children ran squealing out of the house.

Late one afternoon, after the rains, I sat on the pig fence trying to write a letter while chewing on a stick of sugar cane. Anna came down from the hut and jumped up next to me.

'What are you doing?' she asked.

'Nothing much,' I said. 'What happened to your nursery?'

'Oh, mum came down and took them away. Said they had bothered us enough for one day. Look,' she said, holding out her arm, 'one of the little girls made me a bracelet.' It was rather elegant; made from woven strands of brown fibre.

We watched a two-year-old pass by with his new toy: a torn plastic bag which, like all our rubbish, had been eagerly fought over and distributed about the village. 'He's been dragging that about on his foot for almost half an hour now thinking it's a shoe,' I said as the boy began his second circuit of our little village. 'I suppose most of them have never seen outsiders before. What effect do you think we've had on them?'

'I don't know,' Anna said as she propped her chin on her hand. 'I think they're very ashamed of how little they have. That older women who speaks Indonesian; you know her?'

'Yes. The one who wears the T-shirt?'

'Yes, she was looking at one of the magazines and said that the city must be like a second heaven, where everyone lives in bliss because they have so much.'

'If only she knew.'

'And she assumed that I spoke Indonesian naturally. She thought that was the language the whole world spoke. I tried to explain about different countries, like England and Holland, and she asked me how many days' walk they were from each other. And every time I came to a picture of a white man or woman in the magazines she asked me if it was my father or mother. I don't think they can imagine how big the world really is.'

'What amazes me is the number of words that didn't exist before outsiders came. Like clock, spoon, knife, read, nation, metal.'

'And all the numbers. There are only a handful of numbers in the Nduga language. The silliest thing is,' Anna laughed and put her hand to her mouth, 'they know the word kitty. The woman said it when she saw a picture of a cat. Maybe the missionaries had one. But you know what's really sad – after she called our world the second heaven, she called this place empty. It was the empty land, almost as if their life was empty.'

'Empty?' I said, surprised. 'In a way this place has everything.

The women are strong and charismatic. The men are gentle and caring. And what a place to grow up in: I've never seen such happy children.'

The sun was breaking through beneath a low band of black cloud. It caught the tree stumps standing in the garden below. They were like statues; relics of the forest that had stood before the village began, and some were quite tall where the men had climbed up and cut the trees above their buttress roots. The valley was filled with a golden glow and the birds began singing a second chorus from the woodland around.

A troop of girls came skipping by with long sticks in their hands and disappeared into the head-high grass. 'What was on those sticks?' I asked.

'Haven't you seen?' asked Anna. 'They collect grasshoppers.'

'What? To eat?'

She shrugged. 'I guess.'

'Do they taste nice?'

'I haven't had the pleasure.'

A sweet Nduga melody wafted across the gardens. We cocked our heads and listened.

'I'll see you later,' I said picking up my sugar cane and leaving my letters on the fence. A young man was sitting on a log in a meadow of yellow-flowered grasses, strumming his homemade banjo. Two of the strings were made from rattan while one was a rare piece of steel wire. He began singing again and I beat a rhythm on the log with my stick of sugar cane. A younger boy came laughing through the garden and sat down next to us. He began carving at the log with a tiny knife sharpened from a piece of corrugated-iron roof. The young man sang again and the boy joined him in duet. I improvised a bass line and the three of jammed away in the sunset.

Navy and Adinda began to make plans for a big party to be hosted by their parents on our return to Jakarta. They would give the details to the ICRC at the meeting the next day so that everything would be ready for our release. The guest list was passed around for us to make our own additions. Anna refused to be involved. 'Touch wood we'll be released,' she said touching the side of the hut. 'But don't you think this kind of tempts fate?' Bill was less reserved. The chances were so good that he had finally allowed himself to become hopeful. For days the two of us had been racing to conclude our Scrabble championship and finish the pile of good books that had arrived in the last two weeks. Annette spent much of her time apart from us, either socializing gregariously in the other hut or sitting on the porch looking over the valley in contemplation. I think, like me, she battled with the concept of release.

Three days and I would be free. Through my captivity that magic word had drawn me on with its promises of untold pleasure. Now I began to wonder if it might not be a little disappointing. I missed my family and I longed for a pint with my friends, but what else drew me? I did not crave the ugly towns and ringing telephones. I no longer missed the home comforts. The loo with a view of the mountains was perfect. The river with its waterfalls and spa baths was refreshing. The hut was comfortable and warm and I had even become used to the fleas. As for food, the ICRC had recently sent in five boxes of stock-piled parcels all cheekily labelled 'Club Med' by Sylviane. We had been eating Philadelphia cream cheese, jelly and crisps non-stop and I was stuffed.

It was six months since I had arrived in Mapnduma yet still I had difficulty grasping the reality of the world around me. I kept double-taking at the soaring mountains or the men in penis gourds. Was I really here or was it a dream? The bombardment of new sensations and emotions made my life more vivid than it had ever been. But in the confusion I struggled to make sense of it all.

Women and children left every morning to clean the church and prepare for the party. Murip's stubbornness finally yielded and he came to ask us for our address in Europe so that he could visit us one day. Petrus had relapsed and was insistent that we would not be released until Martha's baby was born. The ICRC went to collect Kwalik and the flag by helicopter and returned with Kwalik's father as well. He was carried up to our village like a hero but then Kwalik insisted the ICRC take him home before the party. The

Amungme troops stayed away but even more Dani men arrived over the mountains. We wondered why they were showing such a sudden interest just as everything was coming to an end. The men began to build a big shelter in the forest nearby. They said it was for all the extra guests but I passed it every day on my way to the river and it was always empty. Markus began to type documents for our representatives. We watched helicopters fly across the valley with pigs and potatoes strung beneath in great string bags. And the old Dani man sat with us constantly.

NINETEEN

8 MAY

Angry Papuans had filled my dreams. They had taunted me and danced around me in the darkness. I had woken tense and alert, unsure which side of midnight it might be. Alone outside, as the sky began to pale, I had tried to focus on a last farewell, but anxiety and cold had distracted me. So I had paced the path, longing for the day to begin.

Now, just after sunrise, the air was clear and bright and I was relieved that the feast day had finally come. I jumped off our porch and walked down the short grassy bank to the bottom hut. It was already billowing smoke as Petrus boiled water for tea.

'How are you doing?' I called in. They were busy filling bags with soap, clothing, medicine and other things to be distributed among the village women. 'Are you giving everything away?'

'Might as well, although Murip said we shouldn't,' said Martha, opening one of the plastic bags to put in an extra T-shirt. 'They won't have room on the helis for much of our stuff anyway. You and the others want tea?'

Back in our house, everyone was asleep except for Anna. She was sitting up against the wall, still inside her sleeping blanket, sorting through the threads she used to make her braids and bracelets.

'Hiya,' she said. 'Did you have a good night?'

'In parts. You?'

'I had a horrible dream. They didn't have room for me on the helicopter.'

'Oh no,' I laughed sympathetically.

'Who are you giving those to?' I asked, pointing to the coloured threads.

'The woman with the T-shirt. Are you leaving everything?'

'Yes. Except my notebook. And my torch – but I'll give that to the Dani man when I see him in the village.'

'Teatime,' I called loudly to the others, shaking Tessy. 'It's ready now. Come and get it.'

Soon after breakfast we heard the first helicopter arrive with the ICRC and shortly afterwards the first messengers came saying that a representative from each nationality should go down to the village to witness the slaughter of the first pig. The rest of us would be sent for later. Navy, Mark and Bill went on ahead while we swept the empty huts and picked litter from the grass. The ICRC had sent in razors so I had shaved off my beard the day before. Petrus squeezed into a pair of trousers that Bram had sent him as a present. When there was no more to be done we sat on the porch in the sun, dangling our legs over the edge with little to say except that maybe we would miss this happy village. Soon more boys came running up across the gardens.

'This looks like it,' Annette said, getting up slowly. The boys signalled for us to follow and I stayed at the back of our group to help Martha along the path. She was almost seven months' pregnant now and found it hard to see her feet.

By the time we had entered the woodlands whooping and cheering resounded through the forest and soon a column of forty men appeared, trotting along the path. The whoopers filed in behind us, jumping and thrusting their bows in the air with every cry. The cheerers gathered in front to lead. The two groups threw their calls back and forth across our heads.

The men wore the same mask-like expression I had seen on the 8 January, exactly four months before: fierce, detached and slightly crazed. Although many of the faces were familiar, I felt a tremor of fear. Nervously I joined them: chanting, jogging on the spot, throwing my right arm into the air. I looked around for their approval or amusement but they didn't notice me.

We continued along the path until we could hear a much larger crowd whooping from the village far below. Our entire procession began cheering, sending its cries through the forest in reply. All of us had joined in now. Martha was smiling, enjoying herself, though Tessy and Lita were still reserved. Anna glanced back at me along the line and smiled but I was caught in the hypnotic rhythm. I felt powerful and unafraid.

As we came down the steep hill into the village we could see a hundred people ahead. Mark, Navy and Bill were among them, being buffeted and manhandled, and quickly the crowd engulfed us too. I began to feel vulnerable and frightened. Why were they being so aggressive? It was as if something terrible was about to happen.

Silas was up ahead with Bill, Mark and Navy pointing this way and that in the commotion. He signalled for us to join him. We pushed through and he lined us up. Grass skirts were tied around the women's waists. For a dreadful moment I thought we would have to strip and wear penis gourds, but instead we went bare-chested except for shoulder sashes made from coloured *nokin* string. 'These are traditional,' Silas said, but there were only four, so Navy and Tessy went without.

The front row of men moved forward and the crowd surged behind. For a moment the Dani man was next to me, rattling his arrows in the air. He gave me one from his sheath and urged me to copy. I was moved that he had singled me out.

The crowd jogged up through the village, churning the deep mud; cheering and whooping discordantly. We moved past the clinic and church and filtered into a swirling mass of men running in a giant circle around the gravel helipad. On the periphery four or five women were running back and forth in semi-circles, stopping occasionally to jump up and down and wave bunches of leaves in the air. They wore beads, flowers, grass skirts and black lacy bras brought in by the ICRC. A hundred people hopped and stamped with their arrows dancing in the air as we ran and shouted in this mad, May Day rave.

Then suddenly the crowd began to disperse over the grass into small groups. They strolled up the slope casually, talking quietly among themselves. I, too, abruptly stopped dancing and walked calmly over to the church.

René, Ferenc, Sylviane and three men were chatting with the other hostages.

'Hello, Daniel,' Ferenc said. 'Are you well? Here, have you met Henry Fournier yet? He is head of the delegation.' He turned to a large, animated man in a straw hat, who was talking to Bill. I was also introduced to John Broughton, Jan de Graaf and Iyang Sukandar from the British, Netherlands and Indonesian Red Cross Societies respectively.

'ABRI would not give security clearance for your government representatives or CNN. But we have two video cameras so we will film and do a press release later.'

After a brief chat I went to drop my shirt just outside the church, balancing my precious arrow against the wall. I saw several metallic camera boxes, a video camera mounted on a tripod, battery packs, many bags and several large boxes.

'Is this party food?' I asked, tapping a box.

'Absolutely,' Ferenc replied as he passed by. 'Sweets here, two large cakes in those. This one is cigarettes donated by the military.'

'And what is the schedule for today? What time are the helicopters due?'

'Mid-day. So you'll be able to ring your parents from the satellite phone later this afternoon when we get to Keneyam. Then straight to Timika where there's an Airfast jet on stand-by to take you to Jakarta.'

'And how do the OPM feel about no CNN and no government reps?'

'The Nduga don't seem to have any problems but Kwalik has not shown himself since we brought him in by helicopter two days ago.'

Annette was with Mark and Martha talking to the Dutch representative. I joined Anna and Bill who were with John Broughton, a softly spoken, middle-aged man in a smart suit and tie. He looked rather out of place on this wild plateau in highland Papua. The green valley blazed in the mid-morning sun. We could hear the Ilare thundering through the gorge far below. John mopped his brow with a white folded handkerchief. I wiped mine with my bare arm.

'I should have brought a sun hat,' he said.

'Yes,' I replied. 'Me too.'

I spotted the Dani man searching for someone. He saw me and came over but it took me a while to understand that he wanted his arrow back. Feeling very disappointed, I returned it reluctantly but then decided to negotiate a swap for the torch. He was pleased with that and laid his arrows on the ground so I could choose. Some were mounted with long slithers of bamboo. '*Wam, wam,*' he said when I looked at them. I had seen these used for killing pigs. Others ended in three stubby prongs. For these he squawked like a crow and imitated a bird with his hands. The one I liked best was the one he had given me originally. It had sharp barbs and simple carvings. I took it and asked the men who had gathered around what it was for. '*Manusia,*' one whispered in my ear. 'Humans.'

Fifteen pigs were roped by their hind legs to a solitary tree. Some pulled and squealed, the others were content to sleep. Men were chopping logs and giant pyres layered with rocks were beginning to smoulder nearby. The thick smoke rolled across the grass and up the slopes where over a hundred men and women were talking in small groups, waiting patiently for speeches and feasting to begin. Some children were chasing each other around the church, running past the Indonesians who sat sheltering beneath the eaves on a long bench.

Several old faces whom we had not seen since Aptam and the river house came up to say hello. The lieutenant with the white whistle shook us all enthusiastically by the hand. The scowling young guard was smiling and had a soot-free face. And then Anto appeared and there were warm reunions all round.

Yudas, Silas and Daud called the people together. Daud had changed into a penis gourd almost two feet long. His face was painted black and white, his legs were daubed with stockings of yellow clay, the letters O and P were written across his front – a nipple in the centre of each loop – and a large M sat squarely on his back. His tall fur hat sprouted white feathers, pig tusks and leaves. He wore a tiepiece woven from silver thread and a waist sash of coloured paper and feathers. An antique stone axe was on his left shoulder and a huge cassowary brush was in his right hand.

Yudas was dressed in a lurid orange suit with camouflage patterning. His feet were hidden beneath bell-bottom flares. Silas had simply changed into a new balaclava: blue instead of white.

We were lined up in columns: the four British headed by Bill, the two Dutch by Mark, the four Indonesians by Navy. Markus was nowhere to be seen. In fact I had not seen him for over an hour.

'Hostages, Red Cross, representatives of Britain, Holland and Indonesia,' Yudas cried above the noise of the crowd that had gathered behind him. He waited and a hush descended. 'These pigs and chickens we give to you as gifts from Papua, so that you and your countries may never forget our people.' Three piglets were brought forward on leashes and handed to Bill, Mark and Navy who held them warily. Chickens were put in the arms of Anna, Martha and Lita. 'We will slaughter these animals and eat the meat together as a sign of our future unity,' continued Yudas. 'But one pig will remain here to show that the hostages will be welcomed as honoured guests should they one day return.'

Silas and Daud said a few lines, then the other pigs were unleashed from the tree and tied to stakes dotted about the village and the men began the slaughter. We leapt for the safety of the church as the scene turned to chaos. Arrows flew and some pigs fell gracefully to the ground. Others bucked, squealed and broke their tethers. The men ran about the village, dodging the dead to catch the dying.

The stiffening bodies were carried to the fires where the hair was singed and the skin charred. They spilt the rib cages with machetes, prized open each carcass, removed the entrails and stuffed the cavities with leaves. The animals were quartered and the meat was taken to giant cooking pits and buried with hot stones.

At the north end of the village the finishing touches were being made to the parade ground. Benches had been constructed along two sides of the muddy pitch. Men checked the string on two one-hundred-foot flagpoles. Several banners were tied up between posts. A high wooden podium and staircase were decked with West Papuan flags: small rectangles of paper coloured in crayon with a red star and blue stripes. We trudged through the sticky mud and took our seats.

'Daniel, do you know how to use this thing?' asked Henry Fournier, holding a video camera in his hand and sitting next to me in the mid-morning sun.

'Yes. I had one like this in Mapnduma.'

'Kwalik wants us to film his speech. René will film from that side, can you film from here?'

'Fine,' I said, taking the machine and checking to see that I could work it. 'Do you know what the plan is now?'

'Well, Kwalik should appear any minute and make his speech. After that I'm not so sure,' said Henry Fournier, looking about him. 'We have two choppers waiting in Mapnduma. They are due to come back at mid-day but its ten thirty now so at this rate we have to hope the weather holds.'

We sat for a moment in silence watching the clouds collect along the mountain chain.

'You have done an incredible job here,' I began self-consciously. 'For us, the hostages, and for the communities. I never thought the OPM would achieve this much. Thank you.'

Henry laughed and patted me gently on the back. 'For the ICRC it has also been very valuable. We have made good links with the military, the communities and the OPM and can hope to work on humanitarian issues here for many more years. We have been trying to explain to the OPM that we can provide a bridge into the area for other organizations working for community development, land rights and conservation. None of this was possible before, you know.'

'So all fingers crossed for today,' I said, smiling. The day was moving, things were happening, I was confident. 'Where's Markus?' I asked, changing the subject. 'I haven't seen him all morning.'

'Navy says he is finishing some typing for Kwalik.'

Even that didn't shake me.

We waited patiently in the hot sun. I draped my shirt over my head and spoke to no one, staring instead at the dry reeds that covered the ground beneath my feet. Yudas, Silas and Daud had officially released us now. Whatever Kwalik said or did we were on their land and it was they who held the authority. In one and half hours I would be sitting on a helicopter.

Opposite us about eighty standing troops were also waiting patiently. They had turned out in their best and many were in traditional dress: large penis gourds, fur or feather head dresses and painted bodies. Others wore shorts and T-shirts and a couple even had tatty OPM or West Papua T-shirts.

When Kwalik finally appeared from the door of the tin-roofed clinic the troops straightened their backs, stuck out their chests and held their fists tightly against their thighs. Kwalik wore his brown fur helmet and an orange camouflage suit identical to Yudas's. He walked nonchalantly to the desk beneath the nearest flagpole and carefully arranged his thick wad of papers. Murip and several others came with him. Markus had also been in the hut and now joined us at the end of the bench looking sombre. We sat up and watched with renewed anticipation.

A bow-legged sergeant stood to attention in the centre of the parade ground. He shouted commands in short sharp bursts. Four men marched out of the ranks and stood to attention before him. They turned and saluted the troops and saluted the hostages and Red Cross. Several more men lined up behind them in a confused manner. Awkwardly the unit goosestepped to the front of the parade ground. Kwalik was standing between the flagpoles and a mean-eyed bodyguard stood behind him with his feet wide apart, scanning for assassins down the barrel of his gun. The men saluted Kwalik; Kwalik saluted back. Murip and Yudas paraded around for a bit, stamping the ground, saluting to all and sundry. Several other men joined them, bumping into each other. Then Sion appeared and began to read a short speech. He had difficulty with many of the words but I thought it was some sort of formal welcome. Kwalik turned and walked to the podium while the bodyguard side-stepped alongside him. Murip followed Kwalik up the staircase and helped him arrange his speech. There was silence.

'I, Kelly Kwalik, will be President of West Papua!' he boomed. 'My people will fight for our freedom against those who have taken it away!' He pointed an accusing finger along our bench. It made me seethe, first with anger and then despair. Did he still not understand that the ICRC was on his side? That even the hostages, months before, had been working to protect his land? But his tone quietened and I thought rationally: did I really expect Kwalik to stand up and talk sweetly on his big day? To thank the world for taking such good care of his country and people over the last three decades? My mind turned to Frank's comments in the early days, about the murder of Kwalik's brothers. I tried to imagine the bitterness and resentment. For a moment I think I felt it, as a blinding anger, but it quickly dissolved into my own frustrations. Whatever atrocities had been committed before, surely common sense would prevail today?

Kwalik's Indonesian was too formal and complicated for me to understand. I doubted if more than a handful of people present knew what he was saying. I strained to pick out the word 'sandera, hostage' or 'bebas, free,' but all I could hear was 'hak manusia, human rights' or 'ABRI'. This was just a political broadcast for the cameras and for the world. Our real release had come from Yudas, Silas and Daud.

Half an hour on and he was still going strong. The troops opposite stood wavering like a mirage in the heat. My throat was as parched as the grass. I sat burning in the sun, my arm stiff with holding the video camera. His voice washed over me. I didn't care what he said any more. I just wanted him to stop so that I would know at last: would he let us free?

An hour crawled by and the clouds were gathering high in the valley. I was impatient and anxious now. Maybe Kwalik's plan was to win more time so we would have to wait another day. I heard the faint sound of a helicopter and saw a dot approaching from across the opposite ridge. It was mid-day but we hadn't even had the pig feast or flag-raising yet. Sylviane looked worried as she began talking into the walkie-talkie. I watched our helicopter turn away.

'I have spoken! I, Kelly Kwalik, will become the President of West Papua! ' At last he stopped, arranged his papers and climbed carefully down the steps with Murip. Mark, Navy, Sylviane and Henry began to whisper urgently, then Kwalik came up and politely shook hands with the representatives and handed them papers. There were several pages listing the human rights abuses and other justifications for a free Papua.

Henry and the other Red Cross representatives climbed on to the podium and each said a few words of acknowledgement. There was another parade and more saluting and two standard bearers came forward at a slow march. One was holding a brown Samsonite briefcase tied shut with a piece of string. The other held the neatly folded Red Cross flag. With great precision they were lowered on to the tables beneath each flagpole. The briefcase was opened and the precious West Papuan flag brought out and attached to the string of the flagstaff. The Red Cross flag was attached simultaneously and slowly they were raised. Kwalik began to sing the West Papua national anthem, in Indonesian, and the flags reached the top of the poles smoothly, where they flapped in a timely gust of wind.

It was a moving end and I was impressed by how well rehearsed this last part seemed to be. Papuans took their flag-raising very seriously; it was a capital offence under Indonesian law. The military parades had been a sham though, and would have been comic if they were not so sad. Why did the OPM try to imitate the pomp and circumstance of other armies so badly when they had their own fighting heritage to celebrate?

Suddenly the troops fell out and headed off to open the cooking pits and continue with the party. Desperately thirsty, I ran up to the stream, happy that the day was moving forward again. The people seated on the grass were tucking into their meat and potatoes, talking and laughing. Nothing seemed to have been changed by Kwalik's speech and I was unconcerned.

I met Mark on the way down. 'So everything seems to going to plan, doesn't it?' I said optimistically.

'No, everything does not seem to be going to plan,' he replied simply. 'Kwalik declared war on Indonesia and renewed demands for a free Papua. He doesn't want to release us.'

Embarrassment totally overwhelmed my shock. I just raised my eyebrows and walked off. Ferenc quickly intercepted me before the news had sunk in. 'Daniel. When the two helicopters come there will not be room for everyone. Do you mind waiting behind with Mark and me?'

'Okay.' I felt quite honoured and magnanimous. Obviously there was still a good chance everything would work out fine. I went down to the church where our food was being laid out.

'When will the helicopters come back?' I asked Sylviane.

'One thirty. Earlier if the weather moves in.'

'And what about Kwalik?'

'Henry and Ferenc will talk to him after he has eaten,' she said. I was confident of their ability to turn things round. For now it was easier to ignore any fears and concentrate on eating. Anyway, we still had Yudas, Silas and Daud on our side. Kwalik couldn't override them.

'What does Yudas say?' I asked Ferenc quietly as we squatted by the huge spread of potatoes, vegetables and pork laid out on large leaves.

'I'm just about to go and find him,' he said, chewing on a fatty piece of meat. He grabbed a potato and walked off.

Anna, Annette and Bill were eating hungrily. I wondered if I should tell them about Kwalik's speech. They were bound to know already, I decided. In fact I was probably the last to catch on. Their confidence eased any anxiety. The bright sun and party atmosphere had created a bizarre, optimistic air. Sylviane opened the cake boxes and called out: 'Who's for cake, then?' I went around the crowds distributing sweets and chocolates to the groups sitting calmly on the grass. Markus began handing out the packs of cigarettes from

ABRI. Perhaps if we pretended that everything was okay nobody would notice the helicopters returning or think to stop us climbing aboard.

'Of course you'll be going in the helicopter,' I heard Silas say petulantly. He began cutting up the remaining meat into huge chunks and handing it out to us one by one. 'Anna,' he called, 'have I given you meat yet?'

'I'm already full,' she said, shaking her hands.

'Take it,' he shouted angrily, waving it at her.

Our lumps of meat began to pile up behind us and I wondered if he meant us to take them on the helicopter.

Yudas was talking to Ferenc just out of earshot. I watched Yudas shrug as if to say: it's nothing to do with me. Ferenc came over to us shaking his head. 'Yudas says Kwalik is boss so it's nothing to do with him.'

Daud was nowhere to be seen. Nor was my Dani man.

There was a rising desperation within me that I could no longer suppress. I ate some cake but it made me feel sick. Ferenc and Henry headed up to the clinic and I went into the church. The air was dark, cool and soothing. I paced around the perimeter three times, taking long strides over the dusty floorboards. We had just minutes until we would know Kwalik's decision. Could there have ever been a more important moment in my life than this? I imagined myself on the plush purple helicopter seats, lifting off and flying out over the forested hills. I willed it to happen with all my might, but already I knew I was willing a miracle. My whole body was beginning to ache as I wavered between last hope and true despair.

I felt so totally unprepared. I crouched down in the far corner of the dark hall, rested my head gently on my knees and closed my eyes. I put my fingers in my ears. Cocooned in the darkness I listened to the deep, cavernous rumble of my head.

When Bill walked in we didn't acknowledge each other. He sat in the opposite corner and I stood up slowly, sliding my back against the wall. His face was drawn and pained. Everything was retracted deep inside. He was in the place I knew I was heading. I felt closer to him than I had ever done before.

I sat on a window ledge. The cloud was thick and grey; beginning to spit rain. Two men were sheltering below me in the eaves. They shifted self-consciously under my contemptuous stare. I heard Mark's voice and turned. Ferenc and Henry were coming down the hill, striding behind each other, Ferenc's denim waistcoat flapping at his sides. Their faces were hard with anger. I turned again and could hear the faint sound of the helicopter over the valley.

When I reached the door Adinda was crying into her hands. Martha was trying to comfort her with a hug. 'Don't worry,' she said smiling sympathetically. 'It will be here soon.' I watched Annette make eye contact with Ferenc as he arrived. He shook his head and the first tear rolled down her cheek.

'Martha,' she cried out. 'Don't you understand?' She reached out and grabbed her arm. 'We're not going. It's not happening.'

For an instant Martha's face was blank with bewilderment but Mark was quickly beside her. She was in his arms, punching his back, screaming through her tears: 'Why didn't you tell me?'

Silas came up shouting stubbornly and telling us not to cry. He grew distressed and began pleading with Martha then Anna. 'Please stop. You'll go home tomorrow. I promise.'

Anna was with Bill; I went over and held Annette but he and I were too bitter to cry. The first helicopter was hovering down out of the cloud through the rain. Sylviane, Dr Patrick and René were rushing everywhere, holding their hair. Boxes and bags were piled into the helicopters as they cursed and cried.

'I even asked to stay this night with you,' Ferenc said. 'But Kwalik would not allow it.'

Henry was icy. 'The cheating, lying, mean, egotistic, disgusting, self-important bastard,' he spat in his French accent.

'Don't worry, we'll be back tomorrow morning,' said Ferenc, grabbing the video camera and throwing another bag over his shoulder. 'We won't just leave you. We'll keep coming and trying.'

The second helicopter was coming down now as well. He turned to wave and then he, too, was running off towards it. We stood. The helicopters rose and were swallowed by the cloud.

TWENTY

OPERASI MILITER

The village was dark in the shadow of the storm. Only a few men remained; running in circles, chanting and singing as the first rain wet their skin and soaked into the sun-baked mud. The damp air was scented with ash from the burnt-out pyres.

Murip's brother strode up to us with some of the Dani men. 'Back to the forest,' he said jerking his head. 'Now!'

I found my notebook, but forgot the arrow. Petrus helped us to collect our few possessions. He put the meat into his *nokin* and Bill carried the box of sweets. Navy took our pots which had been borrowed for cooking. I looked to see if there were still any cigarettes but they had all gone. I hadn't even thought to take a pack.

The eighth of May was over and we were heading back to the forest as prisoners still. We fell into step behind each other, picking our way along the path and helping each other where we could. There was a familiarity in the slow trudge which brought some comfort. It was like any other walk, on any other day. I had managed before, I told myself, so now would be no different.

Our group was silent. The tears had dried up with the hopeless realization that our optimism had been based on nothing more than a wishful dream. We gritted ourselves against desperation. We knew this type of distress and were becoming more resilient. I comforted myself with the knowledge that the most agonising despair often passed quickly. As for the consequences, I was content to parcel them away and think about them another time. The immediate concern was where we would stay that night and if we would be moved the following day.

When we arrived at our little village the women and children were in tears. The old mama with the T-shirt was wailing, holding our hands and embracing us. I wasn't sure if her anguish was for us or for her family and village. Tabril and his brothers were pacing up and down vengefully and cursing Kwalik and Murip. The empty rucksacks and carefully sorted gift bags were still neatly stacked in the huts. I began to feel the first pangs of humiliation. Murip had told us not to give anything away. Surely he had known.

Murip's brother was behind us again, urgent and distracted. 'No. You cannot stop here. Move on into the forest to the house.' Fifteen minutes below was the large shelter I used to pass on my way to the river. They had said it was to accommodate visitors but I realized it was another sign we had missed. I wondered if even Petrus had known. For the last few days he had tried to tell us that we would not go but we had not believed him.

We arrived and settled ourselves. The mood of the group had changed. We were gentle with each other, speaking softly and kindly, making way when people passed and offering to help with what we could. Just hearing the quiet breathing of others was support in itself and I wondered how I would cope if I was alone.

I tried to read but did not have the will. There was energy enough to sit on the floor, silent and numb, fragile as a bubble. I felt so empty I wondered if I might just float away. At intervals my mind twinged at the memory of the helicopter. Where would I be now? Flying to Timika? Having tea with the Ambassador? And where would I be when May was over, when the summer began, and when Martha gave birth?

That night in the light of the candle we sat about a single pot eating cold pig meat with our fingers, speculating with little conviction. The Red Cross would keep coming, we thought, but for how long no one dared suggest.

I was still full from the feast so I ate little and went to bed. My body was stiff from the sun, my head burnt out by the events of the day. I fell into a long and dreamless sleep. When I awoke the next morning the sun was already high, shining brightly through the canopy. Smoke was creeping above the undergrowth, then climbing silently between the trees. In the cold light of day I felt stronger and life appeared almost normal: Petrus was building steps, Martha and Mark were washing at the stream, children had arrived from the village to sit by our fire and Lita was sorting through the medical supplies.

The famous 8 May had been a cruel deceit. The 'release' feast had served only to renew OPM resolve. Many fresh troops had been brought from Nduga and Dani areas in the north. Kwalik had returned and declared himself President. What could the ICRC possibly do now? Their months of work had been turned against us and all we had to show for it was a box of sweets.

I sat with Annette on the edge of the house, eating compulsively.

'My mother always said it would happen when we least expected it,' I said. 'I should have known.'

'Well, it won't be before Christmas now,' she said adamantly.

I balked at the thought of a year in captivity. 'I think it will add at least three months.' That was the longest period I considered bearable, providing we had food and books. I remembered back to the cold house when I could only take one day at a time. Now I was counting in months. 'Whatever, it means a baby here.'

'Kwalik: what a bastard.' Annette kicked the side of the house angrily with her heels. 'What right has he got to walk over everyone: the local people, the Red Cross, us?'

My anger had not yet surfaced. My disappointment was turning instead to hopeless frustration at the irretrievable delusions of the OPM. 'Sylviane told me that Kwalik wants to make Murip Finance Minister. Daud is to be Foreign Secretary, Silas Home Secretary and Yudas Deputy President. The new parliament will be in Geselema.'

'What, the five of them around a decrepit typewriter in a beat-up hut?'

'I suppose so. And imagine Kwalik running the country. He and his cronies would be as tyrannical as the Indonesians. It would be an Amungme–Nduga autocracy that would drive West Papua into civil war. After all, it's not as if the Papuans have a great history of inter-tribal co-operation.'

We heard the sound of a helicopter. The ICRC had promised they would return and with faint hope I remembered Silas's words, 'you will be released tomorrow'. Two hours later we heard the helicopter return. Soon afterwards an elderly, faintly familiar Papuan man appeared. His broken teeth glinted through a fixed grin and weasel-face. He wore a canvas, schoolboy satchel which matched his knee-length canvas shorts. The dreaded typewriter was in his hands. He placed it down in front of Markus. Thirty more copies of Kwalik's documents were needed by the Red Cross the following day. Markus stared at him in horror, holding out his blistered fingers. The man grinned some more. 'Think of a free Papua,' he said, then turned and left.

I looked more closely at the documents. It seemed Kwalik wanted signatures of support from various heads of state. 'Could the ICRC fake them?' I asked Mark.

'And what would Kwalik's next demand be?' Mark replied. 'Why should he give up when so much has already been achieved?'

'So what do you think would have happened if the Red Cross had never come in and the army and missionaries had stayed away too?'

Mark shrugged. 'Maybe they would have just got bored. But then maybe they would have got frustrated and killed someone.'

We made pig stew for lunch and were about to eat when Silas and Sion appeared.

'Father Silas, you are in time for pig!' Navy called out, evidently pleased to see him.

Silas came and sat among us, drawing us close, while Sion stood behind. We stopped serving the food to hear his news. They were both angry.

'Kwalik has cheated me. Yudas and Daud as well,' Silas began.

Navy shuffled close to him. 'Us as well, Silas,' he said, touching his chest. 'And the Red Cross too. There is nothing more they can do now.'

'We know that,' said Sion sharply. 'The Red Cross have been good to us.' He started walking around the house.

'Now the world will think the OPM are liars,' said Silas. 'Kwalik has undone everything.'

'But you can show the world that the OPM is good by releasing us,' Navy said.

'You are already free,' shouted Silas. 'You have worn the traditional dress. You have eaten pig with us. You will be freed so don't worry and don't think so much,' he said tapping his head. 'Trust me and I will arrange everything.' There was the sound of a helicopter in the air again.

'The Red Cross,' I said instinctively. Silas was silent for a second then continued talking. The ICRC never came in the afternoon. Never. I watched Navy's eyes flick over to Sion who had turned on the walkie-talkie. He was pressing the transmit button but there was nothing but fuzz. A loud crackling sound came through the forest from the direction of the village.

'A tree falling,' someone suggested, but I had never heard a tree fall like that. The crackle came again. I had never heard machine-gun fire, but I wondered if sounded like this. We waited breathlessly and Silas was calm.

A huge boom was followed quickly by another.

'ABRI!' hissed Silas, too afraid to shout. He moved ever so slightly. 'Quickly, quickly!' he said to us.

There was a third explosion, closer this time. It was followed by the sound of sliding rock and debris: a landslide plummeting into the valley below. There was the sound of a helicopter nearby.

'Get out of the house,' I screamed. 'They're bombing the houses.'

There was a small clearing nearby. We jumped out and hid in the undergrowth as we fumbled to put on our shoes. I looked back at the house. Petrus was burying the fire and filling Bill's rucksack with pots.

I was lying trembling on the wet ground next to Mark, Martha, Annette and Bill. Anna was several yards away with the Indonesians.

'Fucking hell,' I said slowly. 'What the fuck should we do?'

'They could be blanks,' whispered Mark.

'Blanks that cause landslides?' I said cynically. 'That helicopter, it's looking for us, yes?' It was sweeping the forest and was slightly closer than before. I thought I could hear at least two more in the distance.

'It's going to find the house soon,' said Bill.

'If it sees it, what will it do?' I asked. 'Will it bomb or will it land?'

'How can it land?' asked Bill scornfully.

'It can lower men down,' said Mark.

A fourth bomb went off much closer than before. Adinda, Lita and Anna started screaming. 'We're going to die, we're going to die,' an Indonesian voice wailed. I closed my eyes and dug my forehead deep into the wet leafy mulch of the forest floor, squeezing a length of rattan and feeling the thorns pierce my skin. The smell of explosives was in the air and I was shaking uncontrollably.

In the terror was the knowledge that within minutes we could be free but so far the possibilities were just a frantic blur. Should we stay, run, hide, fight? I felt myself beginning to panic.

'We have to get this right,' I called out. 'We have to be calm and make the right decisions.' I took several deep breaths and miraculously my mind began to clear. I sat up and looked around calmly. Annette was next to me crying impulsively, holding on to Mark.

'Annette,' I said quickly, 'Don't panic now. Panic tomorrow instead. Scream another time.'

She stopped and looked up. 'Okay.'

I searched for OPM faces. Petrus and the young boys who had been in the house with us had fled. Even Sion had gone but Silas remained, standing uselessly, fearfully, holding his machete in the air.

'You must run now Silas. Go,' I pleaded, 'or the ABRI will kill you.' Navy came over too, keeping low with his back to the trees.

Silas stepped back, looking behind him and then towards us again. He realized he was alone. 'Don't kill me,' he stammered. 'You won't kill me? I did not want this. I have always looked after you.'

'We won't kill you, Father Silas,' said Navy. 'But you must run.'

'No!' he shouted. 'Kwalik's men are coming from the village and they will kill you. I know what they can do.'

I remembered the small forest path which lead from Geselema to the house. With horror, I realized that OPM troops would be on their way as we spoke.

'Let's move down to the river,' I said to Navy in English. He nodded. We didn't even look to Silas. I called to the others. 'Let's move down to the river. Keep down, keep together.'

The search helicopter was coming close again. It sounded as if it would pass directly overhead this time and see the shelter. Would it throw down a grenade or bomb? We started moving through the forest in twos and threes, running from tree to tree, so that we would be protected from any blast. There was an eerie high-pitched whine behind us.

'What is that sound?' I called to Mark. 'Chainsaws? Are they cutting into the forest to land?'

Mark stopped and listened for a moment. It was a motor of some form, maybe electric. 'It could be a winch,' he said.

'Mark, are we doing the right thing? Should we wait?'

Silas was behind us now and he was gaining confidence, threatening with his machete. Our group had separated and I was afraid of him. 'Keep moving, Kwalik's troops are coming.'

'Look, there's a large clearing near the river,' I said to Mark. 'We can signal down a helicopter from there.'

He nodded and we moved on. We came out by the river and crossed. The sky was swirling with thick, dark clouds but it had not yet begun to rain. We could still hear helicopters about but there was none in sight. I focused on the plan. There was a prominent clearing just above the other river. If we continued into the forest the path would take us straight there. It was ten minutes away at the most.

Silas was ahead. The path was confusing. I sensed he was leading us off into the forest.

'Stop,' I called in English. 'The clearing is this way. This is our only chance.'

I watched Navy pleading with Silas, but Silas was pointing into the forest, urging everyone on. Navy shrugged back at me. I could tell that Lita, Adinda and Tessy wanted to stay with Silas. They needed his protection and were afraid to disobey. I remembered that there were two huts by the clearing. How many OPM men would be there? How many other OPM were nearby? What would happen to us, and especially the Indonesians, if there was a confrontation with the army? Silas was the only man we could trust. He needed to come to the clearing with us.

Bill was next to me. 'We've got to end this,' he shouted to everyone. 'Or we'll never get out. We'll just die in the forest if we don't do something now.'

'The villages are being bombed and the people killed. It's us they want,' I said, walking up to Silas. 'We must signal to the army and end this thing.'

'No!' he said sharply, but he was staring into middle distance, faltering and confused.

'For God's sake keep working on him, Mark, Navy,' I said. 'Talk sense into him.'

I looked to the rest of the group for support. The women could do nothing. Silas never listened to them. Markus was cowering under a bush. He was a Papuan and would never show himself to be a traitor. Mark and Navy were uncertain. They had to think of Martha and Adinda, who were weak and slow. While they kept with Silas in the forest they were safe. Signalling from the clearing was just too risky.

'I'll go to the clearing. You lot stay here.' I turned round to go but paralysing fear welled inside me as I took my first step. What if I was seen attempting to signal and someone shot an arrow in my back? Alone in the forest I could not hide behind my Indonesian friends. I would be the one and only target, despite my white skin.

The thought of months running in the forest spurred me on again. We had nothing this time. No medicine, no clothes, no shelter. Surely one of us would die. I took another step. My vision shuddered with each beat of my pulse. The minuitia of the forest were frozen in a timeless scene as the tall, straight trees and tangled vegetation closed in around me.

I turned to the group. 'Well?' I asked, furious at the lack of support. 'Shall I go or not?'

People looked to the ground lamely.

'Dan, wait,' Bill said. 'I'm coming.'

We had gone just a few yards when I spotted three men stalking silently through the trees towards us on the path with their bows drawn. I did not know them but they took our hands, obviously relived that we were safe.

'These are my men,' Silas called down. 'They will not hurt you.' They nodded forward, indicating we should keep moving into the forest. 'There is a house not far from here,' Silas continued. 'Tomorrow at first light we will signal to the army.'

Silas began to move on, the group followed behind. Soon we were scrambling across dead wood thick with moss, climbing steep slopes layered with leaves, dodging patches of thicket and stooping beneath webs of spiky vines. There was no path, so we found our own way; fanning out widely through the forest, calling regularly so as not to lose each other. I ran through the multitude of opportunities that had passed with bitter disappointment. Somehow we had missed our chance. Now we had four strong, armed OPM men with us and we had lost control. Soon another two joined us as well, having followed our tracks. One was the contemptible weasel-faced man who had brought the typing.

Burrowing through the dense forest, deep beneath the canopy, darkness came quickly. We stopped and leaves were laid down for us to sit on. The helicopters has ceased and the night was silent except for the rustling of birds in the undergrowth and scratching of night possums in the branches above. The men spoke in whispers and hid their glowing cigarettes lest the forest had eyes and ears.

'No one move without asking,' Silas warned. 'Or we will arrow them.'

We sat behind each other in rows; our legs crammed to our chests and our hips squeezed tightly together. Already the water was seeping up from the floor, wetting my behind. The rain had held all afternoon and I prayed the night would be dry, too. I shivered and Annette laid her head on my shoulder.

'What should we have done?' I whispered. 'Where did we go wrong?'

'We did everything,' she said. 'There was no choice.'

Tessy had the remains of a packet of cigarettes with him and he shared them around. We had little else between us. Bill found a wet box of matches in his trousers. Mark was wearing his medical kit bum-bag, but it was almost empty. Thankfully, we were all wearing at least two T-shirts and Martha had her red anorak. I thought of the large box of sweets back at the house. We had not even had the chance to eat our lunch.

The night was painfully uncomfortable. I spent much of it re-living the first moments of the attack and the rest trying to come to terms with this dangerous new world in which Indonesian heli-copters bombed tiny villages and men and women ran for their lives through the forest. When first light came we set off at once; climbing through the forest and then up an overgrown landslide.

We were already high up when the first of several helicopters began circling far below.

'Is this the Red Cross looking for you?' he asked.

'Maybe,' we lied.

'When we reach the safe house, higher in the mountain, we will flag them down.'

An hour passed before we heard another explosion echo between the valley walls and again we begged Silas to release us so that the destruction could stop.

We followed a good path for about an hour then Silas and his men split us into pairs and directed us into the forest from different points so that trackers could not follow our trail. We climbed higher and higher until we had came to a narrow ridge which looked west into a new valley. A thick, cold mist had descended, dashing any hopes of being seen, so we huddled together while Silas sent his men to make a house. After two hours they had still not returned and Silas was sure they had run off and left us. 'Build a house here,' he said, 'and tomorrow we will burn it and bring down the helicopters.' But as we began to clear the vegetation the men came back and led us to a small, flat almost leafless roof suspended between two trees.

As dusk fell a procession of exhausted men, women and children trooped out of the mist with babies on shoulders and in their *nokins*. They were filled with cheer to see us and our fire and we greeted them enthusiastically, holding their hands and asking for news of Tabril, his family and the village. All they knew was that Geselema had been razed and everyone was fleeing. Rummaging in their *nokins* they found a *pandana* nut fruit and an *ubi* which they gave to our twenty-strong group. Then, having warmed themselves by the fire, they set off into the darkness again.

Soon after they had gone the weasel-man returned with a brown and white possum he had killed. He placed it on the fire and a blind, hairless baby crawled from the pouch and mewed like a kitten. It clung tightly to his finger but with a quick flick he tossed it into the undergrowth. The mother's meat was tender and tasty and we nibbled thankfully at our small portions. The *ubi* was sliced into slithers and the pandana nut fruit was shared. It was a different species of pandana palm from the *buah merah* but was equally prized for its flavour. It grew only in the mountains and was the size of a football, made of a hundred or so almond-sized nuts which, if opened carefully enough, yielded a fragile sack of milky gel which tasted of coconut but was almost worthless as a food.

Miraculously, another night passed without rain. We dozed and shivered as the chill mountain wind fanned the glowing embers of the fire. In the dawn light I went to a nearby landslip and drank from the spring. I could see for a hundred miles. The eastern sky was aflame with the sunrise and the valleys of the Kilmid, Yugguru, Gul and beyond were filled with peachy mist. As I returned, the first helicopters resumed their search over the impenetrable canopy three thousand feet below.

Silas was shouting. 'Where is Petrus when we need potatoes? My men and I will have to go off and search for food. And what if Kwalik's troops come while I am gone?' So far from Geselema, I was no longer worried about other OPM men and the thought of being left alone filled me with anticipation. If the helicopters searched high enough that day, it might be possible to signal from the open landslip with the red anorak. But after an hour of indecision Silas's mind was made up: we would all leave together.

We descended rapidly, following steep streams gouged from the red bedrock. The men were hungry, tired and nervous. They goaded us aggressively through the forest, pushing us on as we slipped and fell. We lost height and entered well-trodden forest nearer to Geselema. More men appeared and I worried that Murip's or Kwalik's hardcore troops might appear and take us away. At mid-day we came upon a group of families, some of whom I knew. One of the men had been near the clinic when the helicopters came in two days before. The first was white, he said, the same one the ICRC had used and when it had landed they had seen white people on board and everyone had run up thinking it was the ICRC coming back with news. But four white men had brought out machines and laid them on the floor and fired into the crowds. Ten people were dead, including an old man and two children. Murip had been shot in the leg, but Kwalik had left the day before and was already far away.

We were shocked and wondered if the man's story was true. Was it possible that white people, British people, perhaps, had been a part of that first attack? Was it possible they had commandeered an Airfast helicopter and pretended to be the Red Cross? Some of the locals had already begun spreading rumours that it was Sylviane, Ferenc, Henry and René who had come back with guns to take revenge on Kwalik for cheating them.

Although the families shared precious pandana nuts and tobacco with us, I sensed some hostility. The Nduga had always believed that the white people were good but now they had been betrayed. We Europeans had become enemies like the Indonesians and I felt very much more afraid.

We set off again, moving east through patchy forest. The helicopters were circling nearby. As one came overhead parts of the machine were clearly visible through the canopy although we knew there was almost no chance that it could see us.

'Get down,' Silas shouted, swinging round to face us. He jerked the machete over his throat then waved it in the air. 'One move and I'll cut you. I won't hesitate. Understand?'

The noise of the helicopter passed and I heard sobbing. Anna was sitting among the undergrowth several yards away with her hands covering her face. Already Annette was trying to calm her, holding her face close to her chest and stroking her hair.

'What's wrong with the girl?' Silas yelled, still very agitated. 'Well?'

'She is frightened,' Annette shouted back. 'She doesn't want you to cut her up.'

Silas looked at Anna for a moment then crouched down, took her hand and held it. 'You don't need to be afraid of me,' he said gently. 'Just do as I say and I'll never hurt you.'

Anna looked at him, nodded and wiped her eyes. 'It's okay, I'm okay,' she said.

'We'll rest,' said Silas, getting up wearily. 'We need to rest.'

The afternoon remained dry and we continued along a clayey path that crossed a bleached, scrubby plateau which formed the floor of a three-sided basin. Silas sent the faster walkers ahead with the other men while he stayed at the back with Mark and Martha. After several hours Bill, Anna, Annette, Tessy, Lita and I arrived at a small hut surrounded by tall grasses and pandana palms. We sat on logs with a group of the men who seemed remarkably unconcerned by our exposed location. I drank from a stream and was calmed by their relaxed attitude. It was about three o'clock and the sun was still shining. There was the distant sound of a helicopter but otherwise everything was calm except for a high-pitched, almost inaudible whine. I looked up and a tiny dot, perhaps a Cessna, was flying wide circles far above the valley.

After resting for twenty minutes we saw a friendly face approaching with Navy, Adinda and Markus. It was Anto, walking bow-legged along the path. He smiled as he saw us and waved.

'Anto, will we stay here this evening, in this hut?' pleaded Lita. 'We are so tired.'

'I know you are tired. You are always tired,' he said, 'but there is another house on the other side of the ridge where it is safe. Silas says you must keep moving.'

I went over to Adinda as she arrived. 'My head is so hot,' she said, 'and kidney very sore.' She smiled bravely and held on to Navy. She was clearly in pain.

'*Can* we keep going?' I asked them quietly.

'We *must* keep going,' Markus whispered, looking about anxiously. 'They say that ABRI is tracking us. The OPM are very nervous.'

'But what about Mark and Martha?' I asked. 'We mustn't split up.'

Navy shrugged, shaking his head hopelessly. 'Do we have any choice?' he answered. 'Let's go one more hour and then see.'

We carried on across the plateau, stopping regularly to rest. When an hour seemed to have passed we confronted Anto again.

'How can I build a house for you here?' he asked pointing about with the tip of his machete. 'There are no leaves for a roof. You can sleep alone in the forest if you want but I want to reach the proper house.' He turned and walked on. We looked helplessly at each other for a while and followed.

It was dull and overcast, but still there was no rain. We came to the edge of the plateau and climbed steeply. Within half an hour of dusk we had come to a sheer cliff with a scaffolding of ramps and platforms wedged between wooden supports and out-growing trees. Hungry and tired, we helped each other up the rickety framework, balancing ourselves along logs one hundred feet above ground until finally we pulled ourselves on to a flat grassy shelf above.

In the twilight, perhaps 8000 feet above sea level, mist was rolling swiftly across the high moorland. Clumps of stunted shrubs with twisted, gnarled black stems grew from the white clay soil. I was hot from the climb but a cold wind whistled past my ears. We had climbed out of the Ilare and now the tundra dropped gently into the higher reaches of the Kilmid valley: a complex of converging torrents beneath the mountain wall. I stood silently with Bill looking out over the alien terrain. The gorge below was thick with tall, dark-green conifer trees. The ridge crests further up the mountain were a distinctive grey-brown.

'Look, Bill,' I said pointing. '*Notafagus* stands. That must be the highland beech forest we kept reading about.' New Guinea mountains were famous for them. He stood, finger on chin, nodding at all he surveyed.

In the half light a narrow ribbon of smoke curled into the air from the forest below. Anna and Annette arrived and the four of us half ran, half slid down the open slope. We entered the dark woodland, crossed several streams and finally emerged from the trees. In a small, grassy clearing, surrounded by tall, pine-like conifers, a tiny house sat squat and low. It was made entirely of chocolate brown bark; the walls were bulging out, the roof was bending in and it puffed smoke from every orifice. I went up to the kennel-sized entrance and looked inside. It was about fifteen feet long, warm, smoky and extremely cramped. Almost twenty people were packed into the lower level, their dark bodies hidden in the shadows. Above them several more men were lying on a platform almost invisible in the clouds of heaving smoke.

Tabril, a child on his shoulders and a wife by his side, was standing at the back of the house. I greeted him with a hug, shook his wife's hand and patted the heads of various children who were around. They were pleased to see us, but their faces were lined with stress and worry. Even the children, who usually jumped up and down around us, were tense and quiet. Both Tabril's houses had been burnt. His family had escaped into the forest when the army came but it was the next day before he found all his children. He said he might never be able to return to Geselema.

I held Tabril's hand as I listened and by the time he had finished I was angry, not at ABRI, but at Kwalik. He had already run into the forest with the Dani and other OPM men. He could look forward to returning to the safety of his own village far away, knowing full well that it was the Nduga communities who would bear the brunt of his actions. Perhaps he believed it was high time that the Nduga suffered under ABRI just as the Amungme had done. How else was he to create the undercurrent of bitterness that would drive his revolution?

'Are we staying here?' Anna asked.

'It is best if you do not,' Tabril said awkwardly. 'If ABRI come and they find you with us they will shoot every one of my family . . .'

'There is another hut just through the forest,' Angin said, interrupting.

'How far?' Anna asked wearily.

'Just minutes,' Tabril said. He rummaged in his *nokin* and gave her one of three potatoes. His brother came up and offered me some tobacco. This family had no prospect of finding food for days and yet still they were prepared to share their last supplies.

'Come on,' called Anto walking on. 'Before it is pitch black.'

We left and I entered the forest again. It was silent and murky as we stumbled along the dewy undergrowth and down a small, steep stream as the last minutes of daylight faded away.

'How far is this place?' I shouted down to Anto who was already far ahead. We waited as he yodelled through into forest. From the far distance, maybe a mile to the east and a thousand feet below, came the faintest of replies.

'Hurry up,' he called up to us.

'Wait!' we shouted down, scrambling along and struggling to differentiate between the multitude of fuzzy grey forms around us.

'What about Navy, Adinda and Markus?' I cried.

'What?' I heard him reply.

'What the hell is Anto up to?' snapped Annette.

'Why didn't we wait for them at the house?' Anna lamented. 'This is madness.' With a scream she slipped and fell off the path, crashing through a pile of dead wood.

'Be careful!' I pleaded. 'Are you okay?' We stopped and pulled her up.

She was crying. 'What are we doing here? We can't do this. It's too dark.'

'Anto!' Bill cried out angrily. There was a faint yodel and flash down ahead. 'The bastard's got a torch.'

'Anto!' I hollered. 'Come . . . back.'

There was nothing; not a sound now. We stood close together, almost unable to see each other's forms. Anna was sniffing and my clothes were so wet with dew that I was beginning to shake from cold.

'Together Bill.' I said. 'Now.'

'Anto . . . come . . . back!' we screamed. Nothing.

'Have you still got those matches?' I asked Bill. He pulled out the broken box. It was wet and useless. 'This is going to be one long, cold night,' I said. 'Pray it doesn't rain.'

Anna started crying again and as I got colder I considered joining her. 'I don't want to be here,' she sobbed.

'Oh come on,' I said. 'We'll survive. We've seen worse. Maybe we can get back to the house above.' But it was impossible to move without falling on the steep path. We crouched silently on the sodden ground.

There was a crackle of broken twigs above us. 'What's that?' whispered Bill.

I stared as hard as I could through the darkness. 'Probably an animal.'

'Animal?' he asked. 'There aren't any up here that live on the ground.'

'Could be a lizard,' I argued. 'Or a bird.'

'Shhh' said Annette. The sound came again. 'It's people,' she gasped. 'Hello!'

Two Papuan men arrived, feeling their way slowly through the forest. 'Where are you going?' I asked them. They shrugged. 'Can you speak Indonesian?' They shrugged again. 'Oh shit,' I sighed. 'Anna?'

'Oh, well, I can try.' She began stammering in Nduga. '*Eh . . . kit . . . ngge?*' They pointed down the hill. 'I think they're trying to get to the house, too,' she said.

'*They* might be able to but we can't,' said Annette. 'Can you ask them to make a fire for us?'

'*Ma . . . purak?*' Anna strained. They argued among themselves for a moment and then begrudgingly agreed; disappearing into the darkness while we sat crouching blindly in the slimy forest. Ten minutes later they reappeared with a large heap of twigs.

'*Kabo lak,*' one said.

'No machete,' Anna translated, 'so he can't cut any proper wood.'

'*Purak-o?*' he asked.

'*Lak*,' said Anna, shaking her head. 'He wanted a light,' she said to us.

He sighed and pulled a firestick from his *nokin*. I had seen them before: a stick of wood, split lengthways, wedged apart and filled with dry kindling. He lodged the stick under his feet, fed a strip of bamboo underneath and began to saw up and down until the friction ignited the kindling. He brought the twigs close and blew. We squeezed around the tiny fire trying to dry out our cold, wet clothes but it died quickly. The mountainside was growing steadily colder and the next twelve hours presented a miserable prospect. Suddenly, with a crunch of leaves, Anto was upon us, flashing his torch in the darkness. 'You think I would go off and leave you?' he asked, laughing.

Our relief was overwhelming. The men disappeared into the forest with Anto's torch and machete, returning twenty minutes later with burning sticks to light our way. They led us back up the hillside until we reached a small plateau. At the centre of a tiny clearing a furnace, white hot at the core, was billowing superheated air up into the trees above. The flames were fiercely consuming a pile of branches and logs three foot square. It was a magical scene, with a ring of ground palms, tree ferns and gingers painted with yellow flickering light, while around them the forest was crisp and black.

We curled up around the fire on a bed of fresh fern leaves, warm and exhausted. Anto roasted pandana nuts and the two men sang. We had not rested properly for three days and that night my aching body slept deeply for several hours.

It must have been close to midnight when I woke and found Tabril and his family warming themselves nearby. They were on the run again, certain that the army were following our shoe prints. I watched them trail back into the night: mothers, toddlers, babies; stoical and proud, without one ounce of self-pity, as they made their way by the light of a burning branch and a billion tiny stars.

TWENTY-ONE

THE PANDANA HOUSE

The morning revealed our fairy grotto as nothing more than a chilly patch of forest scattered with the debris of pandana shells and coals from the fire. But still, the angels had been watching over us. For three days and nights the rains had held. God knows how we would have survived if they had not.

We continued our climb down the steep stream. The orange soil of the banks glowed warmly under the clear blue sky. Within an hour we arrived at the house we had been heading for the night before. Sitting neatly in a large open clearing of head high grass and towering pandana palms, it, too, was made entirely of bark. The light streamed into the dusty interior through the cracked walls as we curled up on the dirt floor and worried about the others.

Navy, Tessy, Lita, Adinda and Markus arrived within half an hour. The previous night they had reached the top house in the dark and had had no choice but to stay with Tabril. I dreaded to think where Mark and Martha were, and how they might be faring, but by late morning they had appeared: Martha hobbling next to Silas. They had slept in the house where we had rested the previous afternoon, and were at the end of their reserves. Martha's feet were blistered and sore and she began to treat them with a tiny bottle of iodine from Mark's sparse medical bag. Suddenly everyone was borrowing the bottle and applying it liberally to their infected cuts.

'Hey!' shouted Mark. 'That is for Martha if she gives birth here.'

'Has Silas come up with any masterplan?' I asked after a moment's silence.

'He said we can flag down an army helicopter,' Martha said. 'I think he's realizing there is no point in continuing.'

I was hopeful for a second, but doubt quickly filled my mind. When he came to talk to us later in the morning, his plans had already changed. He would send messages to Murip and Yudas while the men fetched potatoes from the gardens in the valley below. Then he took a small notebook and pen from his *nokin* and asked us to write letters demanding that ABRI withdraw.

'I will send one copy to the Red Cross and missionaries in Wamena,' he explained. 'They will send a white helicopter to start negotiations again.'

'Silas, you said we were already free,' I began, 'and that we could flag down a helicopter when we reached a safe place.'

'Never!' he shouted. 'Only Mark and Martha can go free. The rest will have to wait for a free Papua.'

That afternoon, as the rain poured down at last, I sat despairing of our situation. Silas was frightened of Martha because pregnant women could spin powerful curses but what would happen to the rest of us? What insane plans would Murip have after being shot by the army? What chance was there that the note would arrive in Wamena or that the ICRC would be granted the necessary clearance to resume their negotiations? The army would never find us and the OPM would never release us.

The next morning, a Monday and our fourth day on the run, Silas woke us early. 'Did you dream?' he asked us, agitated and scared. He explained that a sacred lake stood nearby. The waters ran deep and held powerful spirits. This was a land where dreams came true.

Bill was the only one who thought of anything to say. 'We waved to a great bird which carried us away leaving the Nduga happy.' But the only 'great bird' that came that day was the tiny whining plane high above us in the sky. I was sitting on a log outside next to Silas looking up into the sky.

'This is the Red Cross looking for us,' he said, nodding knowingly.

I called the others out and we sat gazing at its regular, circular flight path hoping that whatever it was doing, it might see us far down below.

At mid-day the men returned, having failed to reach Geselema or the potato gardens below because of the army. We spent the rest of the day shut in the house while Silas and the men huddled together outside the doorway talking and arguing anxiously in Nduga. There were about ten of them: Anto and two of his friends who I knew quite well; two boys, perhaps sixteen, who sat weaving bracelets, calm and almost detached from the proceedings; the weasel-faced man who crouched with his chin on the handle of his axe, fidgeting nervously; and several others, one of whom was dressed in a smart paisley shirt.

'Do you know who they are?' I asked Navy who was sitting quietly with Adinda asleep on his lap.

'Markus says that one of the boys is Silas's son and that the smart man is a preacher from Geselema.'

'He should understand that taking prisoners is wrong,' I said. 'Maybe he will persuade them to let us flag down a helicopter.'

I watched the weasel-man and others go off with the axe. Silas came in to talk to us. 'The other men want to keep running,' he said. 'They say it is too dangerous here; the army is already close.'

I felt my expectant mood turn heavy. How much longer could we go on? It had been so long since I had eaten that I could no longer feel my stomach. All of us were aching from cold and exhaustion. Adinda lay listless most of the time, Martha was pale and weary. And if malaria or infection struck there would be no medicine.

'Today the rains are already near,' Silas continued. 'The men are building a shelter nearby to hide you tonight. It is too open here.'

Mark went up to see the new house. The roof had holes and there were no walls. It would be wet and freezing. He pleaded with Silas who begrudgingly agreed that we could stay where we were.

Late that afternoon we heard our first helicopter for two days. Bill, Tessy and I were outside when the whirr came across the valley. Tessy made for the door of the hut but Bill and I waited.

'There's no one around, Bill,' I said. The men were all in the new house above. The chopper would pass nearby. I contemplated trying to signal and looked around me again. Still no one. 'This could be it, this could be it,' a voice shouted inside my head. I ran into the bushes on the other side on the house. From there I was hidden from the men but could still see out. I whipped off my shirt and began to flag. The machine was visible, moving across my line of sight. I flagged more in short rapid bursts.

'Get in, get in,' I heard Silas shouting. He was coming down the hill but surely he could not see me. I was terrified of his temper and machete. Squatting on the ground, I put my shirt back on and reappeared from the bushes fumbling with my flies. Silas was stand-ing by the edge of the clearing looking up. He heard my rustling and looked at me suspiciously for a moment. 'What are you doing?' he shouted. 'Get in!' He ushered me to the door and followed me in. 'If a helicopter comes you hide immediately, understand?' He pointed his crooked finger at me. 'Understand, young Daniel?'

'I'm sorry,' I apologised, my heart pounding. 'I was peeing and . . .' I tried to look sullen but I felt almost euphoric. I had tricked Silas and signalled. There had been no response, but maybe they had seen and would return.

Silas sat by the door for a while watching me, then he left and we heard him head back up into the forest.

'So what do we do if there is an opportunity to signal again?' I asked having explained what had happened. There was another whirr in the valley below. We sat rigid. Was this it returning? I imagined it trying to land and the OPM men dragging us away at knife point. In the mêleé someone was bound to be killed. Perhaps I had been foolish to signal. But this second helicopter seemed to be following the same route as the first, maybe travelling from Mapnduma to Geselema with supplies. As the sound passed I was filled with a mixture of disappointment and relief.

That evening Silas brought six whole pandana fruits and roasted them on the fire. I had perfected the art of cracking open the nuts with my teeth and pulling out the tiny sack of milky flesh. I must have eaten over a hundred that evening: crack, crack, scoop the flesh; crack, crack, scoop the flesh; I could not stop. And my mind went round and round with worry. That night it was too cold to sleep, as the wind blew in through the open door. I lay close to Annette, my arms embracing her as we shivered together. On the run, moving constantly, there had been little time to think too deeply about what lay ahead. Now, our second night in the pandana house, I thought of the days ahead spent running, freezing, starving and ill. For the first time I wondered how our group would cope if one of us died of sickness. Annette and I turned over together and I stroked her hair. Now, more than ever, we needed each other's love and support.

At first light the weasel-man was at the door with the preacher and two others.

'Hostages, get up,' he called. 'We are moving.'

Martha's feet were swollen, Adinda's fever was high and Annette and Anna feigned sickness. The thought of heading into the forest again made us bold and stubborn.

'Call, Silas,' said Mark. 'We must speak with him.'

He arrived several minutes later. 'What do you want?' he asked. 'We have to move. We have to keep running.'

'Running, running,' shouted Mark furiously. 'To where? To the moon?' He threw one of Martha's plimsolls to him. 'You think Martha can run in that?' The sole had come right away and it was next to useless. 'Martha cannot walk, Annette, Anna, Adinda have fevers. We have no food, no sleeping bags, no medicine.' His tone calmed. 'Do you think we can survive much longer, Silas? Please, give us one more day to rest.'

'I did not start this,' Silas shouted. 'It was Indonesia who came here and took our land. Now the Lord will decide!' He stormed outside and argued with the other men. They were standing ready to go, looking around nervously. We sat breathless and anxious inside our dark hut. Through the thin bark walls I watched the weasel-man bullying Silas.

'Maybe they'll just give up and leave us,' I whispered hopefully. Then slowly they wandered off; some back up to the forest house, others in the opposite direction. Perhaps, for a little while longer, we had won more time.

I went outside. It was an overcast morning and as cold as an autumn day. I tried to see out over the top of our clearing, but neither the mountains or the valley were in view. I went down the steep muddy bank to the stream to drink and it helped to ease my hunger. Back at the clearing I stood in the long grass with my hands in my pockets. Inside I felt a sheet of notepaper which I had taken from Silas's notebook two days earlier. I began tearing off small pieces and scattering them like ashes all around me. One day someone would find them and think of us.

Sitting in the grass, twisting the long stems about my fingers, I looked down and laughed at the Lorentz 95 project T-shirt I was still wearing. Navy had designed it with a bird of paradise on the front. We had come here to help the Papuans and now we had come to represent everything they were fighting against.

My body felt weak and faint but my mood was hard. I let my mind slip to home and family. What must they be going through so far away? Could they possibly imagine where I was now? I pictured my mother with me as I had done many time before and I felt tears rising. As I sobbed, I covered my face in shame, hoping that I would not be seen but also longing for someone to comfort me.

Navy crouched in front of me. 'Navy,' I said surprised, trying to blink away my tears. I felt embarrassed.

'We are all together, you know,' he said, patting my knee. 'None of us are alone. You remember the children from the missionary school in Wamena who sent in those psalms?' I nodded. 'These are some of the lines that I keep in my head:

Oh, Lord I have so many enemies against me.
Many say that even God cannot save me.
But you are a shield around me; you lift up my head.
I cry out to the Lord and he answers from the hill.
I lie down and sleep; I wake again because the Lord sustains me.
And I will not fear the thousands who are against me.

I smiled although I felt a little awkward, as I always did with Navy.

'So there is always hope,' he said, 'even if it is difficult to see. You just have to know it's there, working behind the scenes. Without that faith sometimes I would just fall down and never get up.'

I laughed. 'That's because you're so big, Navy.'

'Not any more.' He pulled up his shirt. 'See.'

He squirmed as I pinched his waist. 'You've got more fat than me. But still there is room for some fried rice and chilli, I think.'

He went off smacking his lips and patting his stomach and I was struck by the extraordinary thought that one day, maybe in ten years' time, I would visit Navy, Adinda and their children for dinner one evening and we would look back and laugh.

TWENTY-TWO

REVENGE

That afternoon Anto sat alone outside the hut twanging his Jew's harp and teaching me how to play. I wondered if the other men had left us but that evening the preacher visited. He spoke about God's support for Papua's freedom and our important role in that fight. He was a fanatic and I did not like him. Silas appeared soon afterwards and explained his new, almost hopeful, plan. We would descend into the valley the next day and head back towards Mapnduma. From there things were less clear but seemed to involve releasing us to the church. We knew it would be a long trek, at least a week, but for now I was relieved that we would at least be descending to somewhere warmer after six freezing sleepless nights.

We had lost hope of the army following our trail but none the less we broke branches and pummelled the soil with footprints as we left the pandana house that Wednesday morning. We had stayed in a permanent house in an obvious clearing for three whole days and nights but the circling plane had not returned and the helicopters had not seen us. Now, as we prepared to leave, about ten OPM men who I thought had run off and left us reappeared.

Angin led the twenty-five-strong party down through the forest, across a landslide and then to a stream which cascaded its way over a series of smooth, wet rock walls. By mid-morning we were still high up and the air was mountain cold. We were in a deep gorge and the jungle towered above us on either side sending creepers down like streamers. As our group made one precarious climb after another I couldn't help thinking what might happen if someone

310

were to fall. This place was so remote and unknown. The isolation was chilling.

The widening river was lined with large, flat, granite boulders, slippery with lichen. As Mark jumped from one to the other he slipped. His feet flew into the air and he fell heavily on his back with a thud. His spine arched and his face convulsed in agony.

We rushed over to him. I was sure he had broken his back. I imagined him being carried with us, screaming or unconscious in the rain while still they refused to release us to the army. The OPM were fighting a war now. There would be no sympathy.

For thirty seconds he lay paralysed on the rock while Martha held his arm and begged him to be okay. All he could do was gasp, but then he began to breathe more evenly. The waves of pain ebbed away from his face and his body became less rigid.

'You're okay, Mark, you're okay,' we told him as Martha held his head.

'We should all rest,' said Silas curtly. Mark sat up slowly and nodded.

When we resumed walking the mood was grave. We cut back into the forest and made our way through deep undergrowth; suddenly we heard Nduga voices echoing eerily through the valley. They were mournful and inhuman, like cries from hell. It was an Nduga family in trouble, I thought, but then the same voices came again but from a different direction, like spirits floating on the wind. I was confused and our Nduga guides were frightened. They stopped in their tracks and listened wide-eyed. For a moment I thought they would run.

Within seconds the source was clear. A helicopter was hovering in the valley below playing the message through tannoys on its underside. 'Give in, give in. We do not want war!' it repeated over and over in Nduga and Amungme. Slowly and cautiously the men led us on and I wondered if the army knew that we were there beneath the canopy. But listening, I realized that the helicopter was covering the entire valley. It could even be covering other valleys as well. There were hundreds of confusing square miles of forests and gorges. We were just a pinprick in this vast, silent land. There was little hope of being found.

After an hour or so we stopped and the men began to smoke. We had new company: a mama and baby. They had appeared from nowhere as the Nduga do. I sat down next to Anto and the weasel-man gave me some tobacco to smoke. I looked at it helplessly as the men laughed. One took it and rolled it for me in a leaf. Superficially, everything was normal but I could see the men were nervous. Their hands trembled and they whispered in small groups. Would their fear drive them away? Or did they have too much pride to leave us to ABRI?

We moved on, traversing the mountain, heading west. We forced a path across a parched plateau of yellow bush. To the left and the right the high ridges of Kilmid rose up like battlements and descended into the lowlands. As I looked out over the lower reaches of the Yugguru and realized I could see the Gul, I experienced a sudden overwhelming sense of homecoming. The happy memories of Mapnduma flooded back, hazy and embalmed with nostalgia. But they felt so old, as if they were from the depths of my childhood. An aeon seemed to have passed but there was something perfect about returning and closing the circle.

As we came to the edge of the plateau the weasel-man came through from behind. He pushed past and talked anxiously with Silas and the men. We stopped and waited for a while, watching their agitated glances. As we walked on again the weasel-man's news filtered back to us. He had returned to the pandana house where we had been that morning. The army had burnt it to the ground.

I had become used to the OPM's rumour-mongering and ever-present paranoia and I did not believe this news. If the army had been there why had they not caught up with us already? Whatever the truth, I was excited. The pressure was on now like it had never been; surely they would not hold out for much longer.

We began to descend from the plateau and as the afternoon wore on the men came and went more often, perhaps impatient with our slow pace.

'Down there we will find flat land to make a house and palm leaves for the roof,' Silas explained, as we heard the sound of a river flowing through the forest far below.

It must have been past two o'clock when our column halted and word was passed back that we should rest. We crouched where we were on the steep wet slope among the roots and rotting leaves. Mark and Martha were huddled on the red anorak at the front of the convoy, under the watchful eye of Silas. The men were nearby, whispering together. We waited as we had always waited: a quiet unspeaking group, thinking of the impending rain.

'Why are they taking so long?' Bill whispered to me. Silas and the men were still talking intently after twenty minutes.

'I don't know. Maybe they're plotting some ludicrous plan.' I got up and went down the slope to speak with Mark and Martha.

'How is everything?' I whispered, crouching next to them.

Martha had huge bags under her eyes. She smiled bravely and patted her stomach. 'Okay, I suppose.'

'What's going on here?' I nodded to the group.

Mark shrugged. 'I don't know. But Silas has promised to build Martha and me a house near here.'

'You think he's going to run off?'

He shook his head wearily. 'He asked Martha to give him her anorak now, in case there wasn't a chance at the end. Who knows what that man thinks.'

Dew dripped from the vines and creepers around us. A fine mist began to creep down the hill.

Silas came over to our group. 'Daniel?' he said crossly. I looked up to him expectantly. He turned to Mark and Martha. 'There are no places to make a house by this river. We will go back up.'

'Oh no,' Martha sighed. 'How can we? Silas, I can hardly walk.'

'Hey,' Silas replied softly. 'It's not far. Just up there. Anyway, you two stay here and rest for now.'

The men were standing silently. 'Daniel,' said the weasel-man. 'Tell the other hostages to climb back up the hill.'

'How far back up?'

'Just back up; over the ridge again.'

'There is a flat ledge with palms just up there,' I said. 'Is that the place?'

He hesitated and looked around him. 'Yes,' he lied.

They had lost their nerve and wanted to take us far back into the mountains again. By the time they made us a house we would already been freezing in the rain. I despised the weasel-man; he made my skin crawl.

I turned to Navy who was sitting just up the slope. He looked at me rather sadly. Adinda, Lita and Tessy were sitting around him and they looked tired and scared. I could feel the whole mood changing around us and the afternoon turned cold and dark. 'What do you think? Shall I go ahead and make sure they build this house nearby and then come and get you?'

Navy nodded and sighed. 'Yes. Adinda needs to rest,' he said.

The men were not pleased with my plan. They talked for a moment and I watched two of them creep away without the other men seeing. Two down, ten to go, I thought. The weasel-man reluctantly agreed with me and I followed the remaining men up the slope to the narrow ledge; a flat area with several ground palms growing among the trees. The men stood around uselessly.

'We will make a house,' said the preacher, his smart shirt at odds with the dirty rags of the other men. 'Now go and get the others.'

'Only when the house is made,' I said firmly. One of them sat and began to pull feebly at some roots. I felt angry. They had brought us too far down the valley, grown scared with talk of the army and now it was late in the day. I raised my voice. 'If you want to go, just go. Isn't four months enough punishment?'

The weasel-man wriggled his satchel off his back and undid the buckles. He drew out an axe head wrapped in cloth and wedged it on to the end of the wooden handle he was carrying. Anto began to chop reluctantly at a tree with his machete.

'How about here?' I said pointing. 'We could put a floor frame across these two logs.' They shuffled over and looked without interest.

'What's going on here?' Silas called, coming up behind me. I was unnerved. Timidly, I explained that the others would come when the house was built. They were tired. He put his hand on my shoulder. 'Daniel,' he said looking me in the eye. 'Trust me. I will build you a house here even if I have to build it alone. Go and get the others.' As I turned to leave he put his hand on my arm. 'But Mark and Martha should stay. Tell them I will fetch them later.'

I went down the slope to where Anna, Annette and Bill were waiting and relayed Silas's message. They headed up the hill while I went to find the others below. Navy looked up at me expectantly.

'Silas promises he'll build us a house.' I said, 'but it's clear they don't want to. They're very close to running. I don't know why we don't just run off ourselves.'

Navy nodded enthusiastically. 'Yes,' he said emphatically. 'Why don't we? We could just go down to the river. I doubt they'd follow us.' We stared at each other for a moment, silently considering the option. Adinda, Lita, Tessy and Markus became impatient and began to trudge on up the path.

'Maybe they'll go in the night,' I said reluctantly. He nodded and I went down to Mark and Martha who were relieved to be able to wait a while longer.

I ran back up the hill, overtaking everyone and arriving back at the ledge first. 'Okay, they're coming now,' I said smiling, trying to make my peace with them. They nodded quietly as they smoked. 'Can I have a drag?' I asked. They were moody and unfriendly. Even Anto shook his head and shrugged awkwardly. He had never refused me before.

The weasel–man finished smoking, stood up, picked up his axe and walked off, passing Bill as he arrived.

'Going to cut leaves?' Bill asked.

'Yes,' he said, grinning through his cracked lips.

Anna and Annette appeared and came over to me. 'Have you got a cigarette then, Dan?' Annette asked, looking at the men smoking about me. I shook my head and we sat waiting for the others in the dreary forest.

We heard Adinda's voice through the trees about fifty yards below.

'Navy!' she cried out in distress.

'That's Adinda,' said Annette, looking over her shoulder. 'I wonder what's wrong.'

'Oh no, Navy!' Adinda cried again. We looked at each other with rising alarm. I had never heard her cry like that before. It was like a lamentation.

'Has he fallen or something?' I got up and moved towards the sound.

'Where is there to fall?' said Annette. The ground was soft and wet. There were no precipices nearby.

I stopped for a moment. There was silence. 'Maybe he's lost something of hers, like a ring?' I suggested. 'Should we help?'

Bill was sitting bolt upright. 'Did you hear that thud just then?' he asked.

'Oh no, not Navy, not Navy!' It was Adinda again and now she was coming up through the trees and undergrowth, her face drained of colour, her eyes locked straight ahead, her hands clenched on her cheeks. I was shocked. What could be so bad? What terrible thing had done this to Adinda? It was incomprehensible.

'What is it?' I pleaded.

'Daniel,' she cried, her tiny weak frame stumbling towards me, her hands reaching out to claw at me in despair. 'Daniel, they kill Navy. They kill my Navy.'

The words passed over me. I could not believe them. These men would never kill anyone. They wouldn't touch us. Kill? How could they kill?

Then I saw the weasel-man coming casually back up the hill, his axe in hand. He stared at me, a sparkle in his eye, then he jerked his head and the other men closed in around us.

Terror shattered my innocence like a brick through glass. My reality had fractured and I felt both paralysed and detached. My eyeballs seemed to have retracted deep into my head and I peered out with tunnel vision at what surrounded me. I looked over my shoulder. A man was slowly preparing his bow. I looked to the side. The preacher had put down his *nokin* and was picking up his machete. There was no fury in these men, no dancing or ceremony as there had been when we had first been kidnapped. Coolly and calmly, they were preparing our execution.

Markus was nowhere to be seen. Lita was crying, following close behind Adinda. Tessy could hardly walk; his body twisting and turning through the air in anguish. 'No, no,' he moaned. Did he know what was coming next? Was he resigned to it? All three of them were walking back up the hill straight into the arms of their attackers.

'Split into two groups,' the preacher ordered. 'White people here, Indonesian people there.' There were about ten men spread widely in a semicircle before us. Half of them were hanging around near the edges looking unsure while the others moved forward with their weapons. I had an almost uncontrollable urge to run.

'We've got to get out of here,' Bill shouted, but already the preacher had grabbed Tessy and was pulling him by his arm into the centre.

'No!' I screamed, jumping forward and trying to grab at Tessy. The weasel-man came towards me swirling his axe above his head. The glinting metal swished through the air. I jumped back. Tessy stood helplessly by the preacher, his head and body limp, his arms up against his chest. He did not run, or struggle or scream. He just moaned softly in his melodic voice.

The preacher raised his machete and hacked into his exposed forearms with two quick, hard strokes. Tessy's white skin opened and through the light pink flesh I saw his bone. In the shock he did not flinch.

'You can't!' cried Annette. She too jumped forward but retreated as the preacher brandished his machete at her. The preacher aimed again, this time at his stomach, but Tessy crumpled to the floor before he could strike.

'No!' I bellowed. I thought I would run right at him this time but I stopped short. Through the corner of my eye I saw one of the men aiming his arrow at me, knees bent, pulling the bow back quickly, his eyes suddenly alight in fury. I jumped away and looked about the crowd. Where were Anto and his friend? They were backing off from the crowd, picking up their *nokins* and preparing to go. They looked unconcerned.

'Split into two groups,' shouted the preacher again, looking up from his prey.

'You should run,' said Angin's friend, looking calmly at me. 'Go now.'

I stepped back and felt myself drawn to run again, an impulse stronger than any I have known. Adinda was on her knees in front of me. 'Please, please,' she sobbed. 'Protect Lita and me. They kill us, too.' Her eyes were pleading with me.

'Yes, yes,' I said, but already my legs were moving. Bill and Annette were beginning to run as well.

'Wait!' I cried. 'Get Adinda and Lita in front. Bill, Annette, we keep to the back.' I pushed Adinda and Lita forward. 'Run, Adinda, run!' I screamed at her furiously. 'Down to the river. Now!' She was so slow and so weak. Would we all be murdered because of her? Why was I being so foolish? The men were already moving towards us.

We tore through the tangled vegetation battering everything in our path. We jumped from the flat ledge down the steep embankment, sliding down however we could. I looked back. Bill was behind me weaving from side to side to dodge any arrows. Six men were standing at the ledge, considering whether to chase us.

'Silas!' I screamed through the forest. 'Silas!' We had to reach him. He would protect us. 'Mark! Martha!' We had lost the path but I knew they were waiting somewhere below. I bounded ahead of everyone shouting again and again. 'Mark, Martha, Silas! Where are you?'

Suddenly I saw some figures through the trees and it flashed through my mind: what if Silas was one of them too? Why did he not help us? Would he be angry that we had escaped? The three of them were standing there. I knelt down at Silas's feet and begged, 'Please, Silas, Father Silas, please don't kill us, please spare us!' He looked down at me, shaking his head in confusion. Tears were pouring down his face. He looked to Mark and Martha who were alarmed and confused.

'They've killed Navy. They've killed Navy and Tessy,' I shouted, gasping for breath.

Silas began to stagger backwards shaking his head again. 'This was not me, this is not the end. I will release you. I did not want this.'

'Mark, Martha, listen, understand.' They nodded their heads. 'They have killed Navy, maybe Tessy. They may come for us. We have to get out of here as quickly as possible.'

They stood stock still.

'Come *on*,' I grabbed Mark's arm and we began to run again, heading down the open landslip until we reached the flat of the river. There was still an hour or more of daylight left. We would follow the river down as far as we could. Then at dusk we would hide silently in this forsaken forest and wait out the night.

TWENTY-THREE

THE FINAL NIGHT

Thick mist was hanging low in the valley. We scrambled down the river, clambering over boulders and wading through the icy current. I stayed close to Adinda, scooping her up and carrying her when she faltered. We had gone only a few hundred yards when Mark called and pointed. A low black wire was strung between the banks some way ahead. Soldiers were rushing out of the forest, crouching behind rocks and aiming their rifles at us. Their hair was straight and black, their uniforms camouflage green. This was the Indonesian army I had seen in my imagination so many times before.

'Get down,' I shouted, terrified that they might fire at us. They were equally alarmed but as they realized we were alone they began to wave us forward.

'*Duduk disana*, get down over there,' they called nervously, taking hold of our arms and running us to the bank. We sat among the tins and debris from a recent camp meal. Between the trees were several ponchos and sleeping mats. Men were rushing around, pulling on their shirts and boots. Some ran out to join their colleagues in the river while others crouched down in front of us.

'From England, *ya*?' one of the men asked me. He smiled and shook my trembling hand. He pointed to himself. 'I am from Indonesia, *ya*!'

Adinda was next to me, shaking in her wet clothes. 'Are you Adinda?' She nodded. 'Your father is an important man!' He called out to the other soldiers and clapped his hands. 'We've got Adinda Saraswati!'

'OPM,' Adinda stammered, pointing to the hill. 'Very near.'

'Kelly Kwalik, *ya*?' He spat on the ground then ran over to the men in the river. They began to fire randomly into the forest.

'Stop! Stop!' Mark called to them. 'Markus is not here. He is a Papuan; black face with a pink jumper.'

'And where's Anna?' called Bill. I hadn't seen her since they dragged off Tessy.

I grabbed one of the soldiers. 'And Navy and Tessy. They are still on the hillside. The OPM attacked them,' I said in broken Indonesian. Then it suddenly came to me that I must lead the soldiers back into the forest to find their wounded bodies. Maybe they could be saved.

'You want to smoke?' he asked excitedly, calling to his friend who threw over a pack. I took one, fumbled to light it, inhaled deeply then took his arm again. 'Navy and Tessy. We must rescue them. Maybe they are alive.'

'Just a moment.' He ran to his bag, pulled out a camera, called two of his friends over and sat them down among us. 'Photo, photo. Smile, *ya*?' The camera flashed and they all swapped places. 'Ujan!' he called out punching his fist into the air. 'Just say Ujan when they ask.' I looked at his badge and saw that it was the name of his unit.

Suddenly they were pointing and rushing off. We turned and saw Markus, walking nervously down the river, limping and ducking his head. 'That's Markus! Markus!' we cried out and the men led him over. Just as he arrived we spotted another figure on hands and knees coming down the landslip. 'Anna!' we called as she stumbled across the river towards us. 'Anna, thank God, thank God,' we sobbed, holding her close.

'Where have you been?' cried Annette. 'What happened to you?'

'I just ran,' she said breathing heavily. 'When they took Tessy, I just ran and hid in the roots of a tree. Then I heard you all run off, and the shots just now.'

'And Tessy? What happened to him. Could you hear?'

'I just heard him moaning and the men talking.' She lowered her head and began to cry. 'Then everything went quiet.'

I felt my whole body boiling up with emotion at the thought of Anna listening to Tessy die. I wanted to cry, to let everything out, but I couldn't.

'We have to see if they're still alive,' I said as I thought of their bodies again. The commander of the unit came to see us and again we tried to explain about Navy and Tessy.

'We can't go in there,' he said shaking his head. 'Too few men, only twelve of us. The others are in the forest. We must protect you.'

Adinda started to cry uncontrollably and her arms were around Mark and then me in turn. 'Oh, Navy, Navy,' she keened. Lita was next to her, weeping into in her hands, calling Tessy's name.

'They don't have guns, just bows and arrows,' I pleaded. 'There's still an hour of light.'

'No guns?'

'No guns. We must go and find them. We can save them.'

He sighed and patted my knee. 'You are safe here,' he said and left.

I looked at Mark, distraught. Suddenly, as if it had only just sunk in, he threw his arms around me and cried, 'Why? Oh, why?'

The commander came over again and took our names. He was just a young man, no older than me. I looked at his men, rushing around excitedly, brewing up instant food for us on their solid-fuel stoves, bringing more biscuits, taking more photos. Most were in their late teens.

'Tell me what happened to the other two?' the commander asked me quietly. 'They arrow them?'

I shook my head. 'They cut Tessy's wrists with a machete.' I said, showing him where on my own body. 'Maybe the stomach, too.'

'And the other one?'

'Only Adinda and Lita saw.'

Mark was soothing them and trying to feed them biscuits. The commander shook them both gently and spoke to them. Adinda started shaking and sobbing again, then drew breath, and said: 'They had an axe. They hit him on his neck.' She broke down again and the man looked at Lita, touching the back of his neck with the edge of his hand as if to check. She nodded. 'With the sharp side?' he asked. She nodded again. Then he pulled his hand right through, from back to front. She looked down and shook her head. I felt sick.

Adinda stopped crying and sat up. Her face was ashen, drawn but determined. 'He dropped to his knees,' she said. 'They hit him again, in his back. He called out, Praise the Lord, Jesus Christ, then he fell forward on his face and was struck again. After that there was nothing: no sound, just poor Navy, my Navy.' She sat back limply and Lita embraced her again and stroked her hair. The commander got up slowly, turned to his colleagues and shook his head. For a moment there was silence.

We sat exposed in the base of the river valley. The steep hillside rose up around us. There were countless vantage points from which we could be watched or shot at with well-aimed arrows. Would the OPM come for us again? Why be content with two murders when the prize could be even greater? I stared into the darkening forest. What if they had gathered more men and planned to ambush in the night?

The radio operator tried to make contact with the base at Keneyam, about twenty miles to the south. 'Ujan, Keneyam, Ujan, Keneyam,' he repeated anxiously, holding the handset tightly to his ear. 'Ujan, Keneyam. Come in.' There was nothing but the hiss of interference. He looked helplessly to his companions. How long would it be before we were found here; before a chopper could come and take us away?

Finally, there was a voice on the radio and after a few minutes he came over to us. 'I'm sorry,' he said. 'We stay here one more night. The chopper can't come in this weather. Already one chopper came out of the sky because of the mist. Five men dead. Tomorrow you go home.' He stroked Adinda's arm. 'Tomorrow you can see your family.'

Twelve more soldiers appeared, splashing down through the river. They had been out on patrol in the hills above and were returning to the camp for the night. One was a Papuan man. He was wearing Wellington boots. Now we had twenty-four armed men to protect us.

As it began to drizzle, they strung up two ponchos for us near a large boulder and patch of thicket. We crowded around the tree stumps in the mud. They gave us hot noodles and rice and we began to eat ravenously. Although my head was heavy with disbelief there were faint glimmers of relief as I thought of our imminent freedom.

As darkness fell two soldiers positioned themselves on either side of our camp. They brought us fresh army socks, underpants and long johns. Wearing their camouflage jackets and trousers, we huddled close together, rubbing each other warm. Lita and Adinda were in the middle with me on one side and Mark and Martha on the other. Bill, Anna, Annette and Markus squashed together in the row behind us. It began to pour with rain. The ground filled with puddles and the ponchos dripped steadily on top of us.

Lita talked with Mark, and Martha held her hand. She seemed more peaceful now. I held Adinda and the unit medic brought her strong tranquillisers and pain killers. She had twisted her ankle, maybe broken it, during the tumble down the hill and it was swelling up horribly.

'You think Navy and Tessy are still there?' she asked me softly.

'Yes, they are still there,' I said, holding her hand tightly, thinking of the two bodies lying in the rain a few hundred yards away. 'They are just sleeping. We find them tomorrow.'

'You think OPM take Navy and Tessy? Take body away?'

'No. Navy, he is too big.' She laughed quietly.

'You pray for them Dan? Pray they are alive.'

'I will pray for them.'

'Navy is good man, the best. Navy and me make plan to marry when we go back to Jakarta. You know that?'

'Yes, Tessy told me. He said it was a secret. I'm so sorry, Adinda.'

'No other like Navy, Dan. We find him in morning. Maybe alive.' The drugs pumped through her body, her eyelids grew heavy and she laid her head calmly on my knee.

*   *   *

Soon the cigarettes ran out and we sat silently together in the pouring rain. The horrors of the afternoon played through my head all night as I worked over the events again and again. Could I have changed anything? Was Silas innocent or did he know about the murders? He had been there when the men had seen the aerial strung across the river and had huddled together to plot. But was it then that they had decided to kill us or had they planned just to take us back into the mountain? Perhaps our refusal to move had precipitated the executions. I remembered Tessy coming up the hill, waving his arms from side to side. He must have known he was next. Why had he not run? Perhaps he knew then that he must sacrifice himself to save Lita and Adinda. And when the preacher had told us to split into groups, had they planned to kill us all? If so, why did they not chase after us? Maybe two lives were enough for them – enough blood to quench the deep-rooted bitterness of thirty years of occupation and abuse. I wondered what they had seen, what brutality they had suffered to make them turn like that, from the gentle people I had grown to know.

In the forest far away I heard whoops and cries: the OPM. I was filled with terror again. 'Turn out your torch,' the sentries whispered urgently. I was sure I could see movement in the woodland and I imagined one hundred men attacking us with axes and machetes. The morning was many hours away.

When it came there was no respite from the rain. In the sober light of dawn we were calm and quiet. They moved us farther up the riverbank and we ate hot stew and more noodles under a poncho, listening to the patter of the rain. All I could think about were the soaking wet bodies, lying on the hillside where we had left them, among the thorns, creepers and insects. By seven o'clock a new group of men had arrived, trudging up the river, dressed all in black with clanking equipment and bulging muscles. These were the Kopassus special forces troops. Dropping down their heavy rucksacks and sub-machine guns they looked at us with amusement.

'What do you think you are doing here?' One asked in good humour. 'We've been all the way up that mountain looking for you. When we arrived at your house yesterday you had already left. Now you turn up here with these guys.' It was clear that he was a bit disappointed. 'We found your litter and footprints though. We were right behind. We spent the night in the forest only an hour from here.'

'How many troops have been looking for us?' Bill asked.

'One thousand, two thousand. Not sure.' He took off his jacket, dug into his bag, pulled out a metal shackle and hooked it on to the body harness he was wearing. 'I used this to abseil down from the helicopters when we took Geselema. I came down through the trees with my machine gun at the ready but when I got to your big shelter you had gone. Why do you always run away from me?' He laughed raucously and looked to his men. 'We found your lunch though. Pork *ya*? And a big box of sweets.'

'So how did you find us up on the hill?' I asked 'We saw a plane high up and the OPM said you had dogs.'

'The plane was remote control and picked up your body heat. Very clever; it's from Israel. We have some white people here, too. Maybe they will come and see you later.' One of his colleagues came over and talked to him. He turned to us again. 'One of you knows where the bodies are, *ya*?'

I put my hand up slowly. Anna and Annette patted me on the back encouragingly. 'Only if we take lots of men,' I said. 'There could still be OPM about.'

'You scared?' The Kopassus man asked surprised. He pulled a flak jacket out of his bag. 'You can wear one of these and we'll paint your face black.' He stopped and thought for a moment. 'But maybe it's easier if you draw us a map.'

The special forces men went off into the forest while the regular soldiers sat with us and brought us tea and coffee. They pulled out copies of the photographs Silas and the others had taken several months before. ABRI had issued them to all the units. All the OPM leaders were named but the other Papuan faces were labelled GPK: 'Security Disturbance Gang'.

'That's Petrus,' cried Anna in alarm as she looked through them. 'He's not OPM.' We tried to explain but the men just laughed.

'Don't worry,' they said. 'Our job is not finished here. We will go after them and will not stop until we have every last one.'

Within an hour the Kopassus men had returned. They laid the bodies behind a big boulder and one of them spoke to General Prabowo on the radio: 'Yes, sir. We have them. Mutilated. Quite dead, sir.' The he turned to us. 'The helicopters are on their way.'

Lita and Adinda began to weep and Mark and Martha held them gently. The rest of us sat silently, looking at the ground. I felt burnt out, bitter and unable to cry.

We heard a far-off whine and the men took our hands and walked us down the river. I quickly shrugged them off. I wanted to make my own way. Two helicopters had landed close by on an area of open riverbank. With the blades thundering above us, the pilot grabbed my arm, opened the door and placed me inside with Anna, Bill and Annette. We strapped up and they slid the door closed. The noise of the engine increased, the machine lifted and we hovered slowly into the air.

The Kilmid ran like a white ribbon in the valley far below. The mist hung in tatters and the dense green forest rose steeply into the shrouded mountains. Fifty miles away, on the horizon I recognized the sharp, black peak of Mount Trikora tearing through the thick band of dark cloud. The helicopter shook noisily, banked to the south-east and gained height. We passed over the lowland hills of the Yugguru and then the Gul. My eye traced the course of the valley as it wound up into the highlands and there, several miles to the north, perched on a tiny plateau, I could just make out the scatter of tin roofs that was Mapnduma. I hid my face in Anna's chest, and I cried and cried like a child as the land passed away beneath me.

EPILOGUE

When we came down in lowland Keneyam, the forward base for the military operation, a wave of heat and humidity hit us. We changed helicopters for our onward flight to Timika. There, soldiers, carried us victoriously across the expanse of wavering black tarmac and at the doors of the five-star Sheraton photographers and TV cameras jostled excitedly. How could we celebrate when Navy and Tessy lay dead?

Bill and I were led into our air-conditioned room by a smart-suited ABRI official. Kopassus T-shirts and jogging pants were laid out for each of us on the bed. I turned the television on and off, picked at a plate of cold chips and examined the fitted wardrobes. John Beadle from Scotland Yard popped his head around the door and said hello. He and his colleagues had been advising the ICRC on negotiating techniques for four months in Wamena. His cheery London accent was heaven to my ears as we chatted about home and smoked Benson and Hedges cigarettes. He said that ABRI had only expected half of us to come out alive. It seemed everyone was overjoyed at the result.

When Bill had finished with the shower, I rinsed the soot from my hair and scrubbed the ingrained earth from my skin. As I dried myself a man came in trailing a black sack. He picked up my pile of old clothes with tongs, then left without a word. John looked at his watch and said we should go. I scooped the contents of the mini-bar into a plastic bag and signed the tab to ABRI.

The six-hour flight in the cavernous, roaring hulk of the Hercules transport plane felt longer. Adinda and Lita slept silently in the bunks. Bill and I sipped at a can of beer. Markus told his story to several journalists. Annette, Anna, Mark and Martha talked to John

329

and the Dutch embassy representative. Navy and Tessy were on a separate aircraft which followed behind. I felt bitter and confused. ABRI had precipitated the murders, but also our freedom. I could not resent their involvement and I could not honestly say I would rather be back in the forest. My anger shifted to the OPM. They had thrown everything away. ABRI would be internationally praised for their handling of the crisis while the OPM would be shown up as a bunch of savage murderers to be hunted down at all costs. How could they have been so foolish and so naive?

It was late when we touched down in the misty orange glow of a wet Jakarta evening. The streets had been cleared and our entourage was taken in a convoy of wailing motorcycle outriders and black limousines to the presidential military hospital where we were locked into individual rooms and told to sleep. The nurses brought me egg sandwiches and hot milk. Jean and Geoff Harrod from the embassy arrived with mobile phones and I spoke to my family. I didn't really know what to say.

I took a bath but I was sure I could still feel the fleas. Dressed in army-issue pyjamas I persuaded the Sister to let me out to see the others. I padded down the corridor to Bill's room where Anna and Annette were perched on the edge of his bed dressed in nighties drinking champagne with the Ambassador and his wife. There were chocolates and fruit cake, too, and John had been joined by his colleage Bill Gent who was passing around cans of chilled lager. We sat and drank and talked and laughed and for over an hour the murders were forgotten. But when I went to bed the guilt returned.

The next day the nine of us were together again. Adinda's ankle was in plaster, Lita and Markus were also in wheelchairs and Martha looked well. Dressed in Indonesian national costume, the foreign minister handed us back to our ambassadors in an official ceremony. The forestry minister gave us each a huge bouquet of flowers and chocolates. Then the head of the armed forces and several of his generals came to interview each of us for television. They didn't ask us what had happened as the official story had already been fabricated and released through the news agency, Antara. In a brilliant operation a score of crack Indonesian troops had abseiled down through the canopy, killed eight rebels and rescued most of the hostages from under their noses. The whole operation had taken ABRI only six hours.

Navy's and Tessy's funerals were held simultaneously in Jakarta and Bandung that afternoon. Adinda had a ring for Navy but we had arrived too late and the authorities would not let the coffin be reopened. The nine of us united in protest and helped those in wheelchairs to the front of the crowd while Mark negotiated diplomatically with the authorities. It was just as it had always been – a closely knit team pulling together through adversity.

Navy was dressed in a suit and tie and was surrounded by flowers. We picked up Adinda and held her as she slipped the ring on her fiancée's finger. Prayers were said and the coffin was lowered with military honours. We sang and cried, not just for Navy but for Tessy buried without us in Bandung.

We returned to Britain on Sunday 19 May 1996. My elder brother wrote: 'We went to our church this evening and blew out the candle that has been burning for 130 days.'

For the first weeks I was shy and reclusive. I couldn't bring myself to speak on the telephone or watch television. I needed to be alone and spend time in the open space of the Penwith moors. I desperately missed the solitude and slow pace of life in the forest. But I had many new fears as well. While driving, or walking along cliffs, or entering a dark house, I was acutely aware of death and how it could strike suddenly and horrifically at any time.

Quickly the experience began to bifurcate. One part of it, the memory, had become a narrative detached from me. It was as if I was telling a story that had once been told to me. The other part, the emotion, had sunk so deep into my body I thought I would never understand it. So in September I began to write. For six months I became a hostage again, working in solitude, reliving every moment in a struggle to understand what Lorentz 95 had become.

It has been a gruelling and painful process that feels a little like a penance. But it has purged me and begun to clear away the spirits and the guilt that have haunted me since my return. I feel more at ease now when I admit that, despite the tragedy that unfolded, the captivity gave me the depth of experience that I went to Irian Jaya to find. I am very thankful for the opportunities I was given to challenge myself through hardship, to feel the freedom of a wild land and to learn a little about a culture with values very different from our own.

And what of the others? Annette is completing a masters in environmental business studies. Anna worked for a scientific publication for a while and now hopes to teach over the coming summer. Bill set up a small consultancy, Eco Sourcing International, which sources suppliers of sustainably managed tropical timber. Mark and Martha returned to the Netherlands briefly before flying back out to Jakarta to continue their work at WWF and Unesco. On 13 July 1996 Martha gave birth to a very healthy blue-eyed 8lb 7oz baby boy named Mick Lorentz van der Wal. All on a diet of sweet potatoes and frogs! Lita is back at BScC continuing her studies in the Halimun National Park in Java. Adinda has also written a book and is now working in the environmental department of an Indonesian petroleum company. Markus returned to Cenderawasih University and Bram to the Forestry Department in Jayapura. His child is now almost eighteen months old.

In Irian Jaya the situation is not so happy. The Timika military operation has been expanded and now has the largest concentration of forces in Indonesia. ABRI have set up permanent posts in Mapnduma, Geselema and many more Nduga villages. Troops are still searching for OPM supporters. Two 'OPM' have been arrested and two others have been shot after clashes with ABRI near Mapnduma. There has been no sight or sound from Kelly Kwalik who has sensibly gone to ground. Adriaan van der Bijl has been allowed to return to Mapnduma on brief visits and he described to me the situation as being 'better than expected' although there is still much fear and tension. Some local people may still be hiding in the forest but community leaders like Philipus have tried to bring them back to the villages.

The ICRC are not working in Irian Jaya at present and it will be several years before they will be able to return to the Nduga region without military escort. It is difficult to know how well they will be received in the area after the stories undoubtedly circulating about the killings in Geselema by white people in white helicopters. The rumours will be bound to fill the Nduga with even more distrust of the world encroaching on them.

When the military came in on 9 May 1996 they quickly found our hut near Geselema and were able to retrieve what little expedition paperwork we were still carrying around with us. A few rolls of film were salvaged as were Navy's and Tessy's bird data. We were pleased that it could be used by WWF to support the UN World Heritage Site proposal for the Lorentz area that is currently under consideration. If this is successful it is possible that Indonesian National Park status will follow. As well as giving some formal protection to the forests it will support government recognition of the local population's traditional land rights. (Under Indonesian law all unfarmed forest land automatically belongs to the state.) Perhaps here-in lies the greatest irony. The clearest chance the Papuans have of achieving limited autonomy in the near future is through the protected areas that conservationists, such as our group, hoped to promote.

The Papuans do not have many allies yet the OPM chose to baulk the opportunities offered by WWF and then ICRC. First I was filled with fury, then frustration and then sadness. It has taken me many months to begin to understand why they chose to throw so much away.

After returning home I contacted several human rights groups, such as Survival International and TAPOL, which I had not known about before I left. I found Bishop Munninghoff's report which documented the terrible string of abuses that were carried out by ABRI in the Freeport area during 1995. (Some of these, such as the murder of Kwalik's four brothers, are described in the Prologue.) The injustices the Amungme and other peoples have suffered in the conquest of their land fuelled an anger in me. I began to understand how one might be led to murder in cold-blooded revenge.

Kelly Kwalik and his OPM supporters – who I believe to be many – have two main options now. They can encourage ever more Papuans to fight and lose their lives against the Indonesian military machine or they can give up their arms, compromise their aims, work to raise education levels among their people and campaign for their rights in the international area.

From my limited experience I have seen that the Papuans are a proud people and a fighting people with a strong and resolute sense of justice. In their minds there can be only one right and proper course of action. But for their long-term survival, in a world that is neither right or just, I sincerely hope that the OPM will take the less honourable course.

Daniel Start,
March 1997

FURTHER INFORMATION

ORGANIZATIONS:

Survival International, 11–15 Emerald Street, London WCIN 3QL. Tel: 0171 242 1441. Fax: 0171 242 1441. Email survival@gn.apc.org. (A Worldwide organization supporting tribal peoples' rights with a focus on those affected by mining in Irian Jaya/West Papua.)

TAPOL: The Indonesian Human Rights Campaign, 111 Northwood Road, Thornton Heath, Surrey CR7 8HW. Tel: 0181 771 2904. Fax: 0181 653 0322. Email tapol@gn.apc.org. (which publishes the bi-monthly TAPOL bulletin).

Freeport McMoran Copper & Gold, 1615 Poydras St, New Orleans, LA 70112, USA. (Freeport hold exploration rights for much of the central mountain range of Irian Jaya. Future developments will effect many indiginous peoples.)

RTZ, 6 St James Square, Lonodn SWIY 4LD. Tel: 0171 930 2399. Fax: 0171 930 3249. (RTZ is underwriting 40 per cent of Freeport's current exploration costs.)

BOOKS:

West Papua: The Obliteration of a People by Carmel Budiardjo and Liem Soei Liong (1988). In-depth documentation of events in the area since the 1960s available through TAPOL.

Under the Mountain Wall by Peter Matthiessen, Penguin Travel Library. A beautiful book describing two seasons spent with the Dani tribe in the Baliem Valley.

Poisoned Arrows by George Monbiot (1989). An investigative journalist's story.

De Nieuw Guinea Kwestie by Dr P. B. R. De Geus. For those who read Dutch this is one of the most authoritative books written on the 'de-colonization' of Dutch New Guinea.

INTERNET:

The 'reg.westpapua' internet news service is without doubt the best way to stay informed. It is well run and free (of course). Send an email to Charlie Scheiner at csheiner@igc.apc.org to subscribe or unsubscribe. Make sure you mention the West Papua list as he maintains several. A newer service, 'west iranian newslist' can be subscribed to by sending an email to owner-west-irian-newslist@xc.org including subscribe-newslist in the body of the message.

USEFUL HOME PAGES INCLUDE:

http://www.cs.utexas.edu/users/boyer/fp/ (on Freeport and the problems).

http://www.fcx.com/fcx/envpol.html (on Freeport and the solutions).

http://www.twics.com/~boyjah/westpapua/welcome.html (the OPM's home page).

http://www.cs.utexas.edu/users/cline/papua/ (the West Papua Information kit).

http://www.state.gov/www/issues/human_rights/1996_hrp_report/indonesia.html (the US government's human rights report on Indonesia for 1996).

http:/www.komnas.go.id/english/index.html (Indonesia's National Commission on Human Rights).

ACKNOWLEDGEMENTS

Thanks are due to the following.

In the writing of this book: Mark Lucas and Michael Fishwick for persuading me it was possible; Sue Waite for inspiration and support while I worked in Cornwall; Rebecca Lloyd for untangling my infelicitous syntax and for help and patience in the final, crucial weeks; Anna Grapes and Philip Lewis for helping arrange the photographs and maps; everyone else at HarperCollins who helped make a gruelling experience so enjoyable and rewarding; my family and friends for being there when I needed help and giving me space when I didn't.

For those who worked so hard for a peaceful resolution: the Protestant and Catholic churches, in particular Adriaan and Elfrieda van der Bijl and Bishop Herman Munninghoff; the International Committee for the Red Cross including Dr Ferenc Meyer, Sylviane Bonadei, Henry Fournier, René Suter, Dr Patrick Sergy, John Broughton (British Red Cross) and the Airfast and Mission Aviation Fellowship helicopter pilots who flew them in; the New Scotland Yard negotiating specialists DCI Bill Gent, DSI John Beadle, DS Chris Chainey, Commander Roy Ram and others; the members of the Foreign and Commonwealth Office, in particular Colonel Ivar Helberg, Brian Watters, Jean and Geoff Harrod, Graham and Julia Burton in the British Embassy in Jakarta and Geoff Fairhurst and Geoff Higgins from the Foreign Office in London who called our families every single day to keep them up to date; the Indonesian Army, in particular Major-General Prabowo, commander of Kopassus Special Forces, on whose authority the peaceful negotiations were allowed to run their course, and those troops involved in the operation which tried to free us. A special thank you to all those who wrote to us and prayed for us during our captivity, in particular my family.

Those who supported the expedition. Our patrons: HRH The Duke of Edinburgh KG KT; Lord St John of Fawsley; Professor Sir Ghillean

Prance, Director of the Royal Botanic Gardens, Kew; Dr Soetikno Wiroatmodjo, Director of the Institute of Biology in Indonesia. Our supporting institutes: LIPI-Biologi who providing crucial sponsorship, Biological Sciences club who were such an excellent and professional counterpart organization, the Royal Geographical Society and Birdlife International. Our advisors, for their direction: Dr Anthony Whitten, Dr Timothy Whitmore, Dr David Chivers, Dr Gerald Allen, Professor Bob Johns, Dr Jim Jarvie, Dr Elisabeth Widjaya, Jim Paine, Alison Stattersfield, Katherine Gotto, Dr Michael Ounstead, Martin Sands, Brian Law, Ann Rocchi, Dr Ron Lilley, Paul Jepsom, Wandy Swales, Charles Miller, Andy and Gill Wight, Dr John Moore. And, of course, our many sponsors: Jephcott Trust, Bird Exploration Fund, Winston Churchill Memorial Trust, Conservation Foundation, People's Trust for Endangered Species, Gilchrist Educational Trust, A. J. Burton Charitable Trust, Rayne Foundation, Institute of Biology, British Ecological Society, Royal Geographical Society, Adrian Ashby-Smith Memorial Trust, A. S. Butler Charitable Trust, Sir Albert Howard Travel Exhibition, PT Freeport Indonesia Company, BP Indonesia, British Airways, PT Philips Radio, BECO Batteries Ltd, Philips Communications Ltd, Shell International, Conoco Indonesia Inc., Guinness Brewing Worldwide Ltd, KallKwik Centre, Cambridge, BP Conservation Awards, Duke of Edinburgh Trust II, Corpus Christi College, Clare College, Emmanuel College, Pembroke College, the *Jakarta Post*.

Finally: Anna, Bill, Annette, Navy, Tessy, Lita, Adinda, Mark, Martha, Markus and Bram for being my family during our time together.